The Peace and Nuclear War
Dictionary

The unleashed power of the atom has changed everything save our modes of thinking, and we thus drift toward unparalleled catastrophes.
　　　　　　　　　　　　　　—ALBERT EINSTEIN

The nation-state and the split atom could not coexist on this planet. One or the other had to go.
　　　　　　　　　　　　　　—ARNOLD TOYNBEE

THE
PEACE AND
NUCLEAR WAR
DICTIONARY

Sheikh R. Ali
North Carolina Central University

ABC-CLIO

Santa Barbara, California
Oxford, England

Library of Congress Cataloging-in-Publication Data

Ali, Sheikh Rustum.
    The peace and nuclear war dictionary / Sheikh R. Ali.
        p.   cm.—(Clio dictionaries in political science)
    Bibliography : p.
    Includes index.
    1. Nuclear warfare—Dictionaries.   2. Nuclear arms
control—Dictionaries.   I. Title.   II. Series.
    U263.A434   1989   355.02'17—dc20   89-14971

ISBN 0-87436-531-7 (alk. paper)

96 95 94 93 92 91 90 89   10 9 8 7 6 5 4 3 2 1

ABC-CLIO, Inc.
130 Cremona Drive, P.O. Box 1911
Santa Barbara, California 93116-1911

Clio Press Ltd.
55 St. Thomas' Street
Oxford, OX1 1JG, England

This book is Smyth-sewn and printed on acid-free paper ∞.
Manufactured in the United States of America

With the secret of nuclear weapons forever unlocked from the mysteries of physics and loose in our minds, this study is dedicated to my sons—Bappi and Bobby —and granddaughter—Jessica—and all other children of the world, who are fated to wrestle with the paradoxes of the nuclear-armed world forever more.

Clio Dictionaries in Political Science

The African Political Dictionary
Claude S. Phillips

The Arms Control, Disarmament, and Military Security Dictionary
Jeffrey M. Elliot and Robert Reginald

The Asian Political Dictionary
Lawrence Ziring and C. I. Eugene Kim

The Constitutional Law Dictionary, Volume 1: *Individual Rights*
Ralph C. Chandler, Richard A. Enslen, and Peter G. Renstrom

The Constitutional Law Dictionary, Volume 1: *Individual Rights*
Supplement 1
Ralph C. Chandler, Richard A. Enslen, and Peter G. Renstrom

The Constitutional Law Dictionary, Volume 2: *Governmental Powers*
Ralph C. Chandler, Richard A. Enslen, and Peter G. Renstrom

The Dictionary of Political Analysis, Second Edition
Jack C. Plano, Robert E. Riggs, and Helenan S. Robin

The Electoral Politics Dictionary
Peter G. Renstrom and Chester B. Rogers

The European Political Dictionary
Ernest E. Rossi and Barbara P. McCrea

The International Law Dictionary
Robert L. Bledsoe and Boleslaw A. Boczek

The International Relations Dictionary, Fourth Edition
Jack C. Plano and Roy Olton

The Latin American Political Dictionary
Ernest E. Rossi and Jack C. Plano

SERIES STATEMENT

Language precision is the primary tool of every scientific discipline. That aphorism serves as the guideline for this series of political dictionaries. Although each book in the series relates to a specific topical or regional area in the discipline of political science, entries in the dictionaries also emphasize history, geography, economics, sociology, philosophy, and religion.

This dictionary series incorporates special features designed to help the reader overcome any language barriers that may impede a full understanding of the subject matter. For example, the concepts included in each volume were selected to complement the subject matter found in existing texts and other books. Most volumes utilize a subject matter chapter arrangement that is useful for classroom and study purposes.

Entries in all volumes include an up-to-date definition plus a paragraph of *Significance* in which the authors discuss and analyze the term's historical and current relevance. Most entries are also cross-referenced providing the reader an opportunity to seek additional information related to the subject of inquiry. A comprehensive index, found in both hardcover and paperback editions, allows the reader to locate major entries and other concepts, events, and institutions discussed within these entries.

The political and social sciences suffer more than most disciplines from semantic confusion. This is attributable, *inter alia*, to the popularization of the language, and to the focus on many diverse foreign political and social systems. This dictionary series is dedicated to overcoming some of this confusion through careful writing of thorough, accurate definitions for the central concepts, institutions, and events that comprise the basic knowledge of each of the subject fields. New titles in the series will be issued periodically, including some in related social science disciplines.

—Jack C. Plano
Series Editor

CONTENTS

A NOTE ON HOW TO USE THIS BOOK

The Peace and Nuclear War Dictionary is organized so that entries and supplementary data can be located easily and quickly. Items are arranged alphabetically throughout, rather than grouped into chapters. When doubtful about how to locate an entry, consult the general index. Page numbers for terms appear in the index in heavy black type; subsidiary concepts discussed within entries can be found in the index, identified by page numbers in regular type. For study purposes, numerous entries have also been subsumed under major topical headings in the index, affording the reader access to broad classes of related information.

The reader can also fully explore a topic by employing the extensive cross-references included in all entries. Many entries can be found as subsidiary terms, but in each case the concept is related to the main entry.

The author has adopted the format of this book to provide the reader a variety of useful applications. These include its use as (1) a *dictionary* and ready *reference guide* to the global language of peace and nuclear war; (2) a *study guide* for introductory courses in Nuclear War and Peace or International Relations, or for any specialized course in the area; (3) a *supplement to a textbook* or a group of paperback monographs adopted for use in these courses; (4) a *source of review material* for the political science major enrolled in advanced courses; and (5) a *social science aid* for use in business, education, government, policy sciences, and journalism.

PREFACE

The dawn of the atomic age ushered in a realization of the tremendous potential for world annihilation in the artillery of nuclear weapons. The risk of extinction by nuclear war is now the greatest threat humanity faces. The two atomic bombs dropped on Hiroshima and Nagasaki in 1945, both in terms of immediate and long-term effects, provided the most tragic demonstration of what is, by contemporary standards, considered not even a minimum nuclear destructive capability. The devastation wrought by a nuclear war in the 1990s and beyond would be incalculable. A single-megaton nuclear weapon would almost certainly reduce any city in the world to a state of blazing rubble. If the entire stockpile of nuclear weapons—more than 50,000 in the world arsenal—is used, all life on earth will be extinguished.

Throughout much of *The Peace and Nuclear War Dictionary*, the author has brought the facts of life with nuclear weapons into the spotlight, and has cataloged the unique elements of the ominous capability of the superpowers to destroy each other, and all civilization, in the process. To avoid this unthinkable catastrophe, the promise of peace through negotiations, arms control, arms reduction, disarmament, and other highly probable policy objectives of the nuclear weapons states and the threshold nations have been highlighted in this study.

The Peace and Nuclear War Dictionary grew out of the recognition of the urgent need for a clarification of a new technical and global language. The idea for this volume developed during the course of a workshop, "Enlightenment: The Best Security in a Nuclear-Armed World," organized for faculty from many U.S. colleges and universities and held at the University of Miami, Coral Gables, in 1986. However, the final shape of the book emerged at the joint Massachusetts Institute of Technology (MIT) and Harvard University 1987 intensive summer resident program on Nuclear Weapons and Arms Control for nationwide college and university educators. The program's workshops provided the author with an opportunity to update his knowledge base on nuclear arms, war, and peace. The exchange of ideas with such luminaries as Eugene P. Wigner, a designer of the first atomic bomb, enriched the author's understanding of nuclear weapons, broadened his research interests, and expanded his instructional pedagogy. He is grateful to these institutions for their invitation and financial support to participate in these workshops.

Although this work employs the dictionary format, it includes several variations. In addition to a comprehensive definition, each entry features a major paragraph on *Significance,* to assist the reader in understanding the historical roots and contemporary meaning of the defined concept. Throughout this volume, the author has attempted to explain each term as authoritatively, succinctly, and readably as possible. Furthermore, an extensive cross-reference system is used throughout the work, pointing toward additional information on each term.

Over 300 entries, arranged alphabetically, have been systematically selected and organized to complement most standard works on the subject. These entries deal with all categories of nuclear warfare and weapons systems. In compiling the list of entries, the author reviewed more than 60 books and journals on the subject, and cross-checked to ensure that no major term was omitted. The work's highly selective group of entries includes the most important and most relevant concepts, theories, events, policies, programs, inventions, weapons, armaments, and various equipment dealing with the whole spectrum of nuclear subject matter. For each term the author provides a concise definition and an expanded explanation of its significance.

The instructor—or the student—may use this dictionary as a teaching/learning supplement to a core text, or as a tool for unifying courses developed around individual readings. The author welcomes comments as to any sins of commission or omission. However, one should note that this dictionary is discriminating rather than exhaustive; it consists of those salient terms considered to be most crucial to an understanding of the fields of nuclear war, weapons, and peace.

The author wishes to express his appreciation to the many students who, over the years, have challenged and excited his interest in the field of nuclear war, weapons, the arms race, disarmament, and peace. He hopes that his excitement and interest have been contagious. The author extends his thanks to the ABC-CLIO books staff, especially Heather Cameron, Vice President, and Ann L. Hartman, Senior Vice President. Most of all, the author is indebted to Jack C. Plano, Series Editor, who read the manuscript in its entirety and made many valuable comments and suggestions, and whose wise counsel and balanced judgment gave the author the incentive to bring the dictionary to its final form. The author personally thanks Marion C. Salinger, of Duke University, for providing valuable insights and comments on the manuscript, which were indispensable for the completion of the work. He is also thankful to Rolin G. Mainuddin, of the University of Kansas, for his tireless research efforts in the preparation of the manuscript.

Finally, the author wishes to note the sacrifice his wife, Rina, often made during this venture. Concentration on a theme such as peace and nuclear war necessarily became an all-consuming exercise, and the author's immediate family was called upon to display unusual patience and forbearance. In this respect, his wife set an example of understanding, and so the completed volume is as much Rina's as it is the author's.

—Sheikh R. Ali
North Carolina Central University

The Peace and Nuclear War Dictionary

A

Accidental Nuclear War   An inadvertent nuclear attack. An accidental nuclear war may be caused by human fallibility, electronic error, or mechanical failure. It may result from a malfunctioning warning system, such as radar, or from a simple misunderstanding. Nuclear war may begin with the use of a weapon of mass destruction. Inaccurate radar messages may prompt retaliation. A deranged commander, or misguided human behavior, may precipitate nuclear war. The code used by the U.S. Department of Defense (DOD) for an accident involving nuclear weapons is "broken arrows." There have been many broken arrows in the United States and in the Soviet Union. But so far there has never been an accidental nuclear explosion. To prevent accidental nuclear war, an elaborate fail-safe system has been established. Its mission is to avoid the launching of nuclear missiles without the proper instructions and release of codes from the National Command Authorities (NCA) headed by the president. The Accidents Measures Agreement (1971) between the United States and the Soviet Union pledges them to improve safeguards against accidental or unauthorized use of nuclear weapons. The Prevention of Nuclear War Agreement (1973) between the superpowers requires consultation between them if there is a danger of nuclear war. The Washington-Moscow hot line (a Teletype communication link, 1963, updated 1988) has enabled the superpowers to ward off nuclear conflict. Similar hot lines have been established between Paris and Moscow and between London and Moscow. *See also* ALTERNATE NATIONAL MILITARY COMMAND CENTER (ANMCC); FAIL-SAFE; HOT LINE; NATIONAL COMMAND AUTHORITIES (NCA).

Significance   An accidental nuclear war could be touched off by terrorism or by computer-age incidents. The danger of accidental war is always present in a world in which more than 50,000 nuclear weapons exist, with 30,000 of them in the United States stored in 200 locations in 40 states. But since the dawn of the nuclear age in 1945, there have been no accidents that have led to unintended nuclear confrontations. Yet fear of such occurrences persists. Jonathan Schell, for example, believes that the "machinery of destruction is complete, poised for a 'button to be pushed' by some misguided or deranged human being, or some faulty computer chip, to send out the instruction to fire."[1] The development of solid-propellant intercontinental missiles with nuclear warheads and the proliferation of nuclear weapons among several additional nations have increased the danger of accidental nuclear war. However, with the increase in the sophistication of nuclear weapons, there has been a corresponding increase in precautionary measures.

Aggression   The first attack or act of hostility leading to a war or confrontation; a culpable offensive action by one state against another. Aggression is the use of armed forces by one nation against the territorial integrity and sovereignty of another nation. In the legal sense, aggression means the use of armed force by a government in violation of its obligation under international law or treaty. The term "aggression" has appeared in many treaties and official declarations, including the League of Nations Covenant (Article 10) and the United Nations Charter (Article 39). It refers, in a military sense, to an unprovoked attack and, in a political sense, to any manifestation of an expansive policy. International organizations have considered cases of aggression in hostilities that have occurred following the procedure of ordering a cease-fire and have considered a government to be an aggressor only if it failed to observe that order. The League of Nations found Japan to be an aggressor in Manchuria in 1933, and the United Nations found North Korea and the People's Republic of China to be aggressors in Korea in 1950 and 1951. *See also* NUCLEAR WAR; WAR.

Significance   There is no universally acceptable definition of aggression, but efforts by scholars and international organizations to establish an agreed-upon formulation are continuing. On occasions, international organizations have identified and labelled aggressive behavior of nations. The United Nations Charter does not define aggression, although the General Assembly has recognized the need for a definition acceptable to all concerned. The efforts of the United Nations have failed to produce universally acceptable criteria, due to the insistence by some member-nations to include indirect aggressive tactics, such as infiltration, subversion, economic penetration, support to insurgency, and hostile propaganda. Yet, in 1974, the General

Assembly adopted, without voting, a consensus definition of aggression: "the use of armed force by a State against the sovereignty, territorial integrity or political independence of another State, or in any other manner inconsistent with the Charter of the United Nations."[2] With or without any definition of aggression, in practice, states continue to prepare themselves to defend what they consider to be in their vital national interests. That aggression has occurred is determined by affected states or by a majority in an international organ such as the Security Council and General Assembly of the United Nations.

Air Burst   A nuclear weapon detonation above the ground. An air burst is an explosion that takes place in the atmosphere above the earth's surface. The explosion is detonated high enough to ensure that none of the fireball actually touches the ground. This prevents its effects from being dissipated by local geographical factors, such as irregular contours. An air burst could be used against any large-scale concentration of population, namely, large cities and industrial areas. A 1-megaton bomb must be exploded at least 1 kilometer above the ground to prevent contact with earth. The bombs dropped on Hiroshima and Nagasaki in Japan by the United States during World War II were air burst. An air burst is distinct from a ground burst, in which a nuclear weapon explodes on the surface. A 20-megaton ground burst excavates a crater 300 to 600 feet deep and a mile wide; an air burst doubles the area of destruction but carves no crater. *See also* GROUND BURST; HIROSHIMA; NAGASAKI.

Significance   An air burst ensures the maximum production and dissemination of radiation in the immediate areas of the detonation. Nuclear weapon explosions are usually divided into surface bursts and air bursts. Surface bursts would be used against hardened military targets, such as missile silos and command bunkers. Air bursts would be used against soft military targets, such as airfields and submarine-port facilities, and industrial targets, such as factories for building missiles or airplanes. Air bursts produce typically less dust and local fallout, but are far more effective at igniting fires. Only twice have nuclear weapons been detonated over urban areas. Hiroshima was the first city to suffer an atomic air burst, which destroyed the greater part of the city. The second bomb, dropped on Nagasaki, destroyed the innermost portion of the city. These experiences are still vivid in memories all over the world. Such an air burst may create sufficient radiation to cripple computers and other sensitive electronic devices over a wide area.

Airborne Warning and Control System (AWACS)   Aircraft equipped with sensitive electronic equipment and radar that make it possible to locate a plane in azimuth at height and length distances. AWACS surveillance and control are provided by airborne warning vehicles equipped with search and height-finding radar and communications equipment for controlling weapons. Radar is limited to line-of-sight capability and, therefore, is unable to track objects behind solid obstructions, such as mountains. AWACS coverage is also affected by the curvature of the earth, and thus provides the critical gap below the "radar horizon," which all air forces seek to exploit. Recent improvements in electronics have increased the vulnerability of bombers during flight. Fighter aircraft can be guided toward interception by ground-based radar or AWACS flying above the battlefield. AWACS of the United States includes 42 modified Boeing 707 jetliners to fly at 10 kilometers and scan the airspace both upward and downward to detect enemy aircraft and to direct intercepting fighters and surface-to-air missiles (SAM). *See also* NORTH AMERICAN AEROSPACE DEFENSE COMMAND (NORAD).

Significance   The Airborne Warning and Control System has introduced a completely new dimension in warfare. Only the United States has been able to put an effective AWACS into operation. The Soviets have recently begun to introduce a similar system, but they have lagged behind the United States in developing the look-down radar capability. An increase in the effectiveness of air defense surveillance coverage against low-flying threats has been sought by means of multiple and overlapping deployment. However, this still limits effective radar coverage at lower altitudes in the opponent's airspace, due to the basic limitations of radar. AWACS became a household word in 1985, during the Reagan administration's hotly contested sale of five of these aircraft to Saudi Arabia. The aircraft that were sold, despite Israel's opposition, do not carry the joint tactical information distribution system (a jam-resistant system for the transmission of both digital and voice information). But they possess some "nonsensitive" IFF (identification, friend or foe) capability and some encipherment gear. They do not, however, have a signal intelligence of any sort.

Air-Launched Cruise Missile (ALCM)   A cruise missile launched from an aircraft. Air-launched cruise missiles, approximately 15 feet long, could be launched from a variety of platforms: Boeing 747s, Galaxy Transports (C5A), LTV Aerospace, A-7, Navy S-3As and P3Cs, and from short-range attack missile rotary tracks and pylons of B-52 bombers. The ALCM is also compatible with short-range attack missile (SRAM) avionics and ground equipment. Range varies as a function of payload, speed, and full volume; hence cruise missiles can be made to vary from 600 km to 2,000 km. The new ALCM comes in various lengths; some are as short as 6 feet. The United States deploys one type of ALCM, which is delivered by B-52G, B-52H, and B-1B bombers. It delivers a yield of 200 kilotons for its one warhead and flies about 100 feet above the ground. The Soviet Union has two types of ALCMs: the AS-5 Kelt, which is deployed on the TU-16 Badger bomber, and the AS-15, which is not yet ready to be deployed. *See also* CRUISE MISSILE; GROUND-LAUNCHED CRUISE MISSILE; SEA-LAUNCHED CRUISE MISSILE (SLCM); TOMAHAWK CRUISE MISSILE.

Significance   Air-launched cruise missiles are powered by jet engines and transported by airplane. They are guided by a self-contained internal guidance, which is supplemented by a sensor system called TERCOM (terrain contour matching), a device that can steer cruise missiles to their destinations. Their sophisticated terrain-mapping technology offers 100 percent kill probability against military targets constructed to withstand nuclear attack. According to experts the superior U.S. bomber force is equipped with air-launched cruise missiles that can, from well outside Soviet air defenses, strike their targets. In the United States all three military services are deploying cruise missiles. In the air force, missiles are carried on bombers or other aircraft. This ALCM—"Alkem"—can extend the useful life of the B-52s and FB-111 considerably, since its long range allows them to stand off around the Soviet periphery rather than penetrating the Soviet air-defense system.

Air-to-Air Missile (AAM)   A missile launched from an airborne carrier at a target above the surface. Air-to-air missiles are generally defensive weapons, launched against attacking missiles or aircraft. Behind the control of these modern air defenses lie high-speed, high-capacity electronic computers. These missiles are used during dogfights or fired at a distinct aircraft. Air-to-air guided missiles are of two types—short-range and long-range. The French air-to-air missile known as Magic represents a short-range missile; the U.S. Phoenix, a long-range missile. A Magic missile seeks its target and locates it without being dependent on a radar or any other attacking system. The guidance in Phoenix is based on the radar homing system—it attracts the missile to its targets and the system takes over to intercept the enemy aircraft. The U.S. fighter interceptor aircraft—intended to engage hostile planes entering U.S. airspace—have available to them short-range rockets: air-to-air missiles with nuclear warheads that have several missiles of several miles range. Currently, 2,000 of these are on hand. *See also* GUIDED MISSILE; SURFACE-TO-AIR MISSILE (SAM).

Significance   The air-to-air missile provides the effectiveness of a modern air-defense system. This effectiveness depends largely on its network of ground-based radars. The main improvement in the effectiveness of air defense has been due to the post–World War II development of guided missiles, both surface-to-air and air-to-air. Such technological innovations, based on U.S. capabilities in sensor technology and in data processing, have offset U.S. numerical deficiencies with the Soviet Union in air-to-air combat capabilities. The U.S. tactical air forces hold a distinct advantage because of the longer range of its air-to-air missiles, coupled with longer range radar and the ability of shorter-range, heat-seeking, infrared-guided missiles to home in on opposing aircraft from the sides, or even from the front. U.S. technological superiority has made a major contribution not only to its own defense but also to its European allies' defense.

Air-to-Surface Missile (ASM)   A missile launched from an airborne carrier against a target on the earth's surface. Air-to-surface missiles are generally offensive weapons, fired from an attacking aircraft. There are many air-to-surface missiles, ranging from freefalling aerial bombs to air-launched ballistic missiles (ALBM). Modern bomber aircraft carry ASMs, some with ranges of hundreds of miles. The United States deploys one type of ASM capable of delivering a nuclear warhead: The short-range attack missile (SRAM). SRAMs are currently deployed on B-52, FB-111, and B-1B bombers, and, because they are launched when the aircraft is relatively close to the target, they are highly maneuverable. The SRAM has a range of 160–220 km in high altitude and 50–80 km in low altitude, and delivers one warhead with a yield of 170–200 kilotons. The Soviet Union uses five types of air-to-surface missiles: A-2 Kipper, deployed on the Tu-16 Badger bomber; AS-3 Kangaroo, on the Tu-95 Bear bomber; the AS-4 Kitchen, which serves as a strategic nuclear weapon; the AS-6 Kingfish, which can travel up to three times the speed of sound; and the AS-7 Kerry, which is deployed on a tactical airplane. *See also* AIR-TO-AIR MISSILE (AAM).

Significance   The air-to-surface missile was an earlier form of guided missile. Bombs fired from an aircraft and the use of remote control appeared in World War II. The use of air-to-surface missiles of sufficient range enables the launching aircraft to remain out of reach of an opponent's air-defense system, and attack the surface target with minimal risk. An ASM can fly almost any desired distance after being launched. The major limitation of such missiles is the size of the aircraft required to carry long-range ASM. Some of these aircraft, however, can fly at high speed over a distance of a thousand miles— far beyond the usual combat zone.

Alternate National Military Command Center (ANMCC) The alternate to the National Military Command Center (NMCC), to be used in time of nuclear war. The Alternate National Military Command Center is a hardened special facility at Mount Weather, Virginia, 50 miles northwest of Washington, D.C. Several other ANMCCs exist in the country, one of which lies beneath a mountain at Fort Ritchie, Maryland, 75 miles from Washington, D.C. Another is located deep in a mountain at Raven Rock, Pennsylvania. Eight miles south is Camp David (70 miles from Washington, D.C., at Catoctin Mountain in Maryland), which serves as a presidential retreat and has an underground emergency operations center. This center is also a nuclear war command post and is linked by a buried cable to the command post in Raven Rock. During a nuclear war the national command and control could be spread across these facilities; additional mountain hideouts throughout the country could receive various government officials. These alternate military centers would serve as backups to the Department of Defense (DOD) headquarters and the White House, both of which may be first targets in a nuclear war. The National Emergency Airborne Command Post (NEACP) must therefore provide air transport to high government officials, including the president and subordinates. Its fleet includes four "doomsday" jumbo jets, which are windowless planes that can fly above designated locations or above the atmosphere. One of the NEACP aircraft could transport the president if he decided to evacuate. The vice president, as the first to succeed the president, could be transported by another plane to an ANMCC or to one of the mountain hideouts. *See also* NATIONAL EMERGENCY AIRBORNE COMMAND POST (NEACP); NATIONAL MILITARY COMMAND CENTER (NMCC); NATIONAL MILITARY COMMAND SYSTEM (NMCS).

Significance   The Alternate National Military Command Center is considered invulnerable to a nuclear attack. Since any meaningful nuclear attack would doubtless include as targets all airports and command facilities, the ANMCC would also be slated for destruction. Many experts maintain that the continuity of U.S. leadership and the availability of the doomsday aircraft cannot be unconditionally guaranteed. Obviously, some government officials need to be protected in underground and above-ground shelters if they are to be safe from direct or nearby hits. The main problem is that the command centers, despite their hardness, are still vulnerable to the accurate nuclear weapons in the Soviet arsenal or by way of direct attacks on the communications connecting the command centers.

Antarctic Treaty (1959)   An international agreement to demilitarize Antarctica. The Antarctic Treaty prohibits militarization of the Antarctic continent and prevents deployment of any nuclear weapons there. The major provisions of the Antarctic Treaty are: (1) the prohibition of all military activity on the Antarctic continent; (2) the prohibition of nuclear explosions or the dumping of radioactive wastes on the continent; (3) the right to inspect each other's installations to safeguard against violations; (4) the nonrecognition of existing territorial claims; and (5) the responsibility to settle disputes peacefully and to cooperate in scientific investigations of the Antarctic continent. The 12 original signatories—Argentina, Australia, Belgium, Britain, Chile, France, Japan, New Zealand, Norway, South Africa, the Soviet Union, and the United States—agreed to conduct research in Antarctica. The treaty does not forbid the use of military personnel or equipment for scientific purposes in Antarctica. On-site inspections were agreed to, and some have already taken place. With the ratification of the Antarctic Treaty, the Soviet Union accepted the procedure of on-site inspections of its scientific installations in the southern polar region. *See also* TREATY OF RAROTONGA; TREATY OF TLATELOLCO.

Significance   The Antarctic Treaty was a major breakthrough in which the United States, the Soviet Union, and other signatories consented to a ban on the stationing of nuclear weapons in Antarctica. This treaty was the first arms-limitation agreement in the post–World War II era. The implementation of the Antarctic Treaty led to further agreements: (1) prohibition of the stationing of nuclear weapons in outer space—the Outer Space Treaty (1967); (2) in Latin America—the Treaty of Tlatelolco (1967); and (3) on the seabed—the Sea Bed Treaty (1971). Antarctica is the one remaining unexploited continent whose resources are largely unknown and where there are immense problems of mineral extraction through thick ice. This 1959 treaty prohibits military activities in Antarctica and halts the recognition of further territorial claims. The Soviet Union has the majority of research stations in Antarctica and, with new processes of mineral extraction through thousands of meters of ice, promises to make the continent of "hidden treasure" an area of competitive exploitation. Before that happens it is essential for international institutions to develop rules that will make Antarctic resources available to all nations, not just to the powerful few.

Antiballistic Missile (ABM) Treaty (1972)   An agreement initially allowing each superpower to deploy two weapons systems designed to defend against attacking nuclear missiles. The Antiballistic Missile (ABM) Treaty of 1972 limited each country to two missile sites with only 100 missiles for each site. The ABM Protocol of 1974 reduced the number of permitted defensive systems to one. In 1972, the Strategic Arms Limitation Talks (SALT I) agreement was signed at the Moscow summit meeting between U.S. President Richard M. Nixon and Soviet General Secretary Leonid Brezhnev. The SALT II guidelines were worked out at the Nixon-Brezhnev summit in Washington in 1973, and the agreement was signed in 1979. SALT I consisted of four separate agreements, two of major import and two of minor consequence. Under the first agreement, both sides agreed to an arms freeze, promising not to increase the number of nuclear missile launchers for a five-year period. The second agreement placed limits on the number of ABMs either side could deploy. The third agreement was to prevent the deployment of a comprehensive ballistic missile defense (BMD) network. Under the fourth agreement the Washington-Moscow hot line was upgraded. *See also* BALLISTIC MISSILE DEFENSE (BMD) SYSTEM; STRATEGIC ARMS LIMITATION TALKS (SALT I); STRATEGIC ARMS LIMITATION TALKS (SALT II).

Significance   The ABM agreement in SALT I was a formal treaty ratified in accordance with constitutional procedures in the United States and the Soviet Union. SALT I was of unlimited duration. Both SALT I and SALT II were products of a period of détente (a situation of lessened tension between nations) between the superpowers. The ABM treaty is a permanent part of the Strategic Arms Limitation Talks (SALT I), and is a major constraint on the Soviets' building of a ballistic missile defense (BMD). This was, from the U.S. point of view, the treaty's purpose, and it saves the United States from having to invest heavily in weapons to penetrate a Soviet defense system. The United States, however, accused the Soviets of erecting a large radar at Krasnoyarsk, in violation of the ABM treaty. The Reagan administration announced, in 1985, that it was reinterpreting the ABM treaty in a fashion that would, in effect, permit almost any kind of Strategic Defense Initiative (SDI) testing and the deployment of BMD weapons. This action relates to current controversy over whether the ABM treaty is violated by the SDI program, which relates to controversy over applying a loose or a strict interpretation. The Reagan administration favored the former interpretation.

Antisatellite (ASAT) Weapon   A variety of conventional, nuclear, electronic and laser weaponry intended for the destruction of hostile military satellites. Antisatellite (ASAT) weapons were developed because of the militarization of space, which began in 1957 with the launching of the unmanned Sputnik I satellite by the Soviet Union. The first "test" of an ASAT weapon was an accident in 1962, when the United States Air Force and the Atomic Energy Commission carried out a high-altitude nuclear test. The explosion damaged many orbiting satellites. In 1963, President John F. Kennedy authorized an "active anti-satellite capability," and between 1964 and 1967 the United States launched a number of antiballistic missiles as ASAT weapons. Negotiations to ban ASAT weapons were suspended in 1979; the United States has been reluctant to negotiate a treaty with the Soviet Union, claiming that a ban of ASAT weapons would be virtually impossible to verify. Antisatellite weapons are often referred to as "killer satellites." *See also* STRATEGIC DEFENSE INITIATIVE (SDI).

Significance   A ban or limit on antisatellite systems could enhance U.S. and Soviet confidence that they would receive adequate warning of attack and be able to retaliate. The superpowers started new discussions to limit the militarization of space in 1978, but the Soviet invasion of Afghanistan, in 1979, halted progress on an ASAT treaty. President Ronald Reagan viewed that such a treaty would leave the United States inferior in the arms race, and he also felt that the Soviets would cheat. An ASAT treaty would save billions of dollars as well as declare space off-limits to warfare. The Soviet Union has urged a resumption of the ASAT talks, but the United States has been reluctant because it claims a ban on antisatellite weapons would be difficult to verify. The U.S. ASAT weapon is designed to redress strategic asymmetry and deny unilateral Soviet control of space should a conflict occur.

Antisubmarine Warfare (ASW)   The detection, tracking and destruction of enemy submarines. ASW requires three distinct steps: detection and confirmation that an enemy submarine is patrolling; localization—fixing the sub's position; and destruction. Nuclear depth charges and nuclear-armed antisubmarine missiles are among the weapons used to destroy submarines once they have been localized. For years there have been predictions of a breakthrough in antisub-

marine warfare that would make submarines visible and thus susceptible to attack. But it has not happened. The high value of the submarine as a target provides enormous incentive to the Soviets to invest
heavily in its ability to detect U.S. submarines. Soviet weaponry
research and development includes improvements in satellite detection systems and sonar listening devices, but it is not yet at a stage that
would make U.S. ASW vulnerable to attack. The Soviet Union has
proposed, in the Strategic Arms Reduction Talks (START), that
the United States and Soviet Union establish—for missile-carrying
submarines—zones in which antisubmarine activities by the other side
would be banned. *See also* STRATEGIC ARMS REDUCTION TALKS (START).

Significance   Antisubmarine warfare is extremely difficult to conduct effectively. The vastness of the body of waters and the inaccuracy
of detecting objects that lie thousands of feet under water combine to
make the destruction of submarines most difficult. The U.S. ASW
program is much more advanced than the Soviets', but it is still not
completely dependable. A major drawback of ASW is that a nation
must destroy all of the enemy's subs simultaneously, because a single
submarine could launch an effective nuclear retaliation. Yet the basic
strength of the U.S. submarine force is its invulnerability to preemptive attack by the Soviets. At any given time, nearly half of the missile-
carrying submarines of the United States are in locations from which
they could launch their missiles against the Soviet Union. The Soviets'
antisubmarine warfare cannot now locate and destroy U.S. submarines. Thus their interest in the establishment of ASW-free zones is
understandable. It is clearly in their interest to constrain any U.S.
ASW activity in the vast reaches of the ocean depths.

Arms Control   International negotiations or agreements that govern the numbers, types, characteristics, deployment, and use of armed
forces and weapons. Arms control measures seek to reduce the danger of both conventional and nuclear war. Since the end of World War
II a number of multinational arms control agreements have been
reached. These include: a treaty demilitarizing the Antarctic (1959);
the Limited Test Ban Treaty (1963); the Outer Space Treaty (1967);
and the Sea-Bed Treaty (1972). The United States and the Soviet
Union have entered into several bilateral agreements on subjects
ranging from the establishment of a direct communication link (the
Hot Line Agreements, 1963) to limitation on ABM systems (1972) and
on the Intermediate-range Nuclear Forces (INF) Treaty (1987). Challenges for arms control efforts include the reduction of forces in
Europe; the mutual and balanced force reduction talks in Vienna;

dealing with the imbalance of conventional military power in Europe in favor of the Warsaw Pact; and strategic arms reduction talks dealing with the principal elements of the U.S.-Soviet intercontinental nuclear relationship. *See also* DISARMAMENT; NUCLEAR ARMS CONTROL; NUCLEAR DISARMAMENT; UNITED STATES ARMS CONTROL AND DISARMAMENT AGENCY (USACDA).

Significance   Arms control and disarmament are terms often used interchangeably, but a vast difference exists between them. Both efforts, however, seek to reduce tension and the likelihood of war. Even though arms can be used for creating bargaining positions in negotiations, they can also contribute to international tensions, thereby reducing the possibilities of settling critical issues among nations. Arms control can be divided into two categories: arms reduction and arms limitation. Arms reduction, according to Couloumbis and Wolfe, "implies a mutually agreed-upon set of arms levels for the nation-states involved."[3] Arms limitation, on the other hand, "embraces the wide variety of international accords designed to limit the impact of war and to prevent its accidental outbreak."[4] Any arms control short of disarmament will permit the continuation of some military activities while eliminating others. Even in an arms-control environment, both sides will be concerned with defense and deterrence and will seek other methods and weapons to perform functions formerly dealt with by forbidden weapons and methods. U.S.-Soviet arms control negotiations have created an upswing in interest following the conclusion of the INF treaty in 1987. Whether this renewed interest will be permanent or transitory will depend on the success of current negotiations on strategic arms control.

Atomic Weapon   A weapon whose explosive power is derived from atomic fission, the splitting of large, unstable atoms. An atomic weapon results from the rapid fissioning of a combination of selected materials, thereby inducing an explosion caused by the energy released by reactions involving atomic nuclei. These weapons include missiles, rockets, bombs, artillery shells, and land mines. Atomic weapons can be used tactically on the battlefield or strategically to destroy entire cities. They were the first nuclear weapons (a collective term for both atomic [fission] and hydrogen [fusion] bombs) built and were dropped on Hiroshima and Nagasaki, Japan, in 1945. J. Robert Oppenheimer was the scientific director of the Manhattan Project, which built the atomic bomb. The theory was proposed in 1938 from work done by German scientists, and was proved feasible in the laboratory by Enrico Fermi, who produced the first chain reaction splitting of atoms in 1942. The main difficulty in building the first atomic bombs was to produce enough explosive radioactive material, either enriched uranium (U-235 Hiroshima bomb) or an artificial element, called plutonium (Nagasaki bomb). The first test of this bomb at Alamogordo, New Mexico, had a force of 19,000 tons of TNT, or 19 kilotons. *See also* HIROSHIMA; MANHATTAN PROJECT; NAGASAKI; TRINITY TEST.

Significance   The term *atomic weapon* is loosely applied to all nuclear weapons, including those whose power is based on fission and fusion. Atomic weapons were first developed by the United States in the mid-1940s. Many ask of the bomb's first use in warfare: Was it necessary? The atomic bomb was built out of fear that the Germans would develop one first and use it against the United States. It turned out that Hitler's Germany made horrendous mistakes and was nowhere close to building a bomb. Some critics maintain that if the United States had been at war with Japan alone there never would have been such an expensive secret crash program to develop an atomic bomb. But once the money had been invested in the program, it seemed exigent to use it. In the light of what happened to Dresden and certain other German cities, it seems plausible that the United States would have used the bomb against Nazi Germany if it had been developed sooner.

Atoms for Peace Program   A U.S. cooperative effort to seek peaceful development and use of atomic energy. The Atoms for Peace Program was outlined by President Dwight D. Eisenhower in his U.N. speech, "Atoms for Peace," in December 1953. The program called for technical assistance, including the sale of U-235 for peaceful development programs. By 1955, 25 agreements had been negotiated between other countries and the United States. Under the Atoms for Peace Program the United States has given small reactors and fissionable materials to more than 50 countries to promote the application of atomic (nuclear) technology. An international commission urged by Eisenhower was established in 1957: the International Atomic Energy Agency (IAEA). The Atoms for Peace Program was followed by the Open Skies Proposal, which focused on reducing the fear of surprise attack by exchanging blueprints of military installations and allowing each side to carry on aerial surveillance. After India's nuclear test of 1974, a Nuclear Suppliers Group was set up to establish guidelines for transfer of nuclear technology. *See also* INTERNATIONAL ATOMIC ENERGY AGENCY (IAEA); NUCLEAR ENERGY; NUCLEAR SUPPLIERS GROUP.

Significance   The Atoms for Peace Program was the first offer of nuclear technology as a tool of U.S. policy, a practice that has continued to this day. The United States was attempting to change its world image as the nuclear bully, preoccupied with pride in developing and dropping the first atomic bombs. The United States sought to divest itself of this stigma with which it had been tagged. Abetted by Soviet publicity, the world had come to view the United States as the Gulliver interested in destroying the world. Ostensibly, one of the purposes of the program was for the United States to establish itself in the minds of the people of the world as the leader in development of the peaceful atom. The program was indeed rich with promises of peace, international prosperity and goodwill from the standpoint of shared development of atomic energy. The Atoms for Peace Program was presented by the United States as a step in the direction of encouraging general disarmament.

B

Balance of Power   Peace and security secured through an equilibrium of power among rival nations or group of nations. A balance
of power is not easily measurable. It can be translated many ways.
At various times, it has been used to refer to: (1) a condition of equality
or inequality among states in an international system; (2) a particular historical situation; and (3) an analytical device for understanding
the nature of international alliances. The balance of power has no
central organization to guide it, and there may be multiple and bipolar
balances. A multiple balance of power existed from the seventeenth
to the mid-twentieth century, dominated by shifting combinations of
great powers. After World War II a bipolar balance of power emerged,
dominated by the United States and the Soviet Union. In a balance of
power, participating nations form alliances with one acting as a domi-
nating power. *See also* BALANCE OF TERROR.

Significance   A balance of power is an expression with many political meanings. In the global context it is useful as an analytical concept
for assessing the overall power capabilities of states and coalitions.
The basic pattern of the balance of power is that of direct opposition
between the United States and the Soviet Union. The United States
tries to impose its will upon the Soviet Union and vice versa. To
withstand one another the antagonists must wield equal power. An
increase in the power of one requires a corresponding increase in the
power of the other. Thus the two nations, with a view to defending
their sovereignty, must maintain a balance of power. They can pursue
this balance either by increasing their own power or by forming alliances with other nations. While the United States dominates the
North Atlantic Treaty Organization (NATO) alliance, the Soviet
Union controls the Warsaw Pact. So long as near-equilibrium exists,
neither side is likely to launch an attack upon the other.

Balance of Terror   The current equilibrium of power based on the ability of both superpowers to wreak havoc on the other. The limiting nature of the balance of terror stems from a common fear of annihilation in a nuclear confrontation. The term was coined by Canadian Prime Minister Lester Pearson, in 1955, on the tenth anniversary of the United Nations Charter. He said, "The balance of terror has replaced the balance of power." It rests on mutually assured destruction (MAD), should one attack the other. The concept is based on the mutual understanding that each superpower can absorb a nuclear strike and retaliate in kind. Balance of terror is a state of mutual deterrence between the superpowers based on their ability to deliver a devastating blow to the other. The superpowers have been restrained in their policies and actions by this threat of total destruction. *See also* BALANCE OF POWER.

Significance   The balance of terror can keep peace and has kept the peace between the superpowers for over 40 years. The balance of terror describes, negatively, the post–World War II balance of power between the superpowers. Although it has prevented war between the superpowers, it has had little effect in preventing war among the lesser powers. The balance of terror is based on the assumption that if both superpowers can maintain enough "invulnerable" nuclear weapons in bombers, hardened silos, and submarines, then each can inflict "unacceptable" damage on the other, regardless of who strikes first. Critics maintain that the future of humankind should not be based on assumptions of rationality rooted in instincts of self-preservation. This concept is more readily understood through an Old West metaphor: "The balance of terror was never very stable between two gunslingers: whoever was the quickest draw shot first, killed the other, and walked into the sunset unscathed."[5] Even if a balance of terror works perfectly for the superpowers, it does not eliminate the risk of conflict. It just moves the conflict to a lower level.

Ballistic Missile Defense (BMD) System   A weapons system designed to destroy an enemy's offensive strategic ballistic missiles or their warheads before they reach their targets. Ballistic missile defense (BMD) first uses radar to identify and track attacking nuclear weapons, then launches defensive missiles to intercept and destroy them. BMD is a generic term that refers to the measures a nation might take to disable enemy missile warheads. A ballistic missile is propelled by booster rockets into the upper atmosphere, and its name is derived from the ballistic trajectory it follows. Ballistic missiles are distinct from cruise missiles, which are slow, low-flying missiles that resemble pilotless aircraft. Ballistic missiles are extremely versatile, and thousands of them are currently deployed, based in submarines and underground missile silos. They can carry large or small nuclear warheads. The U.S. radar system detects attacking nuclear missiles and notifies authorities if any enemy attack is underway so they can take appropriate action. *See also* ANTIBALLISTIC MISSILE TREATY; CRUISE MISSILE; INTERCONTINENTAL BALLISTIC MISSILE (ICBM).

Significance   Ballistic missile defense has taken two basic forms to date. The first is an antiballistic missile and, as the name suggests, a missile launched to intercept an offensive warhead in flight. The other form comprises laser- and particle-beam defenses, which are much in public discussion since President Ronald Reagan's Strategic Defense Initiative (SDI), or "Star Wars," speech of March 23, 1983. Although the idea of developing a general defense against missile attacks suffered with the signing of the 1972 Antiballistic Missile Treaty, in the 1980s ballistic missile defense supporters resumed promoting high-tech defenses that use space-based lasers and charged-particle beams. Proponents of the system argue that it is the only sensible assurance one can have in a world of nuclear uncertainty. Critics note, conversely, that the alleged factors may lull people into believing that a nuclear war can be won and the nuclear devastation of the United States prevented.

Baruch Plan   A U.S. proposal based on the recommendation of a special Board of Consultants (Acheson-Lilienthal Report) that would have provided for atomic control and disarmament. Named after Bernard M. Baruch, the plan called for an international authority to own and manage all atomic materials. When the newly created Atomic Energy Commission (AEC) of the United Nations met on June 14, 1946, the U.S. proposals were presented to it by Baruch, a financier, philanthropist, and idealist. The first phase of the Baruch Plan would have established an International Atomic Development Authority to exercise a monopoly over the ownership, production and research for the peaceful use of all atomic materials. This authority would have prohibited the manufacturing of any type of atomic weapon, inspected all nuclear activities, and imposed penalties on transgressors by veto-free Security Council decisions. Denouncing the Baruch Plan, the Soviet Union proposed that the United States destroy its own atomic weapons first, and then permit inspection. *See also* ATOMS FOR PEACE PROGRAM; INTERNATIONAL ATOMIC ENERGY AGENCY (IAEA).

Significance   The Baruch Plan was perceived by the Soviet Union as restricting its decision-making influence in the United Nations.

Rejecting the proposal, the Soviet Union countered with its own proposal to abolish all existing atomic arsenals before any discussion of an
international authority to control atomic energy. The United States
turned down the Soviet proposal because it would have limited ability
of the United States to maintain its monopoly on nuclear weapons.
However, the Baruch Plan remained the U.S. official policy until
1949, when the Soviet Union developed its own atomic bombs. At the
time the Baruch Plan was presented the United States held a monopoly over atomic weapons. Thus the Baruch Plan would have held the
Soviet Union to a second-rank status as a nonnuclear nation. The
Soviet Union was already developing its own nuclear capability that
culminated in their first test of an atomic weapon in 1949. The United
States, bargaining from strength, had underestimated the speed of
Soviet progress. When the Baruch Plan wasn't adopted, the United
States sought to prevent the spread of nuclear technology. In 1953,
President Dwight D. Eisenhower launched his Atoms for Peace Pro-
gram, which, when implemented by the creation of the International
Atomic Energy Agency helped control the spread of nuclear weapons
by making fissionable materials available under international control.

B1, B-1B, B-52 Bombers   U.S. strategic, long-range bombers. The
B-1 bomber was cancelled in 1977 by President Jimmy Carter because
of its high cost, but was reintroduced as the B-1B by President Ronald
Reagan in 1981. It is new, destined to replace the B-52, which was first
deployed in 1954. The newest models of B-52 appeared in 1962. All
models have been enormously upgraded in capacity since then, both
mechanically and electronically. The arrival of missiles had brought
the United States three kinds of strategic offensive forces—intercontinental ballistic missiles (ICBMs), submarine-launched ballistic missiles
(SLBMs) and strategic bombers. The bombers are now mostly B-52s.
The older and smaller B-47s were being phased out; later a small but
fast advanced bomber, the FB-111, was added in modest numbers.
Another, the SRAM (short-range attack missile), an air-to-surface missile, was added alongside the B-52 and FB-111 bombers. Each aircraft
carries several short-range attack missiles (SRAMs) in addition to its
"gravity bombs." By firing SRAMs, each aircraft can destroy widely
scattered targets without having to fly over heavily defended targets.
By the 1990s the B-1B will be used as a vital cruise missile launcher. *See
also* STEALTH BOMBER; STRATEGIC AIR COMMAND (SAC).

Significance   The B-52 bomber, the mainstay of the Strategic Air
Command (SAC) for a quarter century, is becoming obsolete. Although B-52s were adequate against a similar system erected by the

Soviets in Vietnam, there is a question about their ability to penetrate Soviet defenses. With these concerns and controversies in mind, President Ronald Reagan considered the matter of the bomber force as part of offensive force modernization. There were three options: (1) build the B-1B, instead of continuing research on the ATB (advanced technology bomber) and converting the B-52 to carry an ALCM (air-launched cruise missile); (2) build the B-1B but discontinue or cut back research on the ATB; and (3) to build the B-1B, continue air-launched cruise missile (ALCM) production, and maintain a serious research effort on ATB or Stealth technology. As of 1988, the third option is being implemented.

C

Central Intelligence Agency (CIA)   The U.S. government agency that collects, researches, and analyzes foreign intelligence and carries out clandestine operations abroad. The Central Intelligence Agency advises the president and the National Security Council (NSC) in matters concerning intelligence activities of the departments and agencies of the U.S. government as they relate to national security. The agency submits recommendations to the NSC for the coordination of intelligence activities of the departments and agencies that relate to national security; collects and processes counterintelligence and foreign intelligence, and conducts foreign counterintelligence activities. It also—without assuming or performing any domestic security functions—undertakes counterintelligence activities within the United States in coordination with the Federal Bureau of Investigation (FBI) as required by procedures agreed upon by the director of the CIA and the U.S. Attorney General. Established in 1947 under the National Security Act, the CIA conducts special activities approved by the president and, as may be directed, by the NSC. *See also* DEFENSE INTELLIGENCE AGENCY (DIA); NATIONAL SECURITY AGENCY (NSA); NATIONAL SECURITY COUNCIL (NSC).

Significance   The Central Intelligence Agency is responsible for assembling a comprehensive worldwide picture and assessment of intelligence relating to U.S. security. Overall intelligence goals of the U.S. government are set by the president, and their implementation requires specification by the NSC. The president is required to approve all CIA clandestine operations. The CIA enjoys freedom from congressional budgetary controls and expenditure audits; its budget is secret. The CIA has been accused by its critics of plotting against foreign governments and participating in various assassination attempts of foreign leaders. It does not have police, subpoena, or law enforcement powers, but does conduct clandestine activities, using its own and foreign agents.

Before the creation of the CIA, U.S. efforts to gather general intelligence and conduct espionage and secret operations were conducted by the Office of Strategic Services (OSS). The National Security Act of 1947 rechristened the OSS as the Central Intelligence Agency, and assigned to it, on a permanent basis, the responsibilities of the previous office.

Central System   Offensive nuclear weapons considered fundamental to a nation's military force. The Central System of the United States currently consists of intercontinental ballistic missiles (ICBMs), submarine-launched ballistic missiles (SLBMs), and strategic bombers. The United States regards its nuclear missiles based in underground silos, on submarines, and on heavy bombers as its Central System. The 1972 Strategic Arms Limitation Talks (SALT I) limited only the number of ICBMs and SLBMs on each side. In 1974 President Gerald Ford and General Secretary Leonid Brezhnev announced the following limitation on the Central System of the two superpowers: an aggregate ceiling of 2,400 on ICBM launchers, SLBM launchers, heavy bombers, and air-to-air missiles with a range in excess of 600 kilometers and a limit of 1,320 on launchers of ICBMs and SLBMs equipped with MIRVs (multiple independently targetable reentry vehicle). The Vladivostok agreement and the SALT II accord that followed placed quantitative and qualitative limitations on the two types of Central Systems (both superpowers maintain different types of ground-, submarine-, and air-launched weapons systems). *See also* INTERCONTINEN-TAL BALLISTIC MISSILE (ICBM); STRATEGIC BOMBER; SUBMARINE-LAUNCHED BALLISTIC MISSILE (SLBM).

Significance   The Central System is usually thought of as a highly destructive variety of nuclear missiles that can cover large distances and strike deep into enemy territory. It is designed to conduct an all-out nuclear war between the superpowers. A central nuclear war would involve massive, devastating nuclear attacks on the United States and the Soviet Union, whereas a limited nuclear confrontation is restricted to specific regions of the world, such as the Middle East or Africa. Despite SALT I, Vladivostok, and SALT II agreements, which mean to limit strategic weapons, the arms race continues. Sophisticated weaponry is being added to the superpowers' arsenals. The United States has taken advantage of its technological superiority to compensate for the Warsaw Pact's superiority in numbers of men and arms. Given the continual refinements of missile technology, this pattern is likely to continue.

Chemical and Biological Weapons (CBWs)   Armaments, machineries, and equipment involving the employment of lethal and incapacitating munitions/agents. Chemical weapons were used on a large scale in World War I—about 125,000 metric tons. Casualties totaled 1,300,000, 100,000 of which were deaths. Since then scientific and technological advances have increased the destructive potential of chemical agents. Principal types are: (1) nerve agents—colorless, odorless, and tasteless—which poison the nerve system, disrupt vital functions, and kill quickly; (2) blister agents—oily liquids that burn the skin and have general toxic effects; (3) choking agents that irritate the lungs; and (4) psychochemicals that cause temporary mental disturbances and demoralize victims. Recent developments include binary weapons, created from the formation of nonlethal constituents. The Soviet Union, which has been accused of using binary weapons in Afghanistan, announced at the Paris Conference on Chemical Weapons, in January 1989, that it will destroy its stockpile of chemical weapons. The conference, convened at the initiative of the United States, and attended by the representatives of 145 nations, condemned the use of chemical weapons in war and called for an accelerated effort to ban the production and possession of chemical arms. The Geneva Protocol of 1925 bans the use but not the production and stockpiling of chemical weapons. *See also* NUCLEAR WEAPON.

Significance   Chemical and biological weapons are potentially as harmful as nuclear arms since all three are weapons of mass destruction. Tactical use of chemical and biological weapons is "difficult because of their indiscriminate and nonspecific effects. Strategic use of CBW may be easier because of their low cost, CBW agents may be useful as weapons of mass destruction when applied to populated areas."[6] International concern has been directed toward the need to prohibit these weapons. This goal is being pursued by the Conference on Disarmament through a formally organized Working Group. Concurrently, the superpowers are conducting discussions on CBWs; the major stumbling block is the question of conclusive verification of treaty violations. The United States played a leading role in the 1989 Paris Conference on Chemical Weapons, which failed to establish tighter control on technology and material for chemical weapons and sanctions against nations that use them. It was also unsuccessful to condemn, specifically, Iraq or other nations, such as Libya and Syria, that have acquired chemical weapons capability. Third World diplomats at the Paris conference challenged the assertion by the United States that it is entitled to use chemical weapons in retaliation against a chemical attack. The final declaration of the meeting, however, protected Washington's position.

Chemical Laser Weapon (CLW)   A theoretical weapon designed as part of a high-technology system to defend against attacking nuclear missiles. By generating extremely powerful laser beams, the weapon would burn a hole in the surface of attacking missiles and deactivate the sensitive electronic equipment responsible for guiding them to their targets. Laser beams travel at the speed of light, and retain their intensity over thousands of miles of space. CLWs would thus function like super concentrated spotlights: they would focus enormous energy on targets in order to destroy them. The United States is now engaged in research on laser weapons under the Strategic Defense Initiative (SDI). Laser is an acronym for Light Amplification by Stimulated Emission of Radiation. Lasers may be of different types operating at different frequencies, each of which has its advantages and disadvantages: chemical X-ray, free electron, and excimer (ultraviolet). *See also* STRATEGIC DEFENSE INITIATIVE (SDI).

Significance   Laser beams travel at the speed of light (300,000 km/sec) much faster than the 7km/sec of an intercontinental ballistic missile; lasers offer the potential for the very rapid interception of targets. The fast advancement in laser technology over the past two decades has led to the idea of incorporating lasers into defensive systems. Although the Reagan administration emphasized that the SDI program involves nonnuclear weapons, it also acknowledged that research and development for a nuclear pumped X-ray laser is part of the program. Although this system is enormously sophisticated, critics say there are formidable problems that may prove it unworkable. These include, for example, the fact that technologies are unproven, that proposals involve putting weapons into space, that there is the potential for a new arms race in space, and that the new weapons may not work.

Civil Defense   The protection of civilians against the ravages of war, including nuclear war. Civil defense in the United States is the primary responsibility of the Federal Emergency Management Agency (FEMA), which advises the president in times of war and other emergencies. The FEMA has designated many structures as fallout shelters for protection against radioactivity. Civil defense includes all nonmilitary actions that can be taken to reduce harm from enemy military actions. The U.S. civil defense programs, which were started during World War II with coastal blackouts meant to reduce the risk of night bombing, are few, compared to the Soviet Union's program, which seeks to protect 95 percent of its population. Experts believe that well over 50 percent of the unprepared U.S. population would be killed in a major nuclear attack. *See also* FEDERAL EMERGENCY MANAGEMENT AGENCY (FEMA).

Significance   Civil defense is not taken as seriously by U.S. citizens as by the Soviets and Europeans, probably because the United States has not experienced a major war at home, except the Civil War (1861-1865). Many Americans believe that civil defense planning promotes a false sense of security. Military planners also differ over its usefulness in a nuclear war. Supporters of civil defense programs believe a major shelter program would help save millions of civilian lives and permit the mobilization of the population for a second line of defense. They also maintain that civil defense can contribute to crisis management by reducing fear. Opponents argue that because nuclear war is not survivable, civil defense preparedness is futile. They also claim that in a nuclear war civil defense cannot guarantee fewer deaths and casualties.

Cold War   A high level of tension between Western nations and Communist countries, in which diplomatic maneuvering, hostile propaganda, economic sanctions, and military buildups are used as weapons. The Cold War period has been characterized by psychological warfare and a major arms race with much tough talk between the superpowers. The Cold War has been caused by a number of developments: ideological estrangement that created suspicions between Washington and Moscow, conflict between capitalism and communism, and Western apprehension of Soviet expansionism. The Soviet Union's military and political role in East Central Europe further contributed to hostility between the West and the East. Moscow's attempt to gain a firm foothold in emerging Third World countries was another factor responsible for the Cold War. The Cold War, which started after World War II, began to thaw following the Cuban missile crisis in 1962, and a period of détente ensued, followed by a resumption of Cold War attitudes and policies after the Soviet invasion of Afghanistan. *See also* CUBAN MISSILE CRISIS; DÉTENTE.

Significance   The Cold War between the West and the East has involved a synthesis of diplomatic techniques and limited cooperation between the adversaries in areas such as trade and science. The unlimited destructiveness of nuclear weapons helped keep U.S.-Soviet Cold War conflicts from turning into a "hot" war. In view of the occasional flare-ups between the superpowers, some observers have spoken of a continuing Cold War. But superpower relations today are quite different from what they were during the more critical period of the Cold

War. Both powers are more mature in their diplomacy now, and, despite embargoes, trade between them continues, as does tourism and scientific and cultural exchanges. The degree of communication and understanding between them is much greater today than before. The overriding goal of both—the avoidance of a nuclear confrontation—helps, periodically, to moderate the Cold War.

Command, Control, Communications, and Intelligence (C3I) The nerves or central networks for regulating military operations. Command, Control, Communications, and Intelligence includes systems that manage materiel and manpower, including nuclear weapons, during crises and as well as during peacetime. C3I is known as the National Military Command System (NMCS), which is led by the president and the secretary of defense. It serves two basic functions: (1) provides intelligence by evaluating enemy weapons systems, monitoring attacks, and assessing damage inflicted; and (2) oversees the entire military force. Given the danger of a surprise or preemptive "decapitation" attack (knocking out the massively computerized worldwide C3I), at least one of the 17 constitutionally designated presidential successors must be outside of Washington, D.C., in a time of crisis. Since the primary purpose of deterrence is to ensure that no aggressor can profit from starting a nuclear war, protecting C3I assets becomes a priority. *See also* NATIONAL COMMAND AUTHORITIES (NCA); NATIONAL MILITARY COMMAND SYSTEM (NMCS); PRESIDENT.

Significance   Command, Control, Communications, and Intelligence serves to alert each strategic force, and provide military commanders access to their forces in battle. Should a nuclear attack occur, one debilitating effect would be to disrupt the fact gathering that helps guide the leaders of the military. The C3I facilities, (which number only a few hundred) might be destroyed early in nuclear war. If so, each side would be blinded and the effectiveness of the weapons and the military operations would be greatly diminished. Should the president die, a well-defined succession would maintain a viable National Command Authorities (NCA). The order follows the constitutional succession of president: the vice president, the speaker of the House of Representatives, the president pro-tempore of the Senate, and all members of the cabinet from secretary of state to the secretary of veterans administration. The highest-ranking survivor would continue to run the government, and approve the victory or surrender terms. But the increasing devolution of responsibility from human to electronic intelligence contains the risk of an unstoppable accident that could lead irrevocably into nuclear war.

Commander in Chief   The supreme leader of the armed forces of the United States. The commander in chief is the president of the United States, who derives this authority from Article II, Section 2 of the Constitution which begins with the declaration that "the President shall be Commander in Chief of the Army and Navy of the United States, and of the Militia of the several States, when called into the actual Service of the United States. . . . " Civilian control of the armed forces is exercised by the president, although he may delegate some of the powers to the defense secretary, the national security advisor, the Joint Chiefs of Staff, and other military and civilian officials. Modern presidents have not personally led the troops during wartime, but they have made decisions on the deployment of forces and military strategy to be followed. In war as in peace, the president is the commander in chief. The War Powers Act of 1973, which limits the president's power in certain areas, has not served to undermine his authority as commander in chief. Rather, it is a recognition of the broad interpretation of presidential power as the supreme commander of the armed forces. *See also* PRESIDENT; SECRETARY OF DEFENSE; WAR POWERS ACT.

Significance   As commander in chief, the president ultimately conducts U.S. military policy. Authorization of the use of nuclear weapons comes from the president as commander in chief. In the event of his incapacitation, the line of authority runs to the vice president and then to the secretary of defense, not the secretary of state. Presidential authority over the armed forces guarantees civilian supremacy. Although the Constitution is clear in terms of civilian control over the armed forces, it is debatable today whether the president is empowered to send troops into battle without congressional authorization. Perhaps no other area of presidential responsibility has been subject to so much controversy in recent years as the president's role as commander in chief. Presidents Harry S Truman and John F. Kennedy used U.S. armed forces in Korea and Vietnam, respectively, without any formal declaration of war by the U.S. Congress. In both these cases the White House ignored the Congress. There is an acknowledged need to explore military emergencies (including nuclear war) when they arise. But Congress is empowered to declare war and approve funds for any military expenditure. In this controversy the problem of constitutional interpretation is present. This debate over the extent to which the president must consult with Congress will continue. Although the president generally prevails in military and weapons policy, the battles with Congress are not always easily won.[7]

Comprehensive Test Ban (CTB)   Complete prohibition of nuclear testing underwater, underground, in the atmosphere, and in outer space. A comprehensive test ban would seriously limit the development of new nuclear weapons and the improvement of existing ones. A CTB treaty was negotiated among the United States, the Soviet Union, and Britain between 1962 and 1979. The United States at one point announced that the Soviet Union had agreed to permit 10 seismic monitoring stations within its borders to make a CTB feasible, but on-site inspections posed problems. As U.S.-Soviet relations deteriorated, negotiations were suspended. Verification of nuclear tests has been a major obstacle in negotiating a comprehensive test ban treaty. *See also* THRESHOLD TEST BAN TREATY (TTBT).

Significance   Comprehensive test ban continues to elude arms control advocates. There are a variety of arguments for and against a comprehensive test ban treaty. One objection to a comprehensive test ban is that it would, as a form of arms control, halt the development of new weapons technology and scientific progress. Some experts believe that when bans on nuclear tests are discussed, the primary argument to continue testing is that existing nuclear stockpiles become outmoded and need to be checked. Other experts disagree by saying that the problem of corrosion could be detected by tests short of nuclear explosion and can be repaired or parts replaced. However, considerable progress has been made, and at one point a treaty seemed almost within reach. But the Carter administration was busy negotiating the Strategic Arms Limitation Talks (SALT II) and did not believe it could master enough support in the Senate for ratification of a SALT II and a comprehensive test ban treaty. The Reagan administration decided to resume negotiations toward a CTB treaty. Many observers believed, however, that the administration strongly opposed a CTB treaty because such a treaty would have stopped the development of the Strategic Defense Initiative.

Controlled Escalation   An offensive strategy associated with limited nuclear options. Under controlled escalation, decision makers can escalate at the strategic nuclear level in a deliberate and restricted manner, allowing time for the enemy to consider the implications of their actions. Controlled escalation forms the cornerstone of the concept of limited nuclear war, which became U.S. policy in 1974. There are two U.S. strategies: first, maintain the ability to remain continually superior to an enemy, and second, maintain the ability to counter an enemy at every stage of a conflict. Controlled escalation would prevent an all-out nuclear war. It is the mechanism that would make limited nuclear confrontation possible. The technical facilities to effect controlled escalation are called C3I: Command, Control, Communications, and Intelligence. *See also* COMMAND, CONTROL, COMMUNICATIONS, AND INTELLIGENCE (C3I); ESCALATION; LIMITED NUCLEAR WAR.

Significance   Controlled escalation means that an all-out holocaust is not inevitable if nuclear weapons are used in a war. Proponents say it is possible to limit the use of nuclear weapons to specific military targets. Control of escalation of war—conventional or nuclear—depends on the communications of leaders with their military commanders, and the latter with each other. The ability to communicate would be realized with, for example, use of a hot line. But no special arrangements have been made to ensure that the hot line would go undamaged after the outbreak of a nuclear war. If the communication links are destroyed the concept of controlled escalation would be meaningless, because each side would assume the other was about to undertake an all-out nuclear offensive.

Conventional Weapons   Nonnuclear, nonchemical, nonbiological armaments. Conventional weapons have become increasingly complex, sophisticated, and expensive. This is an extremely broad term, encompassing many different types of weapons. Guns, hand grenades, land mines, armored and mechanized divisions, tanks and artillery, tactical aircraft, and naval forces, are examples of conventional weapons and forces. Both superpowers spend about 80 percent of their military budgets on conventional weapons. There are three main purposes for conventional forces and weapons. First, they deter a conventional war. Second, they can be used to intervene in conflicts abroad, notably in the Third World. Third, they are used to maintain domestic law and order. The United States, together with its North Atlantic Treaty Organization (NATO) allies, has proposed a treaty that would reduce NATO and Warsaw Pact forces so as to achieve parity at the levels of 700,000 ground forces and 900,000 ground and air force personnel combined. The treaty also would establish a system of verification and notification of military exercises. Agreement on limiting conventional forces in Europe, however, has not yet been reached. Meanwhile, Soviet President Mikhail S. Gorbachev proposed at the United Nations on December 7, 1988, that he would cut 500,000 troops and 10,000 tanks, 8,500 artillery systems, and 800 aircraft, mostly in Europe. If the Gorbachev proposal ends in an agreement between the two blocs, it would contribute to the lessening to tensions in Europe. *See also* CHEMICAL AND BIOLOGICAL WEAPONS (CBWS); NUCLEAR WEAPON.

Significance   Conventional weapons have been sanctioned by agreement or prior usage and conform to standard international agreements on their acceptability. One of the purposes of the ongoing nuclear arms race is to back up uses of conventional armed forces. Both superpowers use nuclear strategic forces as a cover for conventional military activities in peripheral areas. It can also be argued that nuclear conflict arising from the escalation of conventional war may occur; avoiding a major conventional war is therefore vital. Maintaining credible conventional forces and weapons may be a crucial component of the prevention of nuclear confrontation. Although a superpower nuclear war is unlikely, a conventional attack on U.S. allies in Europe is considered to be a possibility that could lead to a major nuclear confrontation.

Counterdeterrence   A nuclear threat to weaken another power's threat to employ nuclear retaliation against limited aggression. In counterdeterrence, no nation can pursue aggressive policies without the danger of inviting nuclear reprisals. It is based on the possession and deployment of intercontinental ballistic missiles (ICBMs) and submarine-launched ballistic missiles (SLBMs). The purpose is not to win nuclear wars, but to avoid them. Counterdeterrence purports to describe an ineffective process between the defender of a commitment and a challenger to be. The defender is expected to define and publicize this commitment and instill fear in the enemy. In this way both superpowers have deterred one another from launching a nuclear attack. A repetitive cycle of test and challenge is established so that both sides understand each other's position and interests. Counterdeterrence is sometimes called self-deterrence. *See also* COUNTERFORCE STRIKE; INTERCONTINENTAL BALLISTIC MISSILE (ICBM); SUBMARINE-LAUNCHED BALLISTIC MISSILE (SLBM).

Significance   Counterdeterrence is a condition in which nations are restrained from engaging in nuclear war. It may lead to international stability, since no nation can profit from aggression in a nuclear war, realizing that nuclear weapons are too damaging. However, such a "trump card" can only be held at a constant consumption of human, natural, and economic resources in maintaining the nuclear capability that makes counterdeterrence possible. As practiced by the United States, the policy is thought to be "extended deterrence": the spreading of its nuclear umbrella beyond its own frontiers to those of its

NATO (North Atlantic Treaty Organization) allies. A nuclear weapon is a war deterrent, a peace-keeping force. Nuclear weapons, however, obviously could be used destructively. Currently, mutual deterrence seems to exist, but most observers agree that a major conflict between the superpowers has been prevented by the specter of counterdeterrence. They maintain that the price of peace in the nuclear age is the threat of nuclear war.

Counterforce Strategy   The targeting of enemy forces, particularly those that could be used in retaliation to another's initiatory attack. Counterforce strategy is to employ the strategic air and missile forces to destroy the military capabilities of an enemy force. Former Secretary of Defense Robert S. McNamara stated in 1962 that, in the event of a nuclear war, the principal military objective should be the annihilation of enemy military forces. Bombers and their bases, intercontinental ballistic missiles (ICBMs), antiballistic missiles (ABMs), Command, Control, Communications, and Intelligence (C3I) centers, and nuclear stockpiles are typical counterforce targets. This idea has served as the basis for modern theories of limited nuclear war. There are at least three Soviet counterforce strategies: (1) an attack on the U.S. ICBM forces, designed to reduce U.S. options in a limited war; (2) an attack on U.S. strategic forces, designed to shift decisively the balance of nuclear power in favor of the Soviet Union; and (3) an attack on U.S. strategic forces, designed to limit damage to the Soviet Union in an all-out nuclear war. *See also* INTERCONTINENTAL BALLISTIC MISSILE (ICBM); SUBMARINE-LAUNCHED BALLISTIC MISSILE (SLBM).

Significance   Counterforce strategy involves the possibility of a nuclear strike against the enemy's military forces and weapons rather than its cities and populations. If the superpowers could restrict themselves to counterforce strategy, cities and industrial centers could survive a nuclear war. But military installations are not always restricted to areas isolated from civilian centers. In any discussion of counterforce strategy it must be remembered that a major nuclear war would be a colossal catastrophe. However, it is difficult to imagine how a nuclear war would be the least miserable option facing leaders of nuclear nations. Because nuclear war would be so devastating, prudence demands that the factors that might contribute to its occurrence be seriously considered in all nuclear strategic considerations.

Countervalue Strike   An attack at enemy cities or industries. A countervalue strike includes concepts, plans, weapons, and actions directed toward destroying or immobilizing selected opposition population centers, industries, resources, and institutions. If an effective countervalue strike was launched, millions would die and many economic centers would be destroyed. The U.S. use of atomic weapons on the Japanese cities of Hiroshima and Nagasaki in 1945 are examples of countervalue strikes. These two cities were destroyed and many people were killed, crippled, or died lingering deaths from the radioactivity. In the nuclear language, the cities and industrial districts on both sides came to be called countervalue targets. To threaten them was to counter what each side most valued. It has been primarily the submarine-launched ballistic missiles (SLBMs) component of the U.S. triad that has received this mission. Countervalue is distinct from counterforce, which refers to a nuclear attack designed to destroy enemy military installations. *See also* BALANCE OF TERROR; COUNTER-FORCE STRATEGY; HIROSHIMA; NAGASAKI.

Significance Countervalue strike is targeted at enemy cities and other resources that constitute the social fabric of a nation. This strategy, with its concomitant balance of terror holding an enemy population hostage, forms the basis of the mutual assured destruction (MAD) policy, which dominated the superpower strategies in the 1960s. While counterforce targeting might intend to avoid civilian centers, the inextricability of military installations and the populations around them renders such a premise unrealistic. On the other hand, in countervalue strike, no nation can pursue aggressive policies without risking a devastating nuclear attack on its own cities and industrial centers. SLBMs have long been thought of as satisfactory for attacking soft countervalue targets such as cities where high accuracy is not crucial, but they have had limited effects on hard counterforce targets. Supporters of assured destruction strategy do not consider this a particularly damning shortcoming, but those who favor counterforce strategy do.

Coupling The linking of one area of conflict to another. Coupling is an essential part of the North Atlantic Treaty Organization (NATO) strategy usually known as strategic coupling. With strategic coupling, forces of all NATO allies would be combined to counter any enemy attack on Western Europe or North America. The Warsaw Pact's geography and political structure ensure that the coupling of Soviet security to that of its allies is not an issue. For NATO this linkage is a perennial problem, and the cruise and Pershing missiles were supposed to help by coupling a defense of Europe on land with U.S. nuclear forces. But this situation was changed with the signing of the

Intermediate-range Nuclear Forces (INF) Treaty (1987) between the two superpowers. The INF treaty provides for the elimination of two classes of weapons systems: longer range INF and shorter range INF. *See also* INTERMEDIATE-RANGE NUCLEAR FORCES TREATY; NORTH ATLANTIC TREATY ORGANIZATION (NATO); WARSAW PACT.

Significance   Associated particularly with NATO strategy of coupling, in Soviet eyes, is a Soviet conventional invasion of Europe with the threat of retaliation by U.S. strategic weapons. It is a policy that links a low-level conflict (for example, any signs of Soviet or Warsaw Pact aggression in Europe) to the immediate justification for U.S. use of strategic weapons. NATO has made it clear to the Soviets and their Eastern European allies that any attack on Western Europe will trigger a response from the United States. The Warsaw Pact countries, on the other hand, persist in attempting to decouple Europe and the United States by promoting European antiwar movements, offering deals that would benefit Western European governments, and capitalizing on fears that the United States intends to fight World War III with nuclear weapons in Europe—thereby saving North America from the immediate destructive effects of nuclear war. The main result of the superpowers' INF agreement is to increase the fears of the European NATO nations that the United States is becoming less willing to couple its defense against a Soviet attack to that of Western Europe.

Critical Mass   The minimum amount of fissionable material that will support a self-sustaining chain reaction under stated conditions. Critical mass is the smallest amount of uranium or plutonium necessary to fuel a nuclear reactor or weapon. By 1939 it was proved that a fission chain reaction was possible if sufficient fissionable material could be brought together. The energy released in the nuclear fission process comes from changes in the nuclei of atoms such as uranium and plutonium. Uranium and plutonium are highly radioactive substances, used to fuel all nuclear weapons. The U-235 and Pu-239 bomb material was produced in the industrial plants at Oak Ridge and Hanford. The designs of the atomic bombs were developed under the direction of J. Robert Oppenheimer in a laboratory in Los Alamos, New Mexico. To assemble an atomic bomb, three things are essential: (1) knowledge of how to make the bomb, which is described in many physics books; (2) a sufficient amount (a critical mass) of fissionable material; and (3) a means of bringing that fissionable material together to start a chain reaction. The first atomic bomb was tested at Alamogordo, New Mexico, in 1945. *See also* ATOMIC WEAPON; NUCLEAR WEAPON.

Significance   A critical mass can be formed by a few pounds of uranium-235. If compressed by an explosion—one of the means by which some bombs are triggered—even smaller amounts can become critical. This is because the nuclei are much closer together than in the uncompressed state. The problem facing Oppenheimer's bomb design at Los Alamos was to create a critical mass out of stable, smaller-than-critical (subcritical) masses by bringing them together suddenly enough to avoid premature ignition or a slow chain reaction. An alternative means of detonation is to bring together two pieces of uranium that are each individually less than the critical mass but that equal, or just exceed, this amount when brought into contact. Ever since scientists first realized that an atomic bomb could be built, people have felt there is a big problem with atomic weapons. Antiatomic activism has spread on both sides of the Atlantic. In the United States, Critical Mass, an antinuclear pressure group, was founded by consumer advocate Ralph Nader in 1974, concentrating largely on nuclear safety issues.

Cruise Missile   A missile that flies on a horizontal trajectory, like an airplane. A cruise missile is a small, unmanned airplane that hugs the ground and uses its on-board radar and guidance system to deliver long-distance nuclear or conventional warheads with accuracy. In-flight guidance and control can be accomplished remotely or by on-board equipment. Cruise missiles, powered by jet engines, are highly maneuverable and able to avoid defense. They are air-launched, ground-launched and sea-launched. The concept of a pilotless "drone" weapon dates back to 1915, when Elmer Sperry, inventor of the directional gyroscope, created an automatic flying bomb that travelled 1,000 yards. In World War II, the Germans developed the prototype of the cruise missile, the V-1 flying bomb, thousands of which they dropped on London in 1944 and 1945. In 1970 the current generation of drones, today's cruise, entered full-scale development when the Nixon administration authorized the development of the subsonic armed decoy for the B-1 bomber. The Soviet Union is currently improving its cruise technology. Cruise missiles are distinct from ballistic missiles, which are propelled into the upper atmosphere by booster rockets. *See also* AIR-LAUNCHED CRUISE MISSILE (ALCM); GROUND-LAUNCHED CRUISE MISSILE (GLCM); SEA-LAUNCHED CRUISE MISSILE (SLCM).

Significance   Cruise missiles are slow, low-flying aircraft propelled by an air-breathing engine that operates entirely within the earth's atmosphere and maintains thrust throughout its flight. A breakthrough for the missiles was the terrain-contour matching guidance system. The missile takes pictures of the entire terrain under itself through the use of a radar altimeter. In the United States all three military services—army, navy and air force—deploy cruise missiles. The United States holds a technological lead over the Soviet Union, which is now developing and deploying its own cruises. Cruise missiles are easily concealed, and can carry conventional or nuclear warheads, and thus they complicate arms control negotiations. It is difficult to locate cruise missiles by reconnaissance satellites, radar, or any other current means. Hence, verifying limitation agreements would be difficult. Neither superpower appears likely to permit the extensive and intrusive inspection practices that would be needed to count and track cruises.

Cuban Missile Crisis   A U.S.-Soviet Union confrontation that threatened to lead to nuclear war. The Cuban missile crisis of October 1962 started when President John F. Kennedy, after being shown irrefutable evidence of Soviet missile emplacements in Cuba, demanded they be dismantled. Kennedy considered launching an air strike against the missile sites, an invasion of Cuba, and a naval blockade around Cuba. On October 24, he quarantined Cuba. Kennedy also directed the armed forces "to prepare for any eventualities." His insistence that Soviet missiles be removed from Cuba led to a dangerous superpower encounter. The first break in the crisis came when Cuba-bound Soviet ships carrying missiles altered course. The Soviet Union promised to remove its offensive missiles from Cuba in return for a guarantee that no further invasion of Cuba would be undertaken by the United States. *See also* HOT LINE; LIMITED TEST BAN TREATY (LTBT).

Significance   The Cuban missile crisis was a serious incident. In the words of President Kennedy, the chances of nuclear war were "between one in three and even." From the U.S. perspective, the Kennedy administration's handling of the Cuban missile crisis must surely be ranked as one of the most outstanding diplomatic victories by the United States. The Soviets, claiming the missiles were merely "defensive" and aimed at avoiding another U.S. invasion, also claimed a diplomatic victory. The United States managed the crisis with skill and restraint—offering a compromise to the Soviets and giving them time to call back their missiles and withdraw from Cuba. Among its consequences, the Cuban missile crisis warned people everywhere of the possibility of a direct nuclear exchange. Although initially relations between the superpowers deteriorated, U.S. and Soviet officials made renewed efforts to compromise their differences. Western observers believe that the crisis helped bring about Nikita S. Khrushchev's fall from power in the Soviet Union. Regardless of its domestic impact in both countries, the Cuban missile crisis was the closest humankind has come to triggering a nuclear holocaust. The resolution of the crisis did, however, contribute to negotiations that produced the Limited Test Ban Treaty and the Hot Line Agreement between the two superpowers, and a period of détente followed.

D

Decapitation Attack   A strategy to knock out the central decision-making nerve centers of the enemy. A decapitation attack aims to destroy enemy leaders and command posts. It is intended to wipe out an enemy's ability to coordinate decisions and communicate orders. The purpose of a decapitation attack is to paralyze an enemy in a single nuclear strike. A Soviet nuclear attack might decapitate the massively computerized U.S. Worldwide Military Command and Control System (WWMCCS), which operates from 30 ultrasophisticated centers around the world. Such an attack could also render powerless the Command, Control, Communications, and Intelligence (C3I) facilities, which are essential to waging war. It is estimated that 100 Soviet missiles could destroy vital U.S. government facilities and worldwide communications. A decapitation attack could benefit an aggressor, if that aggressor could seriously cripple the decision process calling for retaliation, but it would involve a potentially suicidal risk for the attacking state if its success were not complete. *See also* COMMAND, CONTROL, COMMUNICATIONS, AND INTELLIGENCE (C3I); WORLDWIDE MILITARY COMMAND AND CONTROL SYSTEM (WWMCCS).

Significance   A decapitation attack is calculated to disable an enemy from coordinating its war effort. If a country believed it could prevent its adversary from coordinating retaliatory plans during an attack, then its inhibitions about launching a first strike would be reduced. In this strategy, instead of weapons sites being the targets, command and control structures that would coordinate a retaliation become the targets. A superpower's retaliatory action might include an attack on political and military leaders and their C3I network. For example, if command and control capabilities are lost early in the war by decapitation, then the war could be extended as local commanders make separate and uncoordinated decisions. But it is unlikely to be in the superpower's interest to produce chaos on the other side because this could make it impossible to negotiate an early end to the war. To preserve the option of a negotiated truce, most observers believe that the superpowers should not maintain a decapitation attack strategy as a viable option.

Decoy   A device to mislead an opponent's defense system. A decoy may accompany a nuclear weapon delivery vehicle in order to divert enemy defensive systems, thus increasing the probability of penetration and weapon delivery to target. A relatively small decoy can be made to appear as large as a bomber on radar screens by electromagnetic techniques. Intercontinental ballistic missile (ICBM) decoys generally must stimulate the radar signature of the actual warhead. Some ICBMs can carry up to 100 decoys. Decoy ships are warships or other ships camouflaged as merchantmen or converted commerce raiders, with their armament and other fighting equipment hidden, and with special provisions for unmasking their weapons quickly. A decoy forces a missile defense system to waste time and ammunition by turning attention away from attacking warheads. After tracking the target, the ballistic missile defense system carries out its next function—discrimination—in order to determine which target should be intercepted. Reentry vehicles (RVs) must be large and heavy enough to carry a nuclear warhead; therefore, to be effective, decoys should be lighter and take up less room on the booster. *See also* INTERCONTINENTAL BALLISTIC MISSILE (ICBM).

Significance   A decoy deceives by appearing to be something it is not. The dummy warheads resemble actual warheads, but carry no nuclear explosive. The objective is to inundate enemy defenses with decoys and RVs configured to pose maximum difficulty to the defender. Making room for these decoys would probably require negligible off-loading RVs from Soviet missiles, meaning little or no loss to the Soviet Union if the decoys failed. If one kill vehicle were allocated to each RV-decoy pair, the efficiency would be halved, since the intercepted object has only a 50 percent chance of being a true RV. No decoy is perfect, although the offense could deploy many more than one decoy with each RV. The defense would have to make a trade-off between intercepting the object judged most likely to be an RV and allowing it to penetrate. Much scientific research financed by the Department of Defense (DOD) is directed at trying to solve the problem of distinguishing lethal ICBM warheads from those on board decoys.

Defense Intelligence Agency (DIA)　　An agency in the Department of Defense (DOD) responsible for ensuring that necessary intelligence support is available to the unified commands. The Defense Intelligence Agency also has responsibility for supervising the execution of all approved plans, programs, policies, and procedures dealing with general intelligence for the Department of Defense. Established in 1961 under provisions of the National Security Act of 1947 as amended, the DIA operates under the control of the secretary of defense. An assistant secretary of defense supervises the agency. The DIA is responsible for gathering and processing military intelligence. It does this either by drawing on internal resources—through the management, supervision, and tracking of the intelligence functions of other Defense Department activities—or by working with the other U.S. intelligence agencies. The DIA supplies military intelligence for national foreign intelligence and counterintelligence endeavors, and staff support for the Joint Chiefs of Staff (JCS). *See also* CENTRAL INTELLIGENCE AGENCY (CIA); DEPARTMENT OF DEFENSE (DOD); NATIONAL SECURITY AGENCY (NSA); NATIONAL SECURITY COUNCIL (NSC).

Significance　　The Defense Intelligence Agency reviews and coordinates those DOD intelligence functions retained by the military services. The three military services—army (G-2), navy (ONI), and air force (A-2)—still maintain skeleton intelligence organizations for gathering intelligence about other nations' ground, naval, and air forces. These separate intelligence services—originally assigned to the various military departments—were partially divested from the DIA. As divisions among the services sometimes contribute to operational difficulties, multiple intelligence agencies within the same department, although mutually reinforcing, may sometimes—as in the case of the DIA and its rival or competing agencies—cause conflicts associated with perceived functions.

Defense Nuclear Agency (DNA)　　A Department of Defense agency that manages nuclear weapons, and provides assistance to the Joint Chiefs of Staff (JCS). The Defense Nuclear Agency coordinates research, development, testing, and stockpiling of nuclear weapons. The Atomic Energy Commission assumed responsibility for the Manhattan Project in 1947, and the project's military staff were assigned to the Armed Forces Special Weapons Project (AFSWP). In 1959, the AFSWP was reorganized and redesignated as the Defense Atomic Support Agency (DASA), which in 1971 was renamed the Defense Nuclear Agency. The DNA is headed by a director who reports to both the under secretary of defense for acquisition and the chairman of the Joint Chiefs of Staff. Headquartered in Washington, D.C., the DNA retains the management of Johnston, an atoll in the Pacific, as a test site. The DNA's Field Command is in Albuquerque, New Mexico, and it operates the Armed Forces Radiobiology Research Institute in Bethesda, Maryland. *See also* DEPARTMENT OF DEFENSE (DOD); DEPARTMENT OF ENERGY (DOE); JOINT CHIEFS OF STAFF (JCS).

Significance   The Defense Nuclear Agency plans and supervises activities associated with nuclear weapons research and testing. These include tests analysis, building and operation of simulation facilities, and field experiments. The DNA manages the Defense Department's nuclear stockpile and its associated report system. In addition to being the central organization for coordinating nuclear weapons development and testing with the Department of Energy, the DNA also carries out technical investigations and field tests to enhance the safety and security of theater nuclear forces. It provides advice and assistance to the Joint Chiefs of Staff (JCS) and the military services on all nuclear matters, including site security, tactics, vulnerability, radiation effects, and biomedical effects. The DNA is the oldest agency in the Department of Defense, having its origins in the Manhattan Project, which was formed in 1942 to supervise the development of the first atomic bomb.

Defense Strategy   A series of discrete but interrelated policy objectives concerning national security. The defense strategy of the United States is a component of its overall national security, which includes assurance of the survival of the country as an independent nation, with its fundamental values and institutions intact and its people secure. For this reason, the principal objectives of the United States are: (1) deter foreign aggression against itself and its allies and friends; (2) deny an enemy its objectives and bring a rapid end to the conflict on terms favorable to its own interests; (3) promote meaningful and verifiable mutual reductions in nuclear and conventional weapons; (4) inhibit further expansion of Soviet control and military presence; and (5) avoid subsidizing or supporting the Soviet military buildup by preventing the flow of military technologies and material to the Soviet Union.

While reverse aims are mainly true of Soviet defense strategy, it is also concerned with the nature of future war preparation of its people and armed forces for conducting such a war. The Soviet military strategy deals with definition of the strategic tasks of its armed forces, assessment of the military potential of its principal adversary, the

United States, and the determination of the size and composition of military forces necessary to wage a nuclear war. The defense strategy of the superpowers is influenced by such common factors as geography, national interest, technological developments, economic considerations, and the demands of the respective military-industrial complexes in the two countries. *See also* NUCLEAR WAR; STRATEGIC BALANCE.

Significance   The basic defense strategy of the United States is to safeguard its own and its allies' interests against all odds, by deterring aggression or, if necessary, waging war. Deterrence works only by convincing potential adversaries that the probable costs to them of their aggression will exceed any possible gains. The United States seeks not only to deter actual aggression but also to prevent coercion through the threat of aggression. Against such U.S. allies as Western Europe and Japan, the Soviet threat has shown to comprise overt attack as well as other tactics—all designed to intimidate and to psychologically seduce. Soviet policy seeks to persuade allies of the United States to distance themselves, to neglect their military capabilities, to adopt passive policies such as unilateral disarmament, and, ultimately, to destroy the North Atlantic Treaty Organization (NATO) and the mutual defense treaty with Japan. While recognizing the competitive and predominantly adversarial character of the superpowers' relationship, it is the superpower strategy to pursue a dialogue in order to seize opportunities for more constructive relations.

Delayed Radioactive Fallout   Debris from a nuclear explosion that remains in the atmosphere for weeks or months before falling to the ground. Delayed radioactive fallout is carried by winds over a wide area, spreading harmful effects. Fallout radiation consists of residue created by a nuclear blast. When a nuclear weapon explodes, it pulverizes any objects in the area and contaminates the debris with a radioactive substance. As the debris rises, fallout is saturated with radiation from the blast. Fallout radiation may take weeks, months, or even years to return to earth. It returns to the earth under its own weight or in rain or snow. Delayed radioactive fallout is sometimes called global radioactive fallout and worldwide fallout. Delayed radioactive fallout should be distinguished from early radioactive fallout, which settles within a day. *See also* EARLY RADIOACTIVE FALLOUT; IONIZING RADIATION; NUCLEAR RADIATION.

Significance   Delayed radioactive fallout may be very dangerous. It may cause genetic damage, cancer, internal bleeding, hair loss, and nausea. The genetic effects of radiation arise through damage to those intracellular bodies in the germ cells that are the material basis of heredity. These are the chromosomes with their constituent genes. The role of large doses of radiation in increasing the incidence of cancer cannot be exaggerated. It has been demonstrated in animals that the onset of cancer can be delayed by many years following radiation exposure. Delayed radiation may eventually cause millions of deaths and contaminate the earth's food and water supplies. It is possible that exposure of the entire population of the world to radiation may lead to many types of diseases, including leukemia and various forms of cancer. The Soviet Chernobyl nuclear power plant disaster in the spring of 1986 has already taken dozens of lives, and the impact of the delayed radioactive fallout on the Soviet Union, on Western Europe, and the world is almost certain to cause thousands or even tens of thousands more cancer deaths. Terrible as the Chernobyl catastrophe was, it was nothing compared to what the catastrophe of a nuclear war would be.

Demirving   The process by which multiple warheads, or MIRVed (multiple independently targetable reentry vehicle) missiles, are redesigned to carry only a single warhead. MIRV missiles were developed by the United States in the 1960s and deployed in the 1970s. The Soviet Union developed its MIRV system in 1975. These developments of multiple warheads were breakthroughs in nuclear technology. During the Strategic Arms Limitation Talks (SALT I) in 1972, the United States enjoyed a considerable lead in MIRV technology. It was testing, producing, and deploying MIRV systems. The Soviets were still in the early stage of development of MIRV. Neither side wanted to constrain MIRV. Demirving has posed problems because meaningful MIRV constraints do not provide the most cost-effective means for increasing target coverage. But under SALT II both superpowers agreed not to produce submarine-based or land-based launchers for heavy ballistic missiles. *See also* MULTIPLE INDEPENDENTLY TARGETABLE REENTRY VEHICLE (MIRV).

Significance   Demirving was proposed by the United States during the Strategic Arms Reduction Talks (START) as a means of resolving the arms control dilemma. MIRVs have complicated arms control negotiations because it is extremely difficult to verify whether a missile is MIRVed. Unlike a missile with a single warhead, a multiple-warhead missile can spread damage over a wide area containing several targets. Given the missiles' increasing accuracy and multiple warheads, it is possible that missiles launched from one side could destroy the land-based missiles of the other in a sudden attack. With MIRV, one missile can carry destruction to two or more targets within its footprint—the large land area over which warheads can be delivered by one missile. If some of the missile's propulsive energy is first used to extend the range at which warheads are delivered, however, there will be insufficient energy to disperse warheads at a later time. Size of the footprint at extended ranges will be smaller. Footprinting MIRVed missiles for many different options can be a demanding exercise.

Denuclearization   An agreement to eliminate the deployment of nuclear weapons. Denuclearization is a disarmament policy aimed at denuclearizing a geographic region or the entire world. After extensive discussion on denuclearization of the world in the United Nations General Assembly, four nuclear-free zones were established. The Antarctic Treaty (1959), the Treaty of Tlatelolco (1967), and the Treaty of Rarotonga (1985) have denuclearized Antarctica, Latin America, and the South Pacific respectively. The seabed and outer space have also been denuclearized. The United Nations and its Disarmament Commission have discussed the possibility of denuclearization of many areas such as the Arctic, the Bering Strait, the Adriatic, the Balkans, the Mediterranean, the Middle East, the Indian Ocean, and Scandinavia. Denuclearization may entail two actions: prohibition of the introduction of nuclear weapons into an area, and the removal of nuclear weapons from a territory where they are already developed—such as Europe. *See also* ANTARCTIC TREATY; NUCLEAR-FREE ZONE (NFZ); TREATY OF RAROTONGA; TREATY OF TLATELOLCO.

Significance   Denuclearization of the world, if accomplished, will render nuclear weapons irrelevant and obsolete. This could be the only effective means of making the world safer from the danger of nuclear conflagration. The alternate view is that nuclear weapons are a reality that cannot be wished away. The proponents of this second view maintain that a policy of deterrence (steps taken to prevent an enemy from initiating armed actions and to inhibit escalation if combat occurs) is the best way to avoid nuclear confrontation. This viewpoint favors a policy of limited nuclear options. There are also those who believe that the assured-destruction scenario is a reality and that this awareness is the prime inhibitor for any nation with nuclear ambition. Both superpowers have supported, in principle, the establishment of nuclear-free zones. Latin American countries implemented a U.N. resolution calling for them to denuclearize their continent when they signed the Treaty of Tlatelolco in Mexico City. But a similar U.N. resolution, calling on all African states to agree to denuclearize their continent, has not been accepted by the Organization of African Unity, which was given the responsibility to do so.

Department of Defense (DOD)   A cabinet-level agency of the U.S. government charged with responsibility to defend the country against aggression. The Department of Defense recruits military forces for its component units of the army, navy, air force, and Marine Corps (actually, each branch does its own recruiting). These consist of two million persons on active duty, with reserve components numbering about 2.5 million. The department coordinates logistics; the general administration of the armed forces; and supervises the Joint Chiefs of Staff (JCS), which, by the National Security Act of 1947, acts as the coordinating mechanism for the armed services. JCS is the principal military advisory body of the secretary of defense and the president. The secretary of defense, by law, must be a civilian. The National Security Act of 1949, as amended in 1974, unified the armed forces under the secretary of defense. The department oversees three agencies: International Security Affairs, the Defense Intelligence Agency, and the National Security Agency. The headquarters of the department is located in the Pentagon. The department engages in massive research, and procures technological weapons, including nuclear arms, through contracts with private companies. *See also* JOINT CHIEFS OF STAFF (JCS); SECRETARY OF DEFENSE.

Significance   The Department of Defense is the largest agency of the U.S. government in number of employees and size of budget. It is the third-ranking executive department after the departments of State and the Treasury in, *inter alia,* the line of presidential succession. Who in the DOD is the master planner, who makes fundamental choices and trade-offs, ensures the survivability of the command system, and makes it tolerant of error and uncertainty? A careful examination of the U.S. governmental system would reveal that no single mastermind manages the nuclear operations, although the president alone has the authority to decide the use of nuclear weapons. In practical terms, the authority is divided among many departments and agencies of the U.S. government, the DOD playing the major role in defense policy matters. Whether this division of authority is a strength or a weakness of the U.S. political system is a key question for further policy research.

Department of Energy (DOE)   A major federal agency responsible for policies, programs, and administration in the field of energy. The Energy Organization Act of 1977 consolidated within its jurisdiction the responsibilities of the Energy Research and Development Administration, the Federal Energy Administration, the Federal Power Commission, and the Alaska, Bonneville, Southwestern, and Southeastern

Power Administrations. The DOE administers research-and-development programs concerning fission energy. These include programs relating to civilian and naval nuclear reactor development; nuclear fuel cycle; space nuclear applications; and uranium enrichment. The Energy Department also manages the Remedial Action Program, which treats or stabilizes radioactive wastes and performs decontamination and decommissioning at DOE surplus sites. The department conducts technical analyses and provides advice concerning nonproliferation; assesses alternative nuclear systems and new reactor and fuel cycle concepts; and evaluates proposed advanced nuclear fission energy concepts and technical improvements for possible application to nuclear power plant systems. *See also* NUCLEAR REGULATORY COMMISSION (NRC).

Significance   The Department of Energy provides the framework for a comprehensive and balanced national energy plan through its coordination and administration of the energy functions of the U.S. government. It has sought to promote public interest in energy conservation, encourage competition in developing alternative sources of energy, and reduce dependence on unreliable energy supplies from foreign countries. After the Arab oil embargo of 1973–1974, two federal agencies were created: the Energy Research and Development Administration and the Federal Energy Administration. These steps proved inadequate to tackle the growing energy problems of the nation. President Jimmy Carter decided to consolidate these agencies, and, subsequently, created the Department of Energy. While the DOE is responsible for devising viable plans and programs to make the U.S. energy supply independent, it also performs certain vital defense-related functions. The Energy Department directs the U.S. nuclear weapons research, development, testing, production, and surveillance. It looks after the production of special nuclear materials used by the weapons program within the department, and handles defense nuclear wastes and by-products. The DOE also oversees research in inertial fusion; safeguards the security program; classification, declassification, and reclassification of documents; test-ban treaty verification and monitoring technology; and energy-related intelligence activities. Critics of the Reagan administration held that the Energy Department failed in its basic mission of providing the nation with a balanced and effective energy plan, and have called for the Bush administration to give high priority to this project.

Department of State   The major agency of the U.S. Government that advises the president in the formulation and execution of foreign policy. The Department of State's first objective in the conduct of foreign policy is to promote the long-range security and well-being of the United States. It evaluates data relating to U.S. interests overseas, makes recommendations on policy and future action, and takes the steps needed to carry out established policy. The department is headed by the secretary of state, who is appointed by the president (with Senate approval) and is the leading member of the cabinet. The Department of State maintains embassies and consulates in almost all the independent nations of the world. It represents the United States in more than 50 international organizations and more than 800 international conferences annually. The department issues passports to citizens, and the consular officers grant visas to foreigners wishing to visit the United States. One of the major agencies of the department is the Arms Control and Disarmament Agency, which is responsible for negotiating arms control treaties, including conventional and nuclear weapons. The Department of State has five geographic bureaus responsible for the various regions of the world: the bureaus of African, European and Canadian Affairs, East Asian and Pacific Affairs; Inter-American Affairs, and Near Eastern and South Asian Affairs. *See also* DEPARTMENT OF DEFENSE (DOD); NATIONAL SECURITY COUNCIL (NSC); UNITED STATES ARMS CONTROL AND DISARMAMENT AGENCY (USACDA).

Significance The Department of State is the oldest and the highest-ranking cabinet department of the U.S. government. The traditional function of the department is supplemented today by a wide variety of activities as foreign and domestic policies become enmeshed, and as the United States assumes a broader role in the world. The department, through the Bureau of Politico-Military Affairs, originates policies regarding U.S. security, military assistance, and nuclear strategy, and provides general direction on other foreign policy matters. It maintains liaison with the Department of Defense and other federal agencies in a wide variety of political/military affairs. Among the chief problems associated with the Department of State's operations is the overlap of functions with other departments and agencies of the U.S. government. The historic conflict between the departments of State and Defense on the question of formulation and execution of the defense of the country has never been resolved, except by presidential interference on occasion. Also, conflicts have often developed between the secretary of state and personal advisers in the White House Office and advisers in the National Security Council over policymaking.

Détente   The lessening of tensions and improvement of relations between nations, under which they agree to disagree peacefully.

Détente is usually applied to relations between the two superpowers. As a result of improved relations between the United States and the Soviet Union, a period of détente followed in the 1960s and the 1970s. Détente began with the Limited Test Ban Treaty and the Hot Line Agreement signed during John F. Kennedy's presidency. Under conditions of détente, the superpowers also signed a number of other agreements and treaties acknowledging the borders and frontiers arranged after World War II, recognition of East Germany as an independent state, and a number of limited arms controls measures such as the Strategic Arms Limitation Talks (SALT I and SALT II). Détente is based on the idea of peaceful coexistence that seeks to create a framework of limited cooperation within the context of an international order. New détente in the late 1980s and 1990s will seek greater measures of superpower activism. *See also* STRATEGIC ARMS LIMITATION TALKS (SALT I); STRATEGIC ARMS LIMITATION TALKS (SALT II).

Significance   Détente was designed to protect U.S. influence in an era of lessened power abroad and increased isolationism at home. The nuclear era demands some mutual understanding and, possibly, attempts to control the arms race. Underlying the objective is the assumption that an extensive relationship and the creation of interdependence make war less likely. Confrontation and crisis management are now too expensive to be the primary means of resuming aggression. Détente relations have been dead since the Carter administration, and especially since the 1979 Soviet invasion of Afghanistan. The subsequent U.S. boycott of the 1980 Summer Olympics and the refusal of the United States to ratify the SALT II agreement regulating strategic armaments contributed to the deterioration of relations between the superpowers. To climax it all, President Ronald Reagan made it clear that his foreign policy had no place for the "evil empire"—a reference to the Soviet Union. However, the signing of the Intermediate-range Nuclear Forces (INF) Treaty by his administration in 1987 and further discussion of other nuclear weapons control treaties indicate that President Reagan responded positively during the last year of his presidency as the Soviets acquiesced to his firm stand. Contributing to the new atmosphere of détente in the late 1980s have been the new Soviet policies of *glasnost* (openness) and *perestroika* (restructuring) ushered in by Soviet President Mikhail S. Gorbachev.

Deterrence   A condition in which nations are discouraged from fighting nuclear or conventional war. Deterrence restrains an enemy from acting through fear of the consequences that are likely to follow.

Nuclear deterrence is based mainly on the possession and deployment of bombers, intercontinental ballistic missiles (ICBMs), and submarine-launched ballistic missiles (SLBMs). U.S. deterrence policy has been divided by Herman Kahn into six levels: [8] (1) minimum: a relatively small deterrent that depends on nuclear taboos—the inconveniences suffered by both sides, the sanctity of thresholds, and a variety of unreliable attack mechanisms; (2) workable: a capacity of inflicting millions of casualties on the enemy and of destroying vital property; (3) adequate: a reliable threat to kill 5 to 10 percent of a population; (4) reliable: the killing of more than 33 percent of the population; (5) approaching absolute: the killing of between half and 200 percent, which, for all practical purposes, means the end of the world; (6) stark: overkill by a factor of ten or more that would convince anyone that their use would be cataclysmic. *See also* INTERCONTINENTAL BALLISTIC MISSILE (ICBM); MUTUAL ASSURED DESTRUCTION (MAD); SUBMARINE-LAUNCHED BALLISTIC MISSILE (SLBM).

Significance   Deterrence in the nuclear age is based on the building and maintaining of a nuclear weapons arsenal. Currently, the idea of mutual assured destruction (MAD) as a forthright threat to the superpowers' existence might lead an observer to expect that they would accept the policy of deterrence. Each has relied on its ability to inflict enormous damage on the other. Deterrence between the two superpowers is based on each side's capacity to absorb a nuclear strike. Both possess a sufficiently large and varied nuclear arsenal to deter attack by the other by the threat of inflicting a devastating second strike military retaliation. This threat is the essence of deterrence. The behavior of the superpowers indicates mutual awareness of this fact and reflects a determination not to permit security, political, and ideological differences between them to escalate into nuclear war. Critics of deterrence maintain that it is immoral because it forces the United States and the Soviet Union to rely on the balance of terror (the superpowers' ability to wreak havoc on each other). The Reagan administration sought to eliminate the need for deterrence through second strike retaliation by developing a Strategic Defense Initiative (SDI) defensive shield. Technical and scientific problems, however, have made such a "Star Wars" program problematical.

Diplomacy   An art and science of negotiation by sovereign nations to reach agreement on such matters as trade and cultural interaction. Although diplomacy involves the application of tact in the conduct of affairs between nations, it sometimes calls for sharp, blatant tactics. It is an instrument of foreign policy and closely identified with bargaining and negotiation that may involve policy formulation and execution. Diplomatic bargaining strategies are subject to constant reformulation on the basis of assessments provided by diplomats abroad. When mutual interests and consensus on an issue exist, a policy formulation process begins. For example, the INF (intermediate-range nuclear forces) Treaty signed in December 1987, between the United States and the Soviet Union, took long periods of time to negotiate. During that time, both superpowers held convictions on the deployment of nuclear weapons. Finally, their negotiations—all the bargaining, threats and promise—resulted in the signing of the treaty. Of all the types of diplomacy—open, secret, bilateral, multilateral, ministerial, summit—the most visible today is summit diplomacy, in which the heads of state meet face-to-face. *See also* INTERMEDIATE-RANGE NUCLEAR FORCES TREATY.

Significance   Diplomacy is often vaguely defined with different meanings. Sometimes it is used to express the whole context of foreign policy and international relations; other times to indicate the manner in which personal affairs are conducted. Often it is used in a derogatory sense, and sometimes a commendable one. However, we are concerned with diplomacy as an instrument of foreign policy and international relations. In a broad sense a nation's diplomacy, foreign policy, and international relations are the same. Some observers think modern diplomacy, especially in its summit conference forms, is not well suited to cope with the problems of international relations because of the glamor of publicity, the fanfare, and the premature expectations of the people. Gilbert Winham maintains that diplomatic negotiation is no longer to outwit and exploit adversaries but to create a framework for resolving disputes.[9]

Directed Energy Weapon (DEW)   A potential weapon designed to function as part of a high-technology shield against nuclear warheads. Directed energy, or beam, weapons include laser beam and particle beam. Lasers are used as "controlled burn-knives" in eye and other types of surgeries. The particle accelerator has been used in nuclear physics research since the 1940s. These are now being used in weapons research. Laser technologies, theoretically, could inflict damage upon a distant target at the speed of light. A laser beam used as a defense against missiles and their warheads could destroy its target by burning a hole in or weakening the "skin" of the designated warhead, thus causing disintegration. The particle-beam weapon is simply an accelerator that sends a stream of subatomic particles, a sort of machine gun firing subatomic bullets almost as fast as the speed of light.

Supporters of laser- and particle-beam development believe that there would be no maneuvering, no escape from weapons. The DEW can either be based on the ground or in space. A study group of the American Physical Society (APS) found a gap in the scientific and engineering understanding of many issues associated with the development of DEW technologies. The study concluded that there is insufficient information to decide whether the required extrapolation can or cannot be achieved. *See also* KINETIC ENERGY WEAPON (KEW); LASER; STRATEGIC DEFENSE INITIATIVE (SDI); X-RAY LASER WEAPON.

Significance Directed energy weapons are currently in varied stages of scientific investigation. One of the many possibilities—the infrared chemical laser—has been under study for the longest period, and several laboratory models have been built. This is good news; the bad news is that there are other difficulties and the scientific community is deeply divided on the feasibility of beam weapons. Many scientists affiliated with the APS, the Union of Concerned Scientists, and the Federation of American Scientists argue that it is technically impossible to build a comprehensive shield against a ballistic missile attack. They express scientific doubt that the technologies proposed for tracking, targeting, and intercepting enemy missiles can actually be made to function. Other critics insist that even if the basic physical principles of DEW were sound, it is unlikely that these technologies would be cost-effective. The reason its proponents and the military are so excited about DEW is that it supposedly could be used to attack ballistic missiles in flight during their boost phase and enemy satellites in orbit. The DEW is part of the Strategic Defense Initiative, which was established by the Reagan administration in the 1980s to erect a space-based, ballistic-missile defense system.

Disarmament The reduction or elimination of armed forces and armaments as a result of unilateral, bilateral, or multilateral international agreement. Disarmament characterizes all measures relating to the prevention, limitation, and elimination of armaments and of military forces. Disarmament has been used to advance distinct ideas: (1) the destruction or reduction of the armament of a vanquished country; (2) bilateral or multilateral agreements applying to specific areas; and (3) universal limitation of armaments by international agreements. The United Nations established a Disarmament Commission in 1952 for the discussion and negotiation of disarmament issues. The Commission called for a World Disarmament Conference which has taken the form of three Special Sessions on Disarmament—in 1978, 1982, and 1988—in the General Assembly and the Security Council.

These sessions were aimed at breaking existing deadlocks in negotiations in critical areas by encouraging most or all nations to participate. The special sessions have also tried to marshal world opinion to pressure the super and big powers into reaching an agreement and to tackle major problems of disarmament. *See also* ARMS CONTROL; NUCLEAR ARMS CONTROL; NUCLEAR DISARMAMENT.

Significance   Disarmament in its absolute form—general and complete disarmament—requires the global destruction of weaponry and the elimination of all armed forces. But the chances of total disarmament are so minimal that its advocates are often dismissed as utopians. Even if all weapons and all potential weapons were abolished, humankind could not do away with the knowledge of how to build them. Complete disarmament is a desirable goal, but it does not seem to be possible in the foreseeable future. The ability to design and produce nuclear weapons cannot be disinvented. One reason that successful disarmament is rare is that it requires a degree of political accommodation that is difficult to achieve. Absolute disarmament would require some form of world government to deter actions of one country against another. The advocates of disarmament argue that: (1) arms races can be the causes of war; and (2) disarmament releases funds needed for the socio-economic betterment of the people. Opponents counter these arguments by pointing out that weapons are not the causes but the consequences of conflictive relationships. Aggression occurs when weak and insecure nations are unable to maintain adequate defense, thereby opening themselves to armed attack by more powerful nations. Hence the argument runs that the best guarantee of peace is a preparation for war.

Distant Early Warning (DEW)   A radar system that detects attacking enemy bombers. The Distant Early Warning line, on or around the 70th parallel of the North American continent, links Alaska and Iceland, and provides about eight hours' warning of any attacking nuclear bombers. The DEW line has been upgraded to monitor cruise missiles. The system can detect high-level flight up to 40,000 feet and 200 miles away, but cannot detect low-flying objects. To complement this effort, the North American Aerospace Defense Command (NORAD) takes reports from the Airborne Warning and Control System (AWACS), from radar stations in Maine and Washington state, and from Regional Control Centers with 46 stations in Canada and the United States and monitors the entire complex of civil and military air traffic. *See also* BALLISTIC MISSILE DEFENSE (BMD) SYSTEM.

Significance   The Distant Early Warning line was the most ambitious of those constructed in the 1950s as a defense against a surprise Soviet bomber attack. A ground-based station such as a DEW line is extremely vulnerable. The system is out of date and under the general plans of the Department of Defense to modernize C3I (Command, Control, Communications, and Intelligence) capacity. Although programs to improve C3I have been disregarded, the subject serves to further the strategic debate. President Ronald Reagan was a firm believer in a robust defense posture. He proposed a marked increase in expenditures on strategic forces. His opponents denied the value of a weapons system as bargaining chips—weapons ideas that can be bargained away at the negotiating table.

Doomsday Clock   A hypothetical timepiece that signifies the danger period for destruction of the world by a nuclear holocaust. The doomsday clock was originally set at 11:52 P.M. in 1947 with midnight as doomsday, at which time civilization would end. It has since appeared in a logo on the cover of the *Bulletin of the Atomic Scientists.* The clock is adjusted when the overseers of the magazine agree the threat of nuclear war has increased or decreased. The clock has been moved forward on several occasions, as in 1960 and 1983, prompted by the breakdown of the superpowers' relationship. The doomsday clock was most recently set in December 1987, when its hands were moved back to 11:54 P.M. because the management of the magazine believed that the possibility of nuclear war receded as a result of the improved relationship between the superpowers. *See also* INTERMEDIATE-RANGE NUCLEAR FORCES TREATY.

Significance   The doomsday clock is a symbolic timepiece that judges the time left before the world is destroyed by a nuclear confrontation. The timepiece changes, not automatically, as is the case with time itself, but when the management of the publication agrees the threat of nuclear war has grown or lessened. Some of the recent events—the U.S.-Soviet Union treaty to eliminate intermediate-range nuclear forces, the improvement in superpower relations, the increase in international and nongovernmental efforts to reverse the arms race—demonstrate that the world's dangerous course can be changed. In recognition of these developments, the authorities in the *Bulletin of the Atomic Scientists* turned the clock to six minutes to midnight.

Dual Key and Two-Man Rule   A double safety measure that requires two different keys, and two separate officers, to launch a nuclear weapon. Dual key and two-man rule means that two crews must separately insert one key each into the release mechanism of a U.S. missile. A launch crew consists of two men, originally senior colonels of the United States Air Force in their forties, now junior officers (usually captains) in their mid-to-late twenties. Upon authorization of a launch of nuclear weapons, each officer would insert a key simultaneously into widely separated keyholes—the distance between keyholes prevents either person from turning the keys alone. The keys must be used at the same time and left in place for at least five seconds. A Soviet launch crew comprises four men—two regular servicemen who launch the rocket, and two KGB soldiers who alone are permitted to arm it. Initially this procedure extended to keeping the warhead physically distant from the rocket, guarded by KGB officials. *See also* INTERCONTINENTAL BALLISTIC MISSILE (ICBM); QUICK REACTION ALERT (QRA).

Significance   The dual key and two-man rule is a "fail-safe" redouble security procedure that requires at least two authorized personnel to be present, with separate keys or codes, for launching nuclear weapons that could trigger an all-out nuclear war. In this way both human and technological safety in the use of nuclear weapons is maintained. Codes that authorize the launching of nuclear missiles are stored in a double-locked safe called the Red Box. Dual keys must be inserted at the same time by two crew officers, so that one person cannot by himself launch a nuclear attack. In addition to this mechanical set-up, the dual key system is a political arrangement with other nations—Britain, West Germany and Italy—to ensure each nation's responsibility for launching nuclear missiles. In the case of NATO, the dual key and two-man system can be used only with both U.S. and Allied consent.

Dual-Track Decision   Refers to the development of new U.S. nuclear weapons in Europe while continuing negotiations to limit such weapons there. Dual-track originated at the meeting of the North Atlantic Treaty Organization (NATO) leaders on Guadeloupe in 1979. French President Giscard d'Estaing spearheaded the concept that NATO deployment of new weapons would proceed alongside continuous arms limitation talks with the Soviets to reduce or eliminate nuclear weapons in Western Europe. President Jimmy Carter supported the idea, and formed two NATO teams: the Special Consultative Group, charged with diplomatic approaches to the Soviet Union, and the High Level Group, responsible for deploying the weapons. The deployment of the U.S. Tomahawk and Pershing II missiles in

Europe was one element of the dual-track decision; the second was the talks between the two superpowers. *See also* INTERMEDIATE-RANGE NUCLEAR FORCES TREATY.

Significance The dual-track decision was meant to reconcile Western European nations divided over whether U.S. weapons might not need to be deployed if the Soviets agreed on a moratorium. But the Soviets responded with their own strategy: if the Americans did not deploy, the Soviets would then reduce or freeze theirs. Unimpressed, the United States began deploying its missiles in Western Europe. In November 1983, the first Tomahawk missiles arrived in England, and the first Pershing missiles in West Germany. As a result the Soviets withdrew temporarily from the INF (Intermediate-range Nuclear Forces) talks. Unprecedented personal acrimony soured superpower relations, and international abuse further complicated arms control negotiations. However, as the superpower relations began to improve slowly, the INF treaty was signed in December 1987, eliminating a generation of intermediate- and medium-range nuclear weapons from Europe.

Dust Defense Consists of nuclear weapons theoretically buried near targets so that when detonated they spew dust and debris up into the paths of attacking warheads. Dust defense is based on the idea that exploding missiles create enormous volumes of dust and debris, thus interfering with the guidance-electronics of attacking enemy missiles. To protect U.S. missiles, nuclear warheads would be planted underground near missile sites. If these sites were attacked, underground warheads would explode to create artificial dust storms and thus interfere with enemy weapons. A nuclear explosion will release a range of radioactive isotopes, from the products of its own fission, neutron bombardment of the weapon materials, and from the plutonium and uranium which did not undergo fission. Altogether, some 300 different radioactive products are formed in fission. As the cloud cools, the stable fission isotopes begin to form on the particles, falling back to earth quickly, according to wind direction. Meanwhile the blast and heat have pulverized the target, reducing it to a rising hot cloud of dust and ash. Dust defense is also known as environment defense. *See also* NUCLEAR RADIOACTIVITY; NUCLEAR WINTER.

Significance Dust has many radioactive effects: the most evident consequence is in the upper air, and the effect on the incoming sunlight. The radioactive effects are known to us not so much from the nuclear detonation as from the natural volcanic eruption of Krakatoa in Indonesia in the 1880s, which filled the world's air with its dust and ash. A few seasons of cooler weather were experienced in the world, and large-scale crop failure was recorded in Europe and the United States. Some studies of modern thermonuclear ground bursts suggest that such an explosion can be expected to place into the air from 1,000 to 10,000 tons of particles—aerosols—per megaton of yield. Voluminous smoke from worldwide industrial sites and the forest fires that would be caused by a nuclear war have been estimated to have even more serious effect than the dust from the explosion.

E

Early Radioactive Fallout   Radioactive refuse that rises into the atmosphere and falls to the earth soon after a nuclear explosion. Early radioactive fallout gets to the earth within 24 hours of a nuclear explosion and is heavily radioactive. When a nuclear weapon explodes, it destroys everything in the area, and the debris is drawn up into the atmosphere. After several tests carried out in 1954 produced fallout measurable on the surface of the entire world, great attention and controversy were aroused with regard to our health and genetic effects. Depending on the decaying isotope (the energy released in the nuclear fission process), likely emissions from nuclear decay processes are: X-rays, consisting of waves used in medicine because of their ability to penetrate the body, slightly dangerous to health; gamma rays, which are similar to X-rays but have a shorter wave length and are more damaging; beta particles, which are electrons that have been freed from the nuclei of atoms—the main risk from these occurs if fallout producing beta particles is swallowed or inhaled; alpha particles, which are the nuclei of helium atoms and, if swallowed or inhaled, can be dangerous to health; and lastly, neutrons, one of the basic particles out of which atomic nuclei are made—these may cause radiation sickness. Early radioactive fallout is different from delayed radioactive fallout, which takes longer to fall back to earth. *See also* DELAYED RADIOACTIVE FALLOUT.

Significance   Early radioactive fallout from fission weapon explosions could be so intense that only persons remaining in underground shelters for weeks could hope to survive such an attack. Usually only the most prominent isotopes in fallout are fission products, but scientists maintain that all materials exposed to nuclear bombs may become radioactive. Depicting a fallout pattern is difficult. When trying to project the fallout pattern that would follow a nuclear explosion, planners must take into account many variables, including weather conditions. The problem is enormously complicated since isotopes have different and sometimes elaborate distribution systems. Isotopes can enter the body by ingestion, inhalation, or injection. Their radiation effects depend on their internal distribution, duration of retention in the body, and rate of radioactive decay. Most of the information on effects has been based on results of studies on laboratory animals. These studies show that babies, children, and the elderly are more sensitive and susceptible to radiation than is the middle-aged adult.

Earth Penetrator   A potential nuclear-tipped missile, with warheads, that can burrow into the earth before detonating. The earth penetrators, or "burrowing nukes" as they are commonly called, are needed if the United States is to hold at risk Soviet command centers under Moscow and other cities. The new weapon is highly classified and the responsibility of the air force. It has been under study for years, but the U.S. Energy Department disclosed in June 1987 that it had begun preliminary development on the warhead for the burrowing missile when the Reagan administration began spotlighting Soviet construction of underground bunkers. (The Soviet Union has been building underground shelters for its leaders for over 40 years.) On August 19, 1988, the U.S. Defense Acquisition Board approved an air force mission statement for an earth-penetrating weapon. Such a statement means that the United States has a need for such a weapon system. The Secretary of Defense, Frank C. Carlucci, directed the air force in the fall of 1988 to provide cost estimates, and predicted performance data. *See also* ALTERNATE NATIONAL MILITARY COMMAND CENTER (ANMCC); COMMAND, CONTROL, COMMUNICATIONS, AND INTELLIGENCE (C3I); STRATEGIC AIR COMMAND (SAC).

Significance   The earth penetrator, if and when developed, should contribute substantially to nuclear deterrence. The Soviet authorities are constructing deep underground shelters to provide protection for all their command and control structures in the event of a nuclear war. As a result, some of their planners may think a nuclear war can be fought and won. The new burrowing weapon would deter them from that notion. The United States does not yet have an earth-penetrating weapon system; it is under study at a fairly low-level of funding. Even then, a "mission needs statement" approval is far removed from approval of an actual weapons program. However, the U.S. Department of Energy will likely step up its work on earth penetrator design, while the air force pursues missile development. In a similar manner, Soviet technologists may be devising a weapons system to penetrate U.S. command and control structures.

Electromagnetic Pulse (EMP)   A burst of radiation released immediately after a nuclear detonation. Electromagnetic pulse is the release
of intense bursts of energy across the electromagnetic spectrum. It
burns out electronic circuitry, destroying electronic instruments,
including computerized communication systems. A limited nuclear
war requires survivable electronic communications. This includes
communication links, ground and satellite observation and warning
systems and linkages between weapons and their guidance systems. In
1962 the EMP, from a high-altitude nuclear blast, caused the failure of
street lights, power-line circuits, and burglar alarms in Hawaii. The
EMP from a high-altitude nuclear explosion can interfere with the
electronic communications needed to run Anti-Ballistic Missile (ABM)
systems. The most effective collectors of EMP in the Command, Control, Communications, and Intelligence (C3I) are long runs of cable,
piping, large antennae and their feed cables, guy wires, support lines,
and many other kinds of equipment and facilities. *See also* ANTIBALLIS-
TIC MISSILE (ABM) TREATY; COMMAND, CONTROL, COMMUNICATIONS, AND
INTELLIGENCE (C3I); SINGLE INTEGRATED OPERATIONAL PLAN (SIOP).

Significance   The electromagnetic pulse is essentially an electric
field and a magnetic field moving away from the nuclear blast. This
phenomenon does not affect people directly and is related to the
ability to control military activities during a nuclear war. The EMP
signal resembles, somewhat, the electronic effects of lighting. But its
electromagnetic spectrum extends farther into the communication
frequencies, as an EMP delivers its energy 100 times as fast as does
lightning. These bursts can temporarily or permanently damage or
destroy all types of electronic equipment, both on the ground and in
space. The EMP that results from a first-strike impact is sufficient
to wreck the greater portion of the United States Single Integrated
Operational Plan (SIOP) as well as cause an electrical blackout across
the whole country. This danger from EMP has gradually been recognized as crucial, if control over nuclear forces is desired. Because of the
ban on above-ground tests, the destructive effect of this phenomenon
is not clearly understood. It is believed by some scientists that a single
Soviet warhead detonated 250 miles above Nebraska might paralyze
the United States and throw U.S. armed forces into total confusion.

Electronic Countermeasure (ECM)   An action taken by an attacker to render ineffective the electronic equipment used by a defender. An ECM includes a variety of actions taken against attacking
missiles. It attempts, for example, to confuse or temporarily disable an
enemy's sensors, satellites or missiles, by jamming their radar. An

ECM involves broadcasting competing radio waves that could cover up the radio waves reflected off the missile. The B-52s bristle with electronic countermeasure devices; one crew member out of six operates ECM to detect all attempts to locate the bombers and to deflect attacking interceptor missiles. A variety of countermeasures have been developed against missiles, such as the SAM-6, including steep dives and other evasive measures, chaff, electronic countermeasure, and heat-flare decoys. The Soviets will take electronic countermeasures to foil missiles equipped with homing devices, thereby degrading the general performance of ECM. Counter-ECM is an area in which the United States and NATO nations need development. *See also* B1, B-1B, B-52 BOMBERS.

Significance   An appropriate improvement in bomber alert capabilities, and in bomber performance through low-level flight and electronic countermeasures, promises a high survival rate for the strategic bomber deterrent as long as it is not attacked by depressed-trajectory (the elliptical path that a ballistic missile could follow as it streaks toward its target) submarine-launched ballistic missiles. Most of the current U.S. bomber deterrent is outdated. The new generation of manned bombers has been planned since 1962. Because the high-altitude plane was vulnerable to attack by surface-to-air missiles (SAMs), the plans changed to the B-1 bomber design, which is a four-engine jet with variable geometric wings. Nonetheless, the logic of technology is seen in current weapons controversy. Some critics believe that by the late 1980s, when many B-1s are expected to be in service, the aircraft will have been made obsolete by a new plane called "Stealth." This bomber, with highly classified design features and special coatings, will be even more radar-invisible.

Emergency Action Message (EAM)   The coded information used for strategic nuclear communications that instructs the crew to launch the weapons. The EAM is transmitted from the National Command Authorities (NCA) to the forces, instructing them to attack, hold fire, or cease fire. The chain of command goes from the president to the secretary of defense to the chairman of the Joint Chiefs of Staff (JCS) to the executing commander. In operations involving nuclear weapons, or in crisis situations, the president may bypass the chain of command and communicate directly with field commanders. The EAM must meet rigid specifications before commanders in the field and launch crew members will accept its authenticity. This message is transmitted over the primary alerting system, commonly known as the Red Phone. An elaborate combination of ground-based, air-based, rocket-based, and satellite-based relay systems ensure that the "go" code is received. There is always at least one SAC (Strategic Air Command) aircraft airborne, with the necessary transmission facilities. In an emergency, this plane is backed up by additional transmission facilities. *See also* COMMAND, CONTROL, COMMUNICATIONS, AND INTELLIGENCE (C3I); NATIONAL COMMAND AUTHORITIES (NCA).

Significance   The coded emergency action message is received by two launch controllers, who must decode and validate it. As coding and decoding goes on, the process can be halted if an EAM fails to satisfy correct codes. Should a nuclear war break out, one of the immediate effects would be severe dislocations in the ability to gather accurate information and to issue appropriate orders to forces. The problem of authentication involves more than simple recognition of the correct coded numbers. Many technicians and other officers involved must decide that the ostensibly correct signal is in fact a valid one. For this reason multiple transmissions are desirable, as are two-way communications to clarify validity of the appropriate series of numbers.

Encryption   The process of coding a message. Encryption is the encoding of telemetry for the purpose of rendering it indecipherable, and thus concealing the message recorded on it. The United States has accused that, contrary to SALT II stipulations, the Soviet Union has encrypted the telemetry from some missile tests. There are also a number of Soviet compliance-related charges against the United States. The approach to encryption was consistent with the SALT I provision that prohibited concealment measures impeding verification by the National Technical Means (NTM) of either party. In 1974 the United States noticed an increase in concealment activity by the Soviet Union which, while not impeding U.S. ability to verify compliance, might have if it had been continued and expanded. The United States raised this concern with the Soviet Union in 1975, after which the United States noted an end to the concealment activities. *See also* NATIONAL TECHNICAL MEANS OF VERIFICATION (NTM).

Significance   Encryption that keeps data secret for that information which is necessary to monitor the treaty is forbidden by the SALT II treaty. Verification demands not only knowledge of the numbers of weapons and their locations but also other details. If such data are essential to the country doing the testing, to determine if its system meets operational requirements, the data are also essential to others to verify whether the characteristics of the new system are compatible with the stipulation of existing agreements. No party is willing to make available such information to the other, yet arms control agreements require access to a good deal of information that can be gleaned only from telemetry. Regarding intercontinental ballistic missiles, a country would like to know their performance and their multiple independently targetable reentry vehicle (MIRV) number. Technicians carrying out weapons tests also need such information. Encoding of telemetry, as such, is not illegal under the terms of SALT II unless deliberate concealment is involved. The distinction is between encoding (translating message for transmission purposes) and encryption to keep the data secret. SALT II prohibits the latter.

Enhanced Radiation Weapon (ERW)   A nuclear warhead that kills mainly by high-neutron radiation, rather than by blast and heat. An enhanced radiation weapon, also called a neutron bomb, kills people but leaves surrounding buildings and areas undamaged. This bomb is designed to maximize damage to enemy troops—specifically, enemy tank crews—and minimize collateral damage to civilian and industrial installations. The neutron bomb was first developed in 1957 by Edward Teller, a distinguished physicist. It was designed to be a "clean" nuclear weapon without massive fallout. The ERW is a thermonuclear (fusion) device that emits a great deal of prompt neutron radiation, while other nuclear effects such as atmospheric overpressure, heat, and residual radiation (fallout) are suppressed. The neutron bomb differs from standard nuclear weapons insofar as its primary lethal effects come from the radiation damage caused by the neutron it emits. The military calls it an "enhanced radiation, reduced blast" weapon. The public perceives the term "enhanced radiation" to be somewhat more deadly than other thermonuclear weapons. *See also* NEUTRON BOMB; NUCLEAR WEAPON.

Significance   The neutron bomb represents a different approach to nuclear weapons, and it has generated controversy. President Jimmy Carter decided not to produce and deploy the bomb, even though the United States had developed it; President Ronald Reagan ordered production of the bomb. It appears to many people that the United States has a bomb in its armory that kills human beings and leaves properties intact. The Soviet Union has tested its own neutron bomb. France has developed a neutron bomb. The neutron bomb is attractive to many leaders because its prompt radiation is directed at enemy soldiers and causes minimal collateral damage to civilian properties. Critics say the ERW is immoral because it places a higher value upon physical structures, including houses and industrial centers, than upon life. The North Atlantic Treaty Organization (NATO) nations will eventually, if surreptitiously, want to use the ERW to offset the Warsaw Pact's superiority in conventional weapons, should there be an invasion of NATO territory.

Enola Gay   The B-29 bomber that dropped the first atomic bombs—on Hiroshima on August 6, 1945, and on Nagasaki in Japan three days later. The Enola Gay was named for the mother of the pilot, Colonel Paul Tibbets. The Hiroshima bomb, code-named "Little Boy," weighed 8,000 pounds, and measured 10 feet in length, 28 inches in diameter. The Nagasaki bomb, called "Fat Man," weighed 10,000 pounds and measured about 10 feet 8 inches in length, 5 feet in diameter. Both atomic weapons were exploded about 1,800 feet (550 meters) over the two Japanese cities. In all, B-29s flew 34,790 sorties during World War II and dropped 170,000 tons of bombs or equivalents on enemy targets, including the two atomic bombs. While the United States lost 414 B-29s—147 of these were attributed to enemy fighters or flak—B-29 gunners destroyed 1,128 Japanese aircraft. This bomber, manufactured by Boeing, was designed as the delivery vehicle for nuclear weapons as they became available during World War II. The B-29 strategic bomber force grew into the Strategic Air Command (SAC), armed with B-36, B-47, and B-52 bombers. *See also* FAT MAN; HIROSHIMA; LITTLE BOY; NAGASAKI.

Significance   The Enola Gay was a high-altitude bomber with a range of 300 kilometers, and is remembered as the aircraft that suddenly ended World War II by dropping two atomic weapons on Japan. The people of Hiroshima had responded to an earlier air-raid siren, but had emerged from the shelters just before the bomb exploded at 8:15 A.M. The fireball (amount of energy released upon detonation) created by the explosion reached temperatures of several million degrees centigrade and, within one second, grew to a diameter of 250 to 300 meters, raising the temperature on the ground to about 5,000 degrees centigrade. It consumed about one-third of the energy created in the explosion, and the thermal radiation emitted by the ball was intense enough to burn at a distance of 2.5 kilometers. Philip Noel-Baker, a British politician involved in the creation of the League of Nations and the United Nations, gives a vivid description of what happened in Hiroshima as the Enola Gay dropped the atomic bomb. "The streets were full of people, people going to work, people going to shop, children going to school. The plane flew across the city and dropped the bomb, which fell for 10 to 15 seconds. Then there was a sudden flash of light and those who looked directly at it had their eyes burnt in their sockets. . . . The greater part of Hiroshima was destroyed and approximately 130,000 people were killed or died later as a result of the first atomic bomb blast. To say the least, it was kind of hell on earth."[10]

Enriched Nuclear Fuel   Refined uranium that can be used in nuclear reactors and weapons. Enriched nuclear fuel is obtained through the process of increasing the concentration of uranium 235. Uranium exists in nature in two forms: uranium 238 and uranium 235. Uranium enriched to about 90 percent, U-235, is considered suitable for nuclear weapons. Many industrialized countries have become involved in the nuclear fuel business for profitmaking. For example, West Germany builds and sells enriching plants for U-235, and Canada sells nuclear plants but retains the reprocessing rights (the technique of obtaining plutonium from the mixture of waste products by a nuclear reactor). Argentina, Brazil, Israel, Pakistan, and South Africa have acquired reactors from various Western nations. India has officially tested a nuclear "device," but several nations—South Africa, Israel, and Pakistan for example—have not admitted developing nuclear capabilities for fear of antagonizing Western donor nations and world public opinion. These nations claim their nuclear reactors are for peaceful purposes, such as producing energy and medical isotopes. *See also* MANHATTAN PROJECT; URANIUM.

Significance   Enriched nuclear fuel is developed through a complex and expensive process, first made available in the United States during World War II. The production of the first atomic bombs in the United States presented scientists with great technical difficulty. The problem with designing World War II bombs lay in obtaining the U-235 by separating it from the U-238 in natural uranium. For the Manhattan Project, which produced the first bomb, it was well recognized that the separation would have to rely on the small difference in mass between the two isotopes. An electromagnetic separation process (combinations of magnetic and electric fields) was used to separate the slightly lighter U-235 atoms from the dominant atoms of U-238. The process cost $444 million. Nations can connect their production of nuclear weapons to nuclear energy through technical expertise acquired in reactor development programs, as was the case for India in 1974. This was that nation's first—and only—nuclear test, and India referred to it as a peaceful nuclear explosion. Confronted with India's nuclear weapons program, Pakistan has been developing its own nuclear option, but, like India, consistently asserts that its nuclear program is entirely peaceful.

Escalation   An increase in scope or violence of a conflict. Escalation occurs when one side in a dispute moves, for example, from a local to a general war or from a conventional to a strategic nuclear strike. Conflict escalation can be achieved in a number of ways: geographic escalation, weapons escalation, and escalation in conflict intensity. The likelihood of escalation is, in part, a function of national security strategy. When dealing with tactical or limited war, the serious questions are those of control and escalation. Controlled escalation is the cornerstone of the doctrine of limited war. Escalation controls seek to prevent an all-out nuclear confrontation. A limited nuclear war would not be feasible if it were likely to escalate into a full-scale nuclear war with its traumatic consequences. Millions of people have been killed in conventional wars since the end of World War II, but no one has been killed in nuclear wars. If any conventional war escalates to the point of nuclear confrontation, it will be a tragic time in the history of civilization. To date, escalation control, *inter alia*, has prevented an all-out nuclear holocaust. *See also* LIMITED NUCLEAR WAR; NUCLEAR WAR.

Significance   Escalation involves crossing a threshold. Studying how or whether escalation might occur requires determining how crucial it is for nations to avoid the firebreak and what is needed to minimize the extent of escalation. There is a tendency for each side to counter the other's pressure with a somewhat stronger one of its own. In all escalation, two sets of basic elements coexist: the political and military issues surrounding the particular conflicts; and the levels of violence or provocation at which they are fought. Few arms control issues are of greater urgency than the need to develop processes that can control the scope of violence involving the superpowers. The obvious goal is to prevent the passage from conventional to nuclear war. Who will decide under what circumstances nuclear forces will be used? In the United States the president makes that ultimate decision. Since any escalation from a conventional to a nuclear exchange is likely to happen suddenly, the president can initiate a nuclear war— without the approval of Congress, his cabinet, or any other person or persons.

Eurogroup   An informal association of defense ministers of the European members of the North Atlantic Treaty Organization (NATO). Eurogroup was created as a means of responding to a desire for closer European cooperation within the Atlantic Alliance. The aim was to make the European contribution to the common defense of the North Atlantic area as strong as possible. European nations taking part are: Belgium, Denmark, West Germany, Greece, Italy, Luxembourg, the Netherlands, Norway, Portugal, Spain, Turkey, and the United Kingdom. Only France and Iceland are not participating. Of the ready forces currently available in the European theater, 85 percent of the ground troops and 80 percent of the air force are supplied by the Eurogroup nations. They also make major contributions to naval forces in European waters and in the Atlantic. Overall, the size of the forces from the European countries amounts to 2.5 million men, compared with over 2 million in the forces of the North American allies (United States and Canada). *See also* EUROMISSILES; NORTH ATLANTIC TREATY ORGANIZATION (NATO); SUPREME ALLIED COMMANDER EUROPE (SACEUR); WARSAW PACT.

Significance   Eurogroup is a pragmatic organization, operating within the framework of the North Atlantic Alliance. Its mission is to reinforce the common security on the basis of partnership and confidence among the European and transatlantic members of the alliance. Changes in the worldwide political and military situation since the founding of the Eurogroup in 1968 have served to strengthen the need for European countries to use their defense resources. As NATO moves forward into the fifth decade of its existence, an alliance with a strong, cohesive European pillar will be able to provide both continents with a guarantee of security and freedom. Working within the framework of NATO, the Eurogroup serves to strengthen the European voice and contribution, and thus undergirds the effectiveness of the Alliance defense system as a whole.

Euromissiles   Short- and medium-range missiles deployed in Europe. Euromissiles are deployed in Europe by the United States, Britain, France and the Soviet Union. The U.S. Pershing II and the Soviet SS-20 are examples of Euromissiles. With their great accuracy, the Pershing II medium-range missiles and the SS-20s are intended to succeed in an attack on the enemy's hardened military targets. Since 1977 the Soviet Union has been deploying the intermediate-range ballistic missile (IRBM), labeled the SS-20 by NATO. This missile is solid-fueled, and consists of the lower two stages of the SS-16 ICBM. One SS-20 can deliver three MIRVs of 150 kilotons each with an accuracy of about 400 meters over a range of 5,000 kilometers. About 210 of the 315 presently deployed SS-20s are thought to be aimed at NATO targets. the United States has 108 Pershing II IRBMs in response to the SS-20. Their accuracy is 40 meters or better, over their range of 1,500 kilometers, and they deliver a single warhead of 250-kiloton yield. Their relatively small size makes them mobile. The

British currently have 64 missiles, carrying three warheads each, on four submarines; the French have 18 land-based missiles and 80 SLBMs carried on five submarines. *See also* NORTH ATLANTIC TREATY ORGANIZATION (NATO).

Significance   Euromissiles have been controversial and have complicated arms control negotiations. U.S. missiles in Europe pose a direct threat quite close to the Soviet Union. Soviet missiles in Europe, on the other hand, are at least three thousand miles from mainland United States. The United States justifies its missile deployment in Europe as being part of the North Atlantic Treaty Organization (NATO) strategy. The Soviets criticize this action since the United States is not a continental part of Europe. The United States contends that the NATO alliance is based on the principle that the defense of the independent and democratic systems of the European allies against the threat posed by the Soviet Union is vital to the health, and even to the survival, of the United States. Not all NATO members agree with U.S. policy. The debate within NATO about the role of the United States in the defense of Europe continues. Great Britain's inventory of nuclear warheads is planned to more than quintuple, reaching 500 by the mid-1990s. During this time, France will also increase its nuclear arsenal, numbering more than 600 warheads. These expansions, when considered with the removal of the superpowers' short- and medium-range nuclear weapons from Europe—in accordance with the Intermediate-range Nuclear Forces Treaty (1987)—imply that the British and French nuclear forces will acquire for them greater bargaining position in NATO decision making.

F

Fail-Safe   A complex mechanism that prevents the launching of missiles without proper orders and release codes. Fail-safe is a system aimed at avoiding a nuclear war triggered "by accident." U.S. bombers have a fail-safe point to which they fly in the case of a given level of war readiness alert, but which they must not pass unless specifically ordered. There exists no check on intercontinental ballistic missiles (ICBMs)—once they are launched there is no way of recalling them. The U.S. president has a variety of methods and targets available to him. These include: (1) major attack options; (2) all-out retaliatory attack; (3) selected attack options; (4) attack on only certain specific targets; (5) limited nuclear target options, aimed specifically at fixed enemy military or industrial centers; (6) regional nuclear options to destroy the military command of a given area; and (7) a preemptive strike. Fail-safe is distinct from fail-dead, which refers to a system that fires nuclear weapons without proper authorization. Fail-safe is also known as positive control. In a 1964 movie, "Fail Safe," a practice launch of SAC (Strategic Air Command) bombers is almost perfectly executed. All but one plane returns to base. The lone aircraft, aimed at Moscow, eventually reaches its target, and drops its nuclear weapon on the Soviet capital. *See also* COMMAND, CONTROL, COMMUNICATIONS, AND INTELLIGENCE (C3I).

Significance   The fail-safe device permits the checking of whether an emergency must lead to war. If warranted, the bombers are ordered back to their base. However, once they pass the fail-safe point, each individual commander will, as directed, deliver his bombs on target. Although the early-warning and command systems of the United States have been planned to eliminate human error, they offer no constraint on a mechanical malfunction. U.S. forces require backup information before executing defensive and retaliatory measures. The confirmation is obtained from more than one early-warning radar source of the potential and approaching threat following a Soviet nuclear missile launch. The proposed Strategic Defense Initiative (SDI) system, if it materializes as envisioned, will require a highly sophisticated computer so massive that it will probably have to be self-policing since it would transcend human ability in its complexity. The great danger is that once ICBMs are launched, they cannot be recalled, and a nuclear catastrophe is certain.

Fallout   The precipitation of radioactive particulate matter that falls to earth from a nuclear cloud. Fallout is radioactive refuse of a nuclear bomb explosion or nuclear power plant malfunction, and the process of the deposition of such refuse on the surrounding land, human beings, and animals. Fallout may be early or delayed. Early, or local, fallout consists of those particles that reach the earth within 24 hours after a nuclear explosion. Delayed, or worldwide, fallout refers to the smaller particles that ascend into the upper troposphere and into the stratosphere and are then carried by winds to remote parts of the earth. The feature that makes nuclear bombs so powerful—the fission and fusion nuclei—also creates the fallout radiation. Fallout can be extremely dangerous; exposure to it can cause genetic damage, radiation sickness, and cancer. Infants, children, and old people are more sensitive to the lethal effects of radiation than are healthy adults. Not all radiation is harmful. Heat and light are forms that normally do no damage at all. *See also* DELAYED RADIOACTIVE FALLOUT; EARLY RADIOACTIVE FALLOUT.

Significance   Fallout is a particularly devastating effect of a nuclear explosion. Created in an all-out nuclear war, fallout can cause millions of deaths and contaminate the earth's food and water supplies. Part of the fallout occurs rather promptly in the vicinity of the blast. Radioactivity that does not reach the stratosphere will drift a few hours or days with the wind, coming down as fallout up to a few hundred miles away. The extent of this fallout differs according to the type of explosion. For example, an air burst will be limited as to local effects but, with greater dispersion into the atmosphere, will have far greater potential as a worldwide pollutant. Helen Caldicott maintains that "in a full-scale nuclear war, the United States probably would be covered by lethal fallout for the first 48 hours. Subsequent consequences would be so devastating that up to 90 percent of Americans could be dead within thirty days."[11] Other nations would also be equally affected. If enough of the nuclear bombs already in existence in the world are exploded, it is possible that the fallout would reach dangerous levels for everybody on earth. There is also major fallout from nuclear power station accidents as happened in 1986 at the Soviet Union's Chernobyl power plant. It affected the environment not only in the Ukraine and Belorussia areas of the Soviet Union but also in countries beyond its borders. The effects of radiation are insidious and long-term and become fully manifest only years after a nuclear explosion or power plant accident.

Fat Man   The second atomic bomb, used to destroy Nagasaki, Japan, on August 9, 1945 at 11:02 A.M. "Fat Man," which measured about 10 feet and weighed about 9,000 pounds, was designed at Los Alamos, New Mexico, by a team of scientists headed by J. Robert Oppenheimer. It was exploded in an air burst 1,640 feet above Nagasaki and had a yield of 20,000 tons of TNT (20 kilotons). This bomb was dropped on Nagasaki by a B-29 bomber. Some survivors of the Hiroshima bombing on August 6 sought refuge in the only Christian center in Japan—Nagasaki. They arrived in time for the second atomic bomb holocaust and here between 60,000 and 70,000 people were killed. Yet Fat Man had only a fraction of the destructive power contained in today's nuclear weapons: Fat Man equalled 20,000 tons of TNT equivalent; a modern hydrogen bomb equals 20,000,000 tons of TNT equivalent, which is one thousand times more powerful. In 1961 the Soviets exploded a warhead of 60,000,000 tons of TNT equivalent. *See also* AIR BURST; HIROSHIMA; LITTLE BOY; NAGASAKI.

Significance   Fat Man was the second plutonium bomb; the first was exploded in the Trinity Test at Alamogordo, New Mexico, in July 1945. To the Japanese, the dropping of atomic bombs on two of their cities was an unnecessary attack on innocent civilian populations. Most military experts believe that the use of the bomb did contribute to Japan's decision to surrender. The attacks were also taken as evidence of the U.S. intention to pulverize Japanese society or demonstrate U.S. strength to the Soviets. However, the decision was made easier by the fact that the United States did not have to fear a Japanese counterattack. Recent advances in both explosive power and delivery accuracy would enable a missile-launched thermonuclear war targeted to major population centers to kill, instantly, millions of people. Even the least powerful nuclear weapon today is more powerful than either of the two atomic bombs used on the two Japanese cities, and the consequences of contemporary nuclear warheads would be far more devastating than anything previously experienced.

Federal Emergency Management Agency (FEMA)   The agency responsible for managing a state of preparedness for emergencies—natural, man-made, or nuclear. Federal Emergency Management Agency (FEMA), an independent agency, was created in 1978 for developing a shelter program; a defense against chemical, biological, and radiological weapons; a warning system; and measures to be undertaken following an attack. This agency has designated many structures as fallout shelters for protection against radioactivity following a nuclear attack and has stocked them with supplies, which range from steel and aluminum to natural rubber, industrial diamonds, selenium, and tantalum. FEMA carries out its responsibility in close coordination with numerous other federal, state, and local agencies. Protection of U.S. citizens from nuclear attack is the agency's primary objective, and it has developed many civil defense programs, such as a warning system, shelter planning and identification, and provision of emergency information through the Emergency Broadcasting System. *See also* CIVIL DEFENSE.

Significance   The Federal Emergency Management Agency is responsible for plans and policies related to peacetime and wartime emergencies and for planning the nation's nonmilitary defense, such as civil defense. It is authorized to plan for the recovery of the United States after a nuclear war. The Reagan administration included in the FEMA various crisis relocation plans for evacuating urban residents to the countryside in the event a nuclear war seemed imminent. The plan was considered ludicrous because Soviet satellites could observe large population movement in the United States, and no means exist to care for millions of Americans transplanted to rural areas. Also, if the Soviets saw the United States evacuating its cities, they would conclude that it was preparing for a first-strike nuclear war. At that point the Soviets could very well initiate their preemptive first strike against U.S. strategic targets and cities. This aspect of the new U.S. strategic program sparked public controversy in the country. Many citizens found the evacuation plan unworkable, and the plan was quietly dropped.

Fireball   The large amount of energy released upon detonation of a nuclear bomb. The fireball is the burning gas that forms immediately after a nuclear weapon explodes. If the bomb is exploded at ground level, it produces a ground burst in which 60 percent of the fallout reaches the ground within 24 hours. Temperatures in the bomb are in the order of tens of millions of degrees, high enough to vaporize all solid materials, its casting, and any material immediately surrounding the blast. X-rays from the explosion are absorbed by the surrounding air and progressively re-radiate on longer wavelengths.

This results in a very bright spherical mass known as the fireball, which grows and rises. A one-megaton burst is about 7,200 feet wide after ten seconds and rises at the rate of 300 feet per second. A large nuclear explosion produces a longer-lived fireball and a mushroom cloud that rises to higher altitudes. *See also* NUCLEAR BOMB.

Significance   The fireball is a mini-sun, intensely hot, which hangs in the sky for as long as ten seconds after a nuclear detonation emits a very bright flash of light and thermal radiation that can cause blindness, burns, and fires. The explosion of a nuclear bomb also leads to a shock wave, as the hot air in the fireball expands. A much larger detonation of the fusion bombs ensures that the much greater areas are covered as the mushroom from the fireball penetrates higher into the stratosphere. The fireball from the explosion is ionized. These ions deflect and absorb radar signals. The high temperatures in the fireball chemically ignite some of the nitrogen in the air, producing oxides of nitrogen, which in turn chemically attack and destroy the gas ozone in the middle stratosphere. The heat effect of the fireball is most effective against densely populated cities.[12] "The fireball will sear the flesh of people in the open, and dry-roast or asphyxiate those in deep shelters."[13] In addition to the violence of the blast wave, the effects of nuclear radiation will account for the vast majority of casualties.

First Strike   The launching of an initial nuclear attack before one's opponent is able to use any strategic weapon. First strike is a massive nuclear attack carried out at such a devastatingly high level of destruction as to nullify an enemy's capability to launch a major counterstrike. This massive first-strike doctrine of the 1950s required only a minimal command control system. A country has first-strike capability if it can destroy so much of the enemy's weaponry in an attack that the retaliatory strike would not inflict unacceptable damage on the attacker. The essential first-strike weapon is the intercontinental ballistic missile (ICBM), which, with its speed and accuracy of delivery, can be used for a preemptive attack, while slower bomber or cruise missiles forfeit that element of surprise required of any first strike. According to deterrence theory, each superpower is able to absorb a first strike and then inflict an unacceptable destructive retaliation. Superpowers have undertaken a variety of measures in order to deter the other from attacking first. *See also* NUCLEAR DETERRENCE; SECOND STRIKE.

Significance   A successful first strike implies the ability to eliminate retaliation by the enemy by counterforce targeting (a nuclear strike against the enemy's military forces and weapons aimed at cities and civilians). It is a hypothetical attack by a state on military and industrial targets of another state. A first strike is, by definition, a preemptive action, launched by a nation when it believes that its national security is at stake. Both superpowers maintain a capability to absorb a nuclear strike and retaliate with an equally or more devastating attack. Thus they are deterred from launching a nuclear attack out of the fear that it will invite a destructive retaliation. Though both superpowers reject any idea of their own launch of a first strike, much of the arms race depends on projecting the belief that the weapons development programs of the other side can only add to mutual distrust. Some argue that stability demands that neither the United States nor the Soviet Union attempt to achieve first-strike capability. Still others see a counterforce capability as essential to deter each other's threat.

Fission   The splitting of an atomic nucleus either spontaneously or under the impact of another particle, releasing substantial quantities of energy. For fission to occur, the atomic particle must be unstable. The energy release in the atomic/nuclear fission process comes from changes in the nuclei of atoms such as uranium and plutonium. In the original A-bombs, uranium 235 or plutonium 239 was used as the fissile material (fissionable material is sometimes called fissile, nuclear, or fertile material). When a U-235 nucleus captures a neutron it becomes a highly unstable U-236 nucleus. The U-236 nucleus decays by flying apart into two large pieces, called fission products. They form part of the waste of the nuclear power and weapons industries. They are highly radioactive isotopes, some of the most lethal being strontium, iodine, and cesium. Fission is much more potent than fusion. It is the essential mechanism of atomic weapons and nuclear power and is used to trigger thermonuclear weapons. *See also* FUSION.

Significance   Fission is initiated by compressing a mass that is slightly less than critical into one that is slightly greater than critical. The chain reaction thus caused reaches a climax in half of one millionth of a second, after 55 generations of subdivision. Inside the core, the fission process is controlled in a nuclear power plant: (1) by the use of control rods, which are inserted into the core among the fuel rods, and (2) by the use of a coolant to control the nuclear chain reaction inside a reactor. The coolant is usually highly purified water. All U.S. reactors, except one, are water moderated. The moderation slows down the neutrons and, in the process, makes fission of the fuel more complete. Two methods of triggering the A-bombs exploded over Japan were used. The gun method was employed on the Hiroshima device, involving the firing toward each other of two subcritical hemi-spheres of nuclear material. When these collided they produced the necessary critical mass. The implosion method, used on the Nagasaki bomb, involved the explosion of a casting of TNT around the fission-able material. This method is used in contemporary bombs.

Fission-Fusion-Fission Weapon   A three-stage thermonuclear bomb with a uranium or fission trigger, a hydrogen or fusion interme-diate state, and an outer case of natural uranium. In a fission-fusion-fission weapon, three basic steps take place. First, an atom-splitting reaction generates very high temperatures. This heat triggers the second step, the combining of atoms. The fusion reaction then trig-gers the final step, the uranium shell that surrounds the core of the weapon. Nuclear fission is the splitting of the nuclei of heavy atoms such as uranium or plutonium. Nuclear fusion is the combination of light atoms such as hydrogen isotopes. In both cases part of the mass of these elements is converted into energy and, if this can be done fast enough, a nuclear explosion would be the result. The atomic bomb—the Hiroshima type—relied on fission for its power with a yield of 12–15 kilotons. A modern thermonuclear bomb works by fusion. *See also* FISSION; FUSION.

Significance   Fission-fusion-fission weapons are the most powerful type of nuclear bombs. The "threat of a large hydrogen bomb com-pared with fission explosions is the potential effect of the large-scale fallout from the uranium fission jacket of the fission-fusion-fission combination."[14] The United States has exploded fusion bombs up to 20 megatons, and the Soviet Union has tested a fusion device with a yield of 58 megatons. Most weapons now in the superpowers' arsenal are fusion bombs, with yields of almost any size—from very great to quite small. Normally, a policymaker is not interested in the type of bomb used, but would like to know the yield of weapons being used so the damage factor can be calculated.

Flexible Response   A strategy of graduated or controlled actions to counter aggression. The flexible response, a policy developed by President John F. Kennedy, held that first conventional weapons, and then nuclear weapons, would be used to repulse a Soviet attack in Europe. This doctrine replaced massive retaliation as official U.S. policy in the early 1960s. It declares that the United States, in consul-tation with North Atlantic Treaty Organization (NATO) allies is pre-pared to use nuclear weapons should other means of protection from

Soviet attack fail. Adopted in 1967 as the official NATO policy, flexible response deters Soviet aggression through a strategy that combines measured reactions and forward defense. The latter is a policy to resist any attack on NATO nations as far forward as possible in order to prevent an aggressor from seizing NATO territory. The essence of the flexible response is to convince the potential aggressor that any attack on NATO nations—whatever its nature, place, or time—would expose the attacker to incalculable and unacceptable risks. This requires NATO to demonstrate its political resolve to act jointly against all forms of aggression, and to have the military capability to respond effectively at all levels of aggression. This strategy does not, however, require NATO to match the Warsaw Pact nations man for man or weapon for weapon. It does require the alliance to maintain a mix of adequate and effective conventional and nuclear forces. *See also* MASSIVE RETALIATION; NORTH ATLANTIC TREATY ORGANIZATION (NATO); WARSAW PACT.

Significance A flexible response policy can be seductive: it makes no preconditions; its flexibility means that there is neither a promise to go nuclear nor any restriction on so doing. The concept of flexible response implies an escalation to meet aggression with suitable levels of counteraggression. The Kennedy administration—made up mostly of men who had fought as junior officers in World War II—offered the concept of flexible response. Through it they sought to remedy the flaws in massive retaliation, particularly the disproportion between means and ends. To European opponents of the policy, flexible response opened the possibility that the United States would stop short of ever using nuclear weapons directly against the Soviet Union. To others, flexible response held up the prospect that the superpowers might fight a limited nuclear war in Western and Central Europe while keeping both U.S. and Soviet homelands out of the nuclear battleground.

Forward-Based System (FBS) A program in which nuclear weapons are deployed beyond one's own territory. A forward-based system is a Soviet concept to denote U.S. and Soviet nuclear weapons placed outside their geographical territories. Attempt is made to place them as close to the adversary as possible, often creating an image of "encirclement" of the potential enemy. These weapons are also known as noncentral systems, and include small, tactical nuclear weapons such as the short-range, medium-range, and intermediate-range ballistic missiles. Proposals to ban forward-based systems go back to Soviet suggestions for banning all foreign bases; the Soviet argument is that such weapons can strike Soviet territory and thus must be regarded as strategic. Although no action was taken on FBS in the Strategic Arms Limitation Talks (SALT II), the United States and the Soviet Union signed a joint statement of principles that would allow either party—in future negotiations—to raise issues related to further limitation of strategic arms. For the Soviets this meant a forward-based system. *See also* COUPLING; TACTICAL NUCLEAR WEAPON (TNW).

Significance   The forward-based system concept was coined by the Soviets during the SALT I negotiations to distinguish it from regionally oriented, alliance-related systems. Accordingly, the FBS exists only to protect the superpowers and to further their interests. Consequently, Pershing IIs, which are part of the North Atlantic Treaty Organization (NATO) panoply, would not be considered a FBS, but nuclear weapons placed in Turkey would be part of it. The Soviet view holds that the FBS is part of the U.S. weapons system because the United States retains direct control over the deployment and use of weapons. The U.S. perspective stresses that even though the United States may have control over the buttons, the weapons themselves are to be used only to defend allies in Europe. Although there appears to be little difference of opinion over the means, the two superpowers disagree over the ends. The Soviet view is that the FBS protects U.S. interests whereas the Americans emphasize its protection of their allies. To the Soviets, the FBS is its first line of defense (or offense), but to the Americans the FBS implies coupling United States security with that of its allies. Consequently, the Soviets believe that the FBS of the United States needs to be included in arms control negotiations.

Free-Electron Laser (FEL)   A theoretical high-technology defensive weapon. A free-electron laser weapon would produce a light beam that is concentrated and is of high speed. The beam would burn a hole in the skin of an incoming nuclear missile and deactivate the electronic gear responsible for completion of the missile's flight path to its target. Such a beam can function as a super-concentrated spotlight that would destroy its targets by focusing tremendous power of energy on them. The laser beam would be aimed at the mirrors, which reflect the beams toward the earth to attack Soviet intercontinental ballistic missiles in their boost phase. Recent advances in free-electron lasers allow scientists to contemplate putting the high-energy lasers on the ground and bouncing the beams around the earth into the engagement battle. In 1986, a team of researchers at the Lawrence Livermore National Laboratory in California demonstrated a device called the experimental Test Facility—a 35 gigahertz free-electron laser—which achieved better than 40 percent electrical efficiency. This advancement in high-energy lasers, in particular in free-electron lasers, shows that we can compensate for the turbulence introduced by the atmosphere. *See also* LASER; STRATEGIC DEFENSE INITIATIVE (SDI).

Significance   A free-electron laser weapon can be deployed both on the ground and in space. In 1987 the U.S. Army offered Fluor Corporation a $197.6 million contract to build facilities for a ground-based FEL experiment. The army also gave the Lockheed Corporation an $80 million contract to provide engineering support services for high-energy laser facilities. Both contracts are part of the Strategic Defense Initiative (SDI) effort to determine whether FEL weapons can destroy enemy ballistic missiles in flight. The experimental and support facilities further demonstrated the Reagan administration's commitment to SDI. Researchers in laser physics know that electrical efficiency is an extremely critical commodity in such devices. Typically, lasers operate in the area of 1, 2, or 5 percent at best. But to achieve 40 percent efficiency, as the Lawrence Livermore National Laboratory did, is quite a success. Scientists outside the government argue that passing a laser beam through the atmosphere, and keeping it focused, is a very difficult problem because of the turbulence in the air due to density variation, which distorts the beam.

Functional Kill   Disabling an enemy space weapon. Functional kill involves deactivating an enemy warhead or satellite. It does not include blowing up an enemy target. The process involves penetrating the outer covering of the target and destroying the sensitive electronic components without causing an explosion. The trick is to cause a malfunction of the target while keeping its outer appearance intact. Directed Energy Weapon (DEW), a hypothetical weapon under the Strategic Defense Initiative (SDI), could be used in a functional kill. The DEWs would destroy their targets by focusing intense beams of energy on the surface of warheads. For this reason a functional kill is also called a soft kill. *See also* STRATEGIC DEFENSE INITIATIVE (SDI).

Significance   Functional kill does not involve an explosion and hence is more difficult to verify. Such weapons will further complicate arms control negotiations because the ability to verify is crucial to arms control progress. The superpowers are already facing problems in resolution of opinions over cruise missiles and multiple warheads; functional kill would present additional obstacles to arms control negotiations. A weapon that can destroy an enemy target may become an effective offensive weapon, raising the specter of a surprise first attack. Thus offense-defense distinction may blur, giving the opponents of SDI a weapon to assail the project. The proposed directed energy systems for functional kill have some difficulty penetrating the atmosphere, but many government scientists view the laser as a promising technology. Although still experimental it has the potential to revolutionize warfare.

Fusion   A type of nuclear reaction in which two or more lighter nuclei are combined to form a heavier, more complex nucleus. This source of the energy of the sun and other stars is one of the fundamental energy-releasing reactions of atomic nuclei. A nuclear-fusion reaction is produced when nuclei of the isotopes of certain light elements collide, resulting in the rearrangement of their constituent protons and neutrons, the formation of reaction products, and the release of energy. Such a process is involved in the explosion of a hydrogen bomb, which is created by using either deuterium or tritium (both are of hydrogen). While deuterium has one extra neutron, tritium has two additional neutrons. The fusion is activated by a nuclear fission, the process involved in an atom bomb explosion.

Energy from nuclear fusion was first tapped in an uncontrolled manner in the hydrogen bomb in the early 1950s. Nuclear reactors now in commercial power plants operate by fission of heavy nuclei, whereas fusion reactors would operate by fusion or fusing of light nuclei. A successful fusion reactor would offer many advances: (1) abundance of low-cost fuel; (2) less radioactivity; (3) no possibility of a nuclear explosion; and (4) fuel would not be usable for making a bomb. *See also* FISSION; THERMONUCLEAR WEAPON.

Significance   A fusion process constitutes the basis of a thermonuclear weapon that is vastly more powerful than the fission-type atomic bombs used on Japan in 1945. While fusion has potential as a cheap source of electricity, it is the crucial mechanism of thermonuclear weapons. If an additional casing of uranium 238 (U-238) is placed around core nuclei, the U-238 absorbs the neutrons created by the fusion process and itself undergoes fission. Such a three-stage fission-fusion-fission mechanism, involving a complex of explosions, produces a highly radioactive dirty bomb. However, the main difficulty lies in preventing the atom bomb (fission) trigger from destroying the entire device long enough for fusion, and the resultant explosion, to take place. The smashing of one nucleus into another has to be done at a tremendously high temperature. The challenge for scientists in producing usable energy is to produce that reaction at room temperature. Muon, which has the properties of an electron but is 207 times heavier than an electron, is as big as the nucleus itself. Muon's negative charge can force the hydrogen nuclei very close together even at room temperature. In 1987, the U.S. Department of Energy selected a subsidiary of KMS Industries for a five-year $77.6 million contract to conduct fusion research.

G

Galosh   The Soviet nuclear-armed antiballistic missile (ABM) defense system. Galosh, first developed in 1964, is also known as the ABM-1B Galosh interceptor, and is designed to intercept and destroy incoming enemy missiles. A Galosh can carry a nuclear warhead over a range of 200 miles but is only capable of terminal-phase interception. The Galosh was first seen in the November 1964 parade when the Soviets deployed the ABM system around Moscow, with rotating antennas. Its very size indicated it was an exoatmospheric interceptor capable of carrying out engagements at long ranges. The Galosh, which is the only currently operational ABM system, is deployed to protect Moscow and much of the western Soviet Union. *See also* ANTI-BALLISTIC MISSILE TREATY; ELECTROMAGNETIC PULSE (EMP).

Significance   The Galosh is the only ABM system deployed by the Soviet Union that is permitted by the 1972 ABM treaty and the 1974 Protocol. The United States formerly deployed a similar system called "Safeguard," designed to defend a missile site in North Dakota. The Galosh system involves a total of 64 missiles in eight batteries, each with eight missiles. By 1980 half the missiles were dismantled leaving only four batteries in four missile sites. A major problem of the Galosh system is that a single enemy missile hitting one missile battery can incapacitate the other batteries by means of the massive electromagnetic pulse (EMP) created by the explosion. The Galosh suffers from other problems, notably that the explosion caused would wreck the power grid and military communications. It would also jam the radar system with a cloud of electrically charged particles that would be released in the air. These shortcomings suggest that the Galosh may soon be replaced with phased-array radars.

Gamma Ray   High-energy short-wavelength electromagnetic radiation. Gamma ray is basically similar to, but of shorter wavelength than, X-ray. It is emitted from atomic nuclei when undergoing changes in energy such as radioactive decay. Gamma ray emission is the most common way for high energy atomic nuclei to drop to their ground (or unexcited) energy level. Gamma ray is not in itself a particle, though its radiation may accompany the loss of alpha or beta particles. It is emitted during exploding stars, generating intense energy and creating heavier elements from lighter ones. In a nuclear explosion, gamma ray is released in two ways. First, it is emitted immediately after the explosion—a stage known as prompt radiation. Second (the stage of fallout radiation), occurs when the explosion creates contaminated debris (by-products) that is sucked up into the atmospheric vacuum and creates another wave of gamma ray. The amount of gamma radiation falls off according to the square of the distance from the source, combined with the absorption effects of the material through which it travels. X-rays and gamma rays are called photons. Strictly speaking, X-rays come from the electron cloud surrounding the nucleus, while gamma rays come from the nucleus. The fireball of a nuclear detonation emits an intense pulse of gamma rays, and fallout dust releases gamma continually. *See also* RADIO-ACTIVE DECAY.

Significance   Gamma ray is of nuclear origin. It causes severe cell mutation and, thus, is dangerously harmful to human beings. Nuclear fission always emits gamma ray. It is highly penetrating, although its force is somewhat diminished by barriers of dense materials such as thick concrete and lead. For this reason nuclear reactor cores require concrete shielding of several meters thick. An intense burst of neutrons and gamma ray is produced during the first few millionths of a second of a nuclear detonation. What happens depends on the energy of the radiation, the nature of the tissue, and whether the radiation is a photon (X-ray or gamma ray), a neutron, or a charged particle. The use of X-rays for medical and industrial purposes add man-made radiation to the natural phenomena.

General Nuclear Response   An all-out nuclear strike against an enemy. A general nuclear response can also be viewed as an all-out or global nuclear war involving the United States and the Soviet Union. It is a high intensity war, with the superpowers using their full nuclear panoply. The possibility of nuclear confrontation has existed for 40 years, ever since the Soviet Union became the second nation to possess nuclear weapons. Once that happened it became evident that the two superpowers could launch a general nuclear response after receipt of a first strike. It is easy to imagine a general nuclear war given the present state of strategic arsenals in the world, yet hard to find an historic example. Obviously there could be a nuclear war by accident, miscalculation, or misunderstanding. What is more certain is that a mutual and general nuclear response by the United States and the Soviet Union would wreak untold devastation on both countries and would severely affect the rest of the world as well. *See also* FIRST STRIKE; LIMITED NUCLEAR WAR; MASSIVE RETALIATION.

Significance   General nuclear response represents the ultimate nadir in the spectrum of the North Atlantic Treaty Organization's strategy of flexible response. The flexible response policy envisions that the scenario of a general nuclear war may result from an uncontrolled escalation of superpower conflicts, and that confrontation may begin at the conventional level (also known as limited nuclear war). The scenario of general nuclear response will result if the superpowers refuse to restrain themselves during a conflict, assuming that each side has a second-strike capability (the ability to destroy each other despite an initial attack). This ultimate form of nuclear warfare will not only be mutually destructive for the superpowers, but will also destroy almost all forms of life on earth. If either of the superpowers were to launch a general nuclear strike, that nation would be gambling that its nuclear weapons would function with perfect accuracy. It would be staking its survival on a flawless execution of a complicated maneuver in which the margin of error would have to be almost nil. Some critics of this strategy suggest that even if the Soviets were confident of unleashing a near perfect general nuclear response, they would be risking everything upon a conjecture of the unwillingness of the United States to launch a massive arsenal of sea- and air-based nuclear warheads.

Generated Alert   A situation in which a nation places all services of its armed forces under a high state of readiness. Generated alert is undertaken when a country prepares for war. It includes all the pillars of the strategic triad: intercontinental ballistic missiles (ICBMs), submarine-launched ballistic missiles (SLBMs), and strategic bombers. Generated alert involves the opening-up of nuclear missile silos, sending submarines out of port, and moving bombers out onto a runway. A generated alert may occur when armed conflicts between adversaries become inevitable. The belligerents then commit their total resources because it is recognized that national survival is in jeopardy. A generated alert, as it is commonly referred to in the United States and the Soviet Union, features nuclear arms, and it could occur even when the two sides have parity in their respective forces and arsenals. Generated alert is not an action-reaction process but the result of two parallel and separate processes driven by independent stimuli in the two superpowers. Decision to organize the general mobilization of the armed forces could be taken in order to satisfy demands of various special interests inside and outside the governments concerned. *See also* GROUND ALERT; TRIAD.

Significance   Generated alert is the all-out state of readiness for a potential superpower nuclear conflict. In a crisis situation such a state of alert may signal to the enemy a country's resolve to protect its national interest, even at the cost of a nuclear war. It is preparation for a war in which all are engaged, and each superpower then makes a series of strikes against the other and its allies. It may be a way to convey to the adversary that the issue at hand is vital to its interests and cannot be compromised. Such a highly charged scenario may force the superpowers to find a mutually acceptable, if not satisfactory, solution to the dispute, and avoid embroiling themselves in a nuclear war. In such a situation the age-old role of bargaining in war may be increased—rather than decreased—both before and after a generated alert. However, nations and individuals may be deluded into believing that the way to increase national security is merely to augment military alertness. Whether one or both sides would take the ultimate step of launching a major nuclear attack—realizing it could be suicidal—remains questionable.

Generation Weapons   Phases of nuclear weapons that reflect technological advances. Generation weapons refer to three phases of nuclear weapons development: atomic, thermonuclear, and specialized weapons. Atomic weapons (A-bombs) are the first generation weapons, which are based on fission (atom-splitting) process. Thermonuclear weapons, also known as hydrogen bombs (H-bombs), are the second generation weapons, which are centered on fusion (atom-combining) technique. Specialized nuclear weapons are fundamentally the same as the second generation weapons in terms of process, but they are modified: a slight modification of the means (instruments) is introduced to produce weapons serving different ends (objectives). One such example is omission of the additional uranium 238 casing after the fission-fusion chain, thereby avoiding a further fission process in sequence. U.S. scientists are developing a third generation of nuclear weapons using extremely small charges that can accomplish highly specialized purposes. Experts at the Lawrence Livermore National Laboratory have cautioned that the Strategic Defense Initiative's kinetic kill vehicles will not be effective against the next generation of Soviet missiles. *See also* ATOMIC WEAPON; FISSION; FUSION; STRATEGIC DEFENSE INITIATIVE (SDI).

Significance   The first generation weapons are the least sophisticated and least powerful nuclear weapons. The A-bombs dropped on Hiroshima and Nagasaki are examples of this generation of weapons. The bomb dropped on Nagasaki had a yield-to-weight ratio of 5,000:1; recent second generation weapons have a 3.5 million:1 yield-to-weight ratio. It follows that contemporary nuclear weapons are likely to be 700 times more destructive than the world's second nuclear bomb. A reflection upon the level of destruction in Japan at the end of World War II gives an idea of potential destruction that a superpower nuclear war can cause, especially since each superpower has many such second generation weapons in its arsenal. While these increased generation weapons produce the most powerful explosion, the explosion of third generation weapons is relatively less powerful, but does, however, emit a great amount of deadly radiation. The neutron bomb is an example of a third generation weapon; it may kill people without destroying buildings or weapons. This makes third generation weapons very controversial on moral grounds. Their potential use in a limited nuclear war, as part of a counterforce strategy, makes them destabilizing weapons.

Graduated Deterrence   A policy of inhibiting aggression throughout a range of force levels. Graduated deterrence is meant to deflect the enemy from further aggression on each rung of the ladder of escalation. The spectrum includes engagement in conventional warfare to all-out nuclear confrontation. Some scholars and strategists even extend the lower spectrum to include counterinsurgency (anti-guerrilla warfare). This concept of graduated deterrence is closely associated with the strategy of flexible response. Graduated deterrence is an incremental application of national power in ways that allow the opposition to accommodate one step at a time. It is a U.S. strategic doctrine of the late 1950s, which sought to supplement the threat of massive retaliation with the additional threat that a relatively large conventional attack on U.S. allies might be met with nuclear strikes in the local theater. *See also* DETERRENCE; FLEXIBLE RESPONSE; INDEPENDENT DETERRENCE.

Significance   Graduated deterrence is designed to convince the enemy that any aggression will be met by blow-for-blow retaliation. However, the intensity of each retaliation will be slightly easier than the corresponding attack, and here lies the essence of a continuous attempt to deter the enemy during a confrontation. In the early 1960s the Kennedy administration adopted the policy of graduated deterrence to counter growing threats of Soviet aggression in Europe and Asia. That policy repeated the Eisenhower administration's policy of massive retaliation in the 1950s. While adequately responding to a Soviet threat, it was believed that graduated deterrence was a more pragmatic way of avoiding all-out nuclear war. A nuclear exchange between the United States and the Soviet Union would almost certainly not be the opening phase of any conflict between them. Rather, it would probably be preceded by intense crises and large-scale conventional war.

Considering the moral incentive for avoiding thermonuclear war, an announcement of a general policy of graduated deterrence might well promote the measure of confidence to sustain effective restraints. This would amount to each nation's adherence to the principle of the economy of force, according to which it would employ a range of military measures proportionate to its perceived threat. However, the graduated deterrence idea of the 1950s and 1960s was valid for a short time only; it depended on the United States being highly superior in nuclear weapons, the ultimate force level.

Ground Alert   A high state of readiness of strategic bombers. Ground alert refers to full-fighting readiness of bombers on the runway. It is a specific component of a generated alert, involving all the legs of the strategic triad. When bombers are on ground alert, they can be sent quickly into the air in the event of a nuclear threat. Both superpowers maintain a number of bombers on ground alert. Ground alert is distinct from airborne alert; under such a scenario some bombers are kept in the air 24 hours a day throughout the year. At the time of the Cuban missile crisis in 1962, SAC (Strategic Air Command) B-52 bombers were stationed at many civilian airports close to major U.S. cities. A rotating fraction of the bombers was kept fueled and armed with bombs, with crews ready to go, in case warnings were received about incoming Soviet bombers. *See also* BALLISTIC MISSILE DEFENSE (BMD) SYSTEM; GENERATED ALERT; STRATEGIC AIR COMMAND (SAC).

Significance   A ground alert is a low-key defense posture. It signals to the enemy a willingness to defend a country's national interest, including armed warfare. While ground alert may be useful to convey intentions, it is vulnerable to a surprise attack. In that case bombers on ground alert may become "sitting ducks." The United States pressed ahead with the fastest possible speed in developing the new radar system called ballistic missile early warning (BMEWS), which was operational soon after Soviet intercontinental ballistic missiles (ICBMs) were deployed. The BMEWS could provide about a 15-minute prior warning on an incoming missile strike, and SAC's ground alert was improved to the point where a substantial number of bombers could become airborne in that same amount of time. Beyond the ICBMs and the BMEWS, both superpowers maintain a round-the-clock force of bombers on airborne alert, but use ground alert in a political crisis. Thus ground alert has more symbolic value than operational utility.

Ground Burst   A nuclear explosion at ground level or in which the fireball touches the ground. A ground burst creates the fireball, which sucks up huge amounts of debris from the subsequent crater. As the debris is drawn up into the atmosphere, it is bathed in radiation from the explosion. Consequently, this falls back to the ground as radioactive particles. A ground burst is also known as a surface burst. The physical effect of a given weapon varies according to the height above the ground at which it is exploded. If the fireball touches the ground, the detonation is called a ground burst. For any height above this, the phenomenon is known as air burst. Ground burst bombs create a much higher level of blast pressure at ground level. Some of this energy is transmitted into the ground to produce an earthquake effect which damages underground rock structures and forms a crater. *See also* AIR BURST; FALLOUT; FIREBALL.

Significance   A ground burst destroys everything in the area of a nuclear explosion, and the resultant radiation is extremely harmful: it can cause nausea, hair loss, internal bleeding, genetic damage, and cancer. While an air burst results in heat and blast over a large area, a ground burst creates a more damaging effect within a relatively smaller area. The debris is irradiated, and it is these radioactive materials that are later swept up into the sky by the inward rushing wind, and then deposited as fallout. The fallout column assumes a ground burst in which 60 percent of the fallout reaches the ground within 24 hours and displays the areas over which a long-term exposure would reach 500 rem (roentgen equivalent in man—a measure of absorbed radiation having an effect on human tissue equal to one roentgen of X-rays). A ground burst may be considered a part of a counterforce strategy in which the destruction of military installations is preferred over destroying vast areas of civilian population. Thus a limited nuclear war scenario will incorporate ground burst as one of its warfighting techniques.

Ground-Based Electro-Optical Deep Space Surveillance (GEODSS)
A high-speed U.S. radar system designed to detect and track enemy missiles and bombers high in the atmosphere or in space. This system uses a technology similar to television—it transmits its images almost instantly. Unlike the less advanced radars, GEODSS does not have a telescope style film camera, hence no film has to be processed. This cuts the time lag between the detection and reporting (and receiving) of information. In 1981 the United States deployed the first GEODSS station in New Mexico. The United States Air Force ground system traces movements in space from stations at Princlik (Turkey), in New Mexico and California, and at St. Margaret's (New Brunswick, Canada), Pulmosan (South Korea), San Vito (Italy), Maui (Hawaii), and Mt. John (New Zealand). It is supplemented by the GEODSS. Five GEODSS sites are planned; three are now operational—at White Sands (New Mexico), Taegu (South Korea), and Maui. *See also* PHASED-ARRAY RADAR; RADAR.

Significance   A ground-based electro-optical deep space surveillance system is designed to notify decision makers very quickly of an enemy attack. The rapidity of information transmission to the decision makers, after detection, will allow for appropriate responses within the short reaction time available. The radar is essential, not only against a surprise nuclear strike but also in preventing any accidental nuclear war. In the latter case, the sooner decision makers are informed about an incoming missile, the quicker they can establish the adversary's intent and, hopefully, have sufficient time to redirect the missile. The hope is to avoid mass destruction. Once the detection has been signaled from the ground-based space surveillance system, which constantly counts and checks all orbiting objects, other ground-based devices are readied to detect nuclear explosions in many points in the United States and to communicate with the president, the commander in chief. In such a crisis, the president is constantly in direct contact with the whole defense system through radio linkages via the officers who always accompany him in carrying nuclear codes nicknamed the "football."

Ground-Based Laser Weapon (GBLW)   An imaginary weapon that would use a laser beam to destroy an incoming nuclear missile. The ground-based laser weapon would be part of a high-speed, high-technology system designed to function as a superconcentrated spotlight. It would be designed to destroy targets by focusing an incredible amount of energy against them. Directing the highly concentrated energy beam against an incoming target involves a two-step process. First, the GBLW would aim its beam at a relay mission high above the earth. Second, the relay mission would direct the beam at a battle mirror, orbiting much closer to the earth. The battle mirror would redirect the beam against an incoming missile, deactivating the missile's crucial electronic components by burning a hole in its outer shell. Along a spectrum of cost-effectiveness the GBLW would probably be placed somewhere between the army's kinetic weapon and the air force's space-based laser weapon. *See also* FREE-ELECTRON LASER WEAPON.

Significance   The ground-based laser weapon was part of the Strategic Defense Initiative scheme of the Reagan administration. The GBLW would be cheaper than space-based laser weapons because the heavy laser producing equipment does not have to be lifted into space. The GBLW, according to its U.S. supporters, would not violate the 1972 Antiballistic Missile Treaty, which prohibits space-based weapons designed to destroy incoming missiles. It is also claimed that it would not violate the 1967 Outer Space Treaty which forbids the use of outer space for military purposes. Thus GBLW would avoid the legal problem of violating any international law for which the United States is a signatory. However, many years, if not decades, of research are required before the planners can begin to proceed from theoretical concepts like the GBLW. If the system is to meet the stated goal of rendering nuclear weapons obsolete, it must work to near perfection.

Ground-Launched Cruise Missile (GLCM)   A cruise missile designed to be launched from a ground-based launcher. A ground-based cruise missile, like the word cruise implies, is a slow, low-flying, highly accurate missile. Unlike ballistic missiles, which are powered by booster rockets, cruise missiles are powered by jet engines. The U.S. GLCM is a modified version of the navy's Tomahawk cruise missile: it is the Tomahawk BGM-109G, with a range of 2,500 kilometers and a yield of 0.3 to 80 kilotons. One battery comprises 16 Tomahawk missiles on four mobile-launchers operated by two launch-control centers. One missile remains on quick-reaction alert status at each base during normal states of readiness. During a full alert each missile is spread out to pre-arranged substations. The Soviet versions are the

SSC-X-4 and SS-20. Deployed within the Soviet Union in the mid-1980s, the SSC-X-4 has a range of 3,000 kilometers. The SS-20 is solid-fueled. The missile normally remains horizontal in the launch tube, but before firing it is raised to the vertical position. The launcher can be reloaded. *See also* BALLISTIC MISSILE DEFENSE (BMD) SYSTEM; CRUISE MISSILE.

Significance   A ground-launched cruise missile has a flexible launch base and is guided by sophisticated terrain contour matching technology (TERCOM). This technology makes it difficult for enemy radar to detect a GLCM. Although the GLCM can carry either conventional or nuclear warheads, 80 percent of the U.S. GLCMs carry nuclear payloads; the Soviet ratio is likely to be similar. The Soviet SSC-X-4 can be launched from a stationary truck, while the SS-20 can be launched from a slow-moving truck. The ranges of the SSC-X-4 and SS-20 allow them to reach targets in Western Europe from inside the Soviet Union. This threat led to the North Atlantic Treaty Organization (NATO) deployment of cruise and Pershing II missiles in Western Europe. Under the 1987 Intermediate-range Nuclear Forces Treaty, both superpowers pledged to destroy medium-range and intermediate-range nuclear weapons.

Guidance System   The complex process that directs a missile to its target. A guidance system evaluates missile flight information, matches this with target data, checks with planned flight path, and communicates the necessary command to the missile flight system to correct deviations from the missile's planned flight. The whole process works on the basis of feedback and control. There are two basic systems: inertial guidance and command guidance. An inertial guidance involves a complete guidance package within a missile; command guidance refers to transmitting instructions through space in the form of electronic signals. The simplest form of guidance is to radio instructions to the missile, basing the directions upon radar observations of its position. The amount of guidance required by a missile depends upon the degree of accuracy demanded. The long-range cruise missile can deliver a nuclear warhead with great accuracy, covering ranges of up to thousands of miles. *See also* CRUISE MISSILE; GUIDED MISSILE; INERTIAL GUIDANCE.

Significance   A guidance system is like the pilot of a missile that navigates it during its trajectory. The inertial guidance system works on the basis of kinetic energy and the laws of motion. It is simpler than the command guidance system, but less sophisticated. Once fired, a missile with an inertial guidance system cannot change its flight path to avoid enemy antiballistic missile defenses. However, a missile with a command guidance system can take instructions from its command center, or may be equipped with information to guide itself. Intercontinental, intermediate-range, medium-range, and short-range ballistic missiles use the inertial guidance system. A cruise missile uses the command guidance system: it is fitted with a contour chart of the terrain to guide itself. The most striking feature of the new generation of cruise missiles is the guidance system. The guidance system, however, is open to electronic countermeasure (ECM); it is possible to jam the radio signal and decode or distort instructions.

Guided Missile   Any missile whose trajectory is continually adjusted during its flight. Guided missiles make up most of the world's nuclear panoply. Depending on the technology of the guidance system, a guided missile can be extremely accurate. Such missiles can be either inertia-guided or command-guided. The former involves internal mechanisms, the latter external stimuli: an inertia-guided missile propels itself following the rules of kinetic energy and the laws of motion; a command-guided missile's trajectory can be changed by external commands. Guided missiles have been developed so that some can perform midcourse corrections by checking their positions with a navigation satellite. An analysis of the intercontinental ballistic missile, for example, shows that it is accurate within a few hundred feet at the end of its 6,000-mile flight. *See also* GUIDANCE SYSTEM.

Significance   A guided missile with an inertial-guidance mechanism cannot change its direction once it is launched. If it is launched accidentally, it will have to be shot down with antiballistic missiles. In contrast, a guided missile with a command-guidance system can be redirected in order to be destroyed safely after an accidental launching. Consequently, command-guidance missiles are safer than inertial-guidance missiles. However, the same technology that allows the command-guidance missiles to be redirected, allows them to be independently directed at different targets. The Soviets have recently produced a new generation of long-range missiles, while the Americans have launched their newest spurt of weapons deployment. Multiple independently targetable reentry vehicles are examples of such missiles that can destabilize superpower nuclear balance and further complicate arms control negotiations.

H

Hair Trigger   The condition in which both superpowers are ready to launch a nuclear strike at the slightest provocation. A "hair-trigger" situation exists at the Command, Control, and Communication headquarters. It often portrays a scenario of launching an accidental nuclear attack. During the 1962 Cuban missile crisis, the superpowers were close to a hair-trigger situation of starting a nuclear war. Operating under a scenario of hair-trigger rules of military engagements, a country may engage in a first strike with nuclear weapons when it feels threatened by anticipated or real hostile enemy moves. *See also* COMMAND, CONTROL, COMMUNICATIONS, AND INTELLIGENCE (C3I); COUPLING.

Significance   A hair-trigger condition reflects the tremendous pressure under which national leaders must make decisions on a nuclear option if there is any indication of an enemy nuclear strike. This is because a crisis situation usually involves a high degree of threat perception, an element of surprise, and a short reaction time. Although it is unlikely that the Soviet Union would launch a nuclear attack without provocation, there are circumstances that could result in a massive Soviet attack against land-based missiles, bombers, and submarines. While it is possible that U.S. land-based intercontinental ballistic missiles could be launched before Soviet missiles destroy them, the United States cannot assume they could be. Therefore, the United States maintains sufficient numbers of nuclear warheads in submarines that could destroy Soviet bases and cities in a counterattack. It is noteworthy that the United States has never declared a no-first use of nuclear weapons policy as a way of ensuring the coupling of U.S. and Western European security interests. Because nuclear weapons are so powerful, and can be invulnerable, only a relatively few nuclear weapons can demonstrate the capacity for assured destruction. Both the United States and the Soviet Union have many more nuclear weapons than is needed for that show of force. The

United States, especially, claims it needs its surplus since it is committed to the protection of Western Europe and Japan.

Half-Life   The time required for the radioactivity in any given substance to decay to half its initial strength. The half-life of any particular radioisotope is the length of time taken for half of the atomic nuclei in a single sample of the isotope to erupt and be transformed into the nuclei of other atoms by emitting radiation. After two half-lives, only one-quarter of the atoms will be left; after three half-lives, one eighth; and so forth. The half-life is a characteristic feature of each radioactive substance and is independent of its amount in the surrounding condition. It differs greatly from one element to another: from a few millionths of a second to billions of years. Each radioactive isotope is characterized by a specific half-life. Tritium (found in minute quantities in water, where it is constantly created by cosmic radiation) has a half-life of 12.3 years. Most of the radioisotopes have very short half-lives, and decay in hours or days. *See also* RADIOACTIVE DECAY.

Significance   A half-life is an indication of the duration for which a given radioactive substance will emit radiation and remain dangerous. This is because the chemical composition of an element itself changes during radioactivity. When its composition changes, following the emission of harmful radiation, it becomes neutral. A nuclear explosion produces many highly radioactive by-products, and many elements produced in a nuclear detonation have extremely long half-lives. The rate of radioactive decay cannot be controlled and it is difficult to gather enough radioactive atoms to make the spontaneously released energy useful. Radiation from any source is dangerous, whether it be from bomb test fallout, the sun, a medical X-ray, or a nuclear power plant.

Hard Kill   This occurs when a target is destroyed by being blown up. Hard kill can be ensured in two ways: by increasing the accuracy of the missile or by increasing the surface area of destructive explosion. The former has been the policy of the United States, and the latter has been the strategy of the Soviet Union. While the United States has attempted to enhance missile accuracy, the Soviet Union has concentrated on increasing the nuclear payload. The Trident and MX missiles are considered first-strike weapons due to their hard-kill capability. The Trident submarine is much larger than its predecessors, with a displacement of 17,000 tons and a length of 170 meters. It is faster, quieter, more reliable, more spacious, and it can accommodate 150 sailors. The MX is the newest intercontinental ballistic missile in the U.S. nuclear arsenal, and is designed to carry 10 multiple independently targetable reentry vehicle (MIRV) warheads, compared to the Minuteman's three. The improved accuracy of the MX missile involves a greatly improved inertial-guidance system. *See also* GUIDANCE SYSTEM; GUIDED MISSILE.

Significance   Hard kill implies destroying an enemy target, rather than merely disabling it. A hard kill can be easily confirmed—consequently, a defense system can use its time and ammunition on other targets. However, it is also difficult to ensure a hard kill, and any battle scenario must bring this factor into planning. Does the United States require certain hard-kill capability? If so, this must be prompt—able to arrive in half an hour on a ballistic missile rather than in ten hours on a cruise missile. The United States can destroy hardened Soviet missile silos and command posts. The Soviets can also destroy U.S. targets. However, the United States offensive forces of the 1990s will have far greater hard-kill capacity than at present, because of the new accurate D-5 warheads on Trident submarines.

Hardening   The process by which a nuclear facility is designed, especially the use of highly strengthened materials to reduce vulnerability to nuclear attack. Hardening is usually done in the form of reinforced concrete and steel defenses and the construction of subterranean bunkers. The U.S. base system was designed so that missile launchers would be hard enough to endure a Soviet attack and be able to return fire. The hardened silos are vertical concrete structures buried in the ground. The basic methods of protecting command system assets are physical hardening, geographic disposition, mobility, secrecy, and active interdiction of attacking weapons. The term *hardening* (or *base hardening*) is also used to mean shielding of delicate electronic parts from an electromagnetic pulse. The method thus protects crucial command centers in which military personnel coordinate the release of nuclear weapons against an enemy target. *See also* HARD-SITE DEFENSE.

Significance   Hardening of underground missile silos is needed because they are particularly vulnerable to a nuclear strike. The process of hardening is essential in the protection of missiles, delicate electronic parts, and command centers; it ensures each superpower a second-strike capability, which is the basis of stable deterrence. Such hardening must be reinforced to keep up with improvements in the destructiveness and accuracy of new weapons. Direct hardening has been used to enhance the protection of command system properties, which are dispersed, numerous, and provide redundant capability. The accuracy of nuclear weapons is such that any single location can be directly destroyed. Therefore, a trade-off exists between hardening and mobility as methods of protecting nuclear missiles.

Hard-Site Defense   A defense system incorporating hardened silos that protect a country's missile sites and other installations against an enemy's nuclear missile attack. Hard-site defense involves silos hardened with concrete and steel, mounted on steel springs, that absorb the shock of nuclear explosion, and fitted with armored blast doors. Hard-site defense installations may be able to withstand the effects of a nuclear blast. The United States first deployed a hard-site defense called Safeguard (an antiballistic missile system to protect U.S. retaliatory capability) in 1974, but it was dismantled two years afterward because of high cost and technical problems. Presently, a hard target is fortified by its physical strength. A missile center, and silos holding the missiles deep underground, is the best known target. Others include various command bunkers provided for the military chain of command, which includes the president. These are situated around Washington, D.C., and the underground Strategic Air Command (SAC) in Omaha, Nebraska. Attacking missiles must be accurate in order to destroy hard targets. In recent years the superpowers have built smaller, highly accurate missiles, with a high degree of destructive power. *See also* HARDENING; HARD KILL.

Significance   Hard-site defense adds a layer of protection for one's own nuclear missiles. A brick house explodes under a pressure of 5 to 10 pounds per square inch (psi); in comparison, a Minuteman silo can withstand a pressure of 2,500 psi. If two missiles aim simultaneously at the same target (assuming that each missile has a 50 percent chance of hitting its target) there is a very good possibility that one of the missiles will make a direct hit. A direct hit reduces the ability of a hard-site defense system to protect its missile sites in the face of the attack. Larger yields and improved accuracy give the superpowers a higher kill probability against hard-site defense. No longer is the buried concrete silo, which holds its nuclear missile, invulnerable to attack. The newest U.S. MX and the Soviet SS-18 are estimated to have a 90 percent chance of knocking out hard-site defenses. Soft targets, such as cities and ordinary houses, will collapse easily.

Heavy Bomber   A multiengine, long-range aircraft. Heavy bomb-ers are essentially intercontinental-range bombers that can deliver both conventional and nuclear weapons. SALT II identifies as a heavy bomber any aircraft that can operate air-to-surface ballistic missiles or air-launched cruise missiles over a range of 600 kilometers of more. The U.S. B-52 and B-1B and the Soviet Tu-95 Bear and Mya-4 Bison bombers are heavy bombers. The B-52 has been the mainstay of the U.S. heavy bomber force for more than three decades. Since its incep-tion in 1955 by the United States Air Force, the B-52 has been modi-fied many times, the latest changes resulting in its ability to carry air-launched cruise missiles with a range of 16,000 kilometers and a carrying capacity of 24 weapons. The B-1B is a new type of bomber, designed to replace the B-52; it is equipped to carry 48 weapons and it has a range of 9,600 kilometers. The B-1B is the descendant of the B-1 bomber, which was cancelled by President Jimmy Carter and later revived by President Ronald Reagan. The Soviet Tu-95 Bear has a range of 12,300 kilometers and can be equipped with either nuclear or conventional weapons. The Mya-4 Bison is similar in size to the U.S. B-52 but carries fewer weapons. *See also* STRATEGIC BOMBER; TRIAD.

Significance   Heavy bombers are designed to carry a tremendous payload of bombs, over long distances. The object of engaging a heavy bomber is to destroy targets that will diminish the enemy's capability or his will to initiate or continue a war. Heavy bombers form one leg of the strategic triad, the other two being ground-based intercontinen-tal ballistic missiles (ICBMs) and submarine-launched ballistic missiles (SLBMs). Heavy bombers are relatively slow-flying and easily detected and are, therefore, the most vulnerable of the three components of strategic deterrence. On the ground they are easy targets for enemy missiles; for this reason a certain number of such bombers are always kept in a state of readiness in the air. Irrespective of their relative effectiveness, heavy bombers do ensure additional credibility in the strategy of nuclear deterrence. A sophisticated weapons system like the heavy bomber is never really complete. A Congressional Budget Office (CBO) study notes, in August 1988, that the air force is already considering B-1B design enhancement to improve the bomber's cred-ibility and mission capability.

Heavy Missile   A large-volume, intercontinental-range ballistic missile with a heavy throw-weight and powerful blast. The precise defi-nition of heavy missile has been a moot issue between the United States and the Soviet Union. However, there is a general understanding to consider the following three criteria: strength of the missile's warhead and the size and weight of the missile. Although no common definition was acceptable, the U.S. Titan-II and the Soviet SS-9 were considered heavy missiles during the SALT I negotiations. During the SALT II negotiations, the Soviet SS-19 was officially used as a yardstick for deciding the heavy or lightness of intercontinental-range ballistic missiles. This large-volume intercontinental ballistic missile (ICBM), with its particularly large volume of throw-weight, is, if accurate enough, capable of destroying fixed, hardened targets. The Titan-II ICBM, first tested in 1962, is being phased out. The development of the solid-fuel Minuteman ICBM by the United States required more radical improvements in technology. The Soviet SS-7, SS-8, SS-9, SS-18, and SS-19 are viewed by the United States as heavy missiles. *See also* INTERCONTINENTAL BALLISTIC MISSILE (ICBM); STRATEGIC ARMS LIMITATION TALKS (SALT I); STRATEGIC ARMS LIMITATION TALKS (SALT II).

Significance   Heavy and accurate missiles can destroy a fixed, hardened silo. Such a scenario envisages a combination of accuracy and throw-weight. Traditionally the Soviet panoply has included more heavy missiles than the U.S. arsenal. Given the Soviet emphasis on throw-weight and warhead size (as opposed to U.S. stress on accuracy), if the Soviets were also to attempt to improve their missile accuracy, it would arouse apprehension in regard to a future Soviet surprise first strike. One of the second generation ICBMs of the United States, called the Minuteman (because it could be fired on about one minute's warning), was destined from the beginning to be launched from hardened underground silos. The other solid-fueled missile was the Polaris, designed to be carried in submarines. If the Soviets were to stage a surprise first strike, they would be gambling on virtually perfect accuracy of thousands of their missiles to destroy 100 percent of the United States missiles. Critics of heavy missiles conclude that the Soviets would have to be insane to take a risk of that order. Similarly, a U.S. first strike would be an insane, suicidal undertaking.

High Frontier   A theoretical system of space-based, antiballistic missile defenses originated by a private study. High Frontier, a private organization, fronted by Lieutenant General Daniel O. Graham, a former director of the Defense Intelligence Agency, issued a report in 1982 urging the United States to build a three-tier space defense system based on existing technology. The first layer will be 432 satellites in orbit, fitted with nonnuclear missiles at an estimated cost of

$15 billion. These may include chemical lasers, which would be used to intercept Soviet missiles in the boost phase (launch phase). The second layer will be comprised of nonnuclear missiles acting as antiballistic missiles around U.S. intercontinental ballistic missile sites. The third layer will consist of particle beam weapons and similar systems. The report was considered part of the Reagan administration's Strategic Defense Initiative (SDI). High Frontier is a lobbying group for the SDI. *See also* BALLISTIC MISSILE DEFENSE (BMD) SYSTEM; STRATEGIC DEFENSE INITIATIVE (SDI).

Significance   High Frontier contends that the technology for deploying a space-based defense system is available. Graham, who had been associated with a study by the right-wing Heritage Foundation, started his own $500,000 study after his differences with Edward Teller, a leading nuclear scientist. While Teller urged waiting for the development of suitable technology, Graham insisted on moving ahead based on available technology. According to Teller, Graham's project would deploy a defense system of limited capability. The U.S. Defense Department estimates the cost could run as high as $1 trillion.

It is not possible to know whether formidable technical obstacles can be overcome to establish a space-based defense system that even its proponents acknowledge is decades away from full development. Many examples can be cited of new weapons originally said to be impractical by some experts; the first atomic bomb and the intercontinental ballistic missile were both considered impossible by a few knowledgeable scientists. The real issue is not technical feasibility, but rather how well it can be made to work and at what cost.

Hiroshima   A southwestern seaport city in Japan, struck by the first atomic bomb. Hiroshima, built on a plateau, was damaged symmetrically in all directions by the atomic bomb blast. On August 6, 1945, at 8:15 A.M., the United States detonated "Little Boy" (the code name of the first atomic bomb) about 600 yards above central Hiroshima. The bomb weighed 8,000 pounds, contained 12 pounds of uranium 235, and set off an explosion the equivalent of 12,000–15,000 tons of TNT (dropped on Hiroshima without prior testing). It completely ruined the city: 80 percent of the 76,000 buildings in Hiroshima were wiped out, and about 75,000 people died in the explosion. Many survivors of the Hiroshima blast died later from injuries, burns, infection, and radiation. Hiroshima has been almost completely rebuilt, and many modern industries have been set up there, including the Matsuda truck factory, Mitsubishi shipbuilding,

and the Mazda corporation. *See also* ATOMIC WEAPON; FISSION; MANHAT-
TAN PROJECT; NAGASAKI.

Significance   Hiroshima was the world's first city to feel the awesome destructive capacity of an atomic weapon. The havoc shortened
World War II by bringing about Japanese surrender. Nevertheless, the death toll was staggering: out of 300,000 persons exposed to
the atomic explosion on Hiroshima, about 130,000 died, including
delayed deaths. John Hersey in his book *Hiroshima* and Michihiko
Hachiya in *Hiroshima Diary* have described the terrible experiences of
the survivors. People were consumed by the furnace of the flash.
Buildings in all directions were leveled. Victims lay in heaps of seven
or eight corpses deep. Deep, long-lasting psychological scars resulted
from the collapse of the Japanese social order after the explosion.[15]
Hiroshima may not serve as a precedent: the bomb used on that city
was much smaller than today's nuclear weapons. Today, the death and
destruction that could result from a single, one-megaton weapon
would be equal to that caused by 80 Hiroshima explosions at the same
time in one place.

Homing   A device by which a missile detects, locates, and moves
toward its target. Homing must involve something that attracts the missile to its object: heat, light, radio waves, or magnetism. It is the same
mechanism that induces a bloodhound to hunt its prey: picking up
and following the target's scent. The smell is the stimulus that produces an automatic response in tracking and catching up to that smell.
Satellites are easier targets than warheads because their trajectories
are predictable. The result is that any ballistic missile defense (BMD)
system that has even a moderate effectiveness against warheads will
offer a much greater effectiveness against satellites. Homing is an
effective way of destroying a target, and can be used with both nuclear
and conventional weapons. *See also* BALLISTIC MISSILE DEFENSE (BMD);
DECOY.

Significance   Homing, used by both conventional and nuclear weapons, is a very useful way to destroy targets. Once the homing signal is
picked up, it is virtually impossible for the target to escape its doom.
A decoy (dummy warhead) with a false homing stimulus may be one
way of overcoming an unwelcome enemy force. A homing device is
likely to be used by missile interceptors to destroy an incoming missile
in flight. On June 10, 1984, the United States conducted, as part of its
research on BMD, a test called "Homing Overplay." The test used an
intercontinental ballistic missile (ICBM) to intercept a single incoming

ballistic missile warhead. It was successful. This action has been compared to hitting a bullet in flight with another bullet. The homing test also demonstrated a degree of antisatellite (ASAT) capability, since detecting a satellite by this method is easier than intercepting a missile warhead. Since the Reagan administration was giving priority to the Strategic Defense Initiative (SDI) research, this meant the administration was conducting research on a defensive system that would have a major ASAT capability.

Horizontal Proliferation   The spread of nuclear weapons to nonnuclear states. Horizontal proliferation refers to spatial or geographical expansion under the 1968 Nonproliferation Treaty (NPT), signed by 110 countries. Nations with nuclear technology pledged in the NPT to safeguard that knowledge against the development of nuclear weapons by nonnuclear weapons countries. In their turn, the nonnuclear countries vowed not to acquire or conduct research on nuclear weaponry. The treaty did not prohibit the peaceful use of nuclear technology, such as for energy purposes. The spread of nuclear weapons ultimately depends upon the capabilities and the intentions of potential nuclear states. So far, six nations—Argentina, Brazil, India, Israel, Pakistan, and South Africa—have been reported to have nuclear capability,[16] either acquired or developed on their own. Israel and South Africa are known to have developed nuclear bombs. Leonard Spector, in *Going Nuclear,* describes the progress the six nuclear-weapons threshold states have made. *See also* VERTICAL PROLIFERATION.

Significance   Horizontal proliferation is also known as the nth (unknown number) country problem. The superpowers and major powers with nuclear weapons feel that the spread of nuclear weapons is destabilizing. Otherwise, it will lead to what came to be known as a "unit veto" system. However, the development of nuclear weapons is useful not only as a deterrent against aggression, but also as a major power status symbol. Certain nonnuclear countries find it contradictory that while the superpowers proceed with their relentless stockpiling of diverse types (vertical proliferation) of nuclear weapons, they oppose the building of nuclear weapons by small nations. For this reason, some potential nuclear powers—Argentina, Brazil, India, Israel, Pakistan, and South Africa—did not sign the 1968 Nonproliferation Treaty (India tested a nuclear "device" in 1974). While relatively stable relationships have emerged among the five major nuclear powers, the spread of nuclear weapons to unstable Third World nations increases the danger that nuclear arms may fall into the hands of terrorists and other anti–status quo forces.

Hot Launch   A method of firing a nuclear missile that damages the underground silo in which the missile is stored. Hot launch involves igniting a missile's booster rockets while the missile is still in its silo. The rockets, which propel and direct the missile to its target, also damage the silo with their heat and force. A hot launch is different from a cold launch, which leaves the silo undamaged. Because the spacing of missile sites is wide, there is no interaction between the events of one site to another. *See also* MISSILE.

Significance   Hot launch has a major handicap: the silo cannot be used for another launch until the damage from heat has been repaired. If a major war results in mass launchings, there would probably be no need to reload. Hot launch is not cost-effective, since the silo has to be repaired before reuse; it is also slow and cumbersome. Traditionally, to protect the stationary, land-based missiles of the United States from attack, the Pentagon has relied on underground, hardened concrete silos. But the new accuracy of Soviet missiles means they might be hit so directly that they would be destroyed. Thus, the land-based missiles of the United States look less like deterrence and more like vulnerable targets.

Hot Line   A direct communication link between the White House and the Kremlin. The hot line, established in 1963, comprises two terminal points with Teletype equipment, a full-time duplex wire (allowing simultaneous two-way communications) telegraph circuit, and a full-time duplex radio telegraph circuit. The wire telegraph circuit runs the following route: Washington-London-Copenhagen-Stockholm-Helsinki-Moscow. The radio telegraph circuit runs from Washington through Tangier to Moscow, and vice versa. Each government is responsible for the link in its own territory, ensuring its continuous functioning, and the prompt delivery to its top political leader of any communications received from the chief political leader of the other country. The 1963 Hot Line Agreement was further improved upon by the September 30, 1971, Hot Line Modernization Agreement. Accordingly, two satellite communications circuits were established, supported by a system of multiple terminals in each country. The United States provided one circuit via the INTELSAT system and the Soviet Union via its MOLNIYA II system. On July 18, 1984, the two superpowers agreed to add high-speed facsimile equipment, enabling the transmission of graphic materials such as maps, photos, and diagrams. The hot line was updated in 1988 with modern computer technology. However, the original wire telegraph circuit remains as a backup system. *See also* NUCLEAR RISK REDUCTION CENTER (NRRC).

Significance   The Hot Line Agreement was the first bilateral arms control agreement signed between the superpowers. It was designed to diffuse international crises, especially those having the potential to embroil the superpowers in a direct nuclear conflict. The emphasis was placed on providing a medium for clarifying misconceptions that, during a crisis, might raise the danger of a nuclear war. Following the October 1962 Cuban missile crisis, the Hot Line Agreement was a manifestation of the realization of potential for nuclear war from such confrontations. The crisis illustrated the need for direct talks between the leaders of the two superpowers. The hot line is proving its usefulness. That it is needed at all indicates that the control of crises through signaling is not as transparent a means of communication between the superpowers as originally thought by critics. Many potential uses of the hot line seem far-fetched, but its cost is low, especially the hope that a last-ditch effort by the superpowers' decision makers to reach an agreement in a crisis might avert disaster. Hot lines have also been established between Paris and Moscow and between London and Moscow.

Hydrogen Bomb   A thermonuclear weapon that derives a large part of its explosive energy from the fusion process. The hydrogen bomb is detonated in a two-step process. First, it involves a fission (atom-splitting) procedure at a very high temperature. Second, this heat activates the fusion (combining or fusing of atoms) stage. This fusion reaction then triggers the optional third step: fission of the uranium shell that surrounds the core of the weapon. Weapons incorporating this third step are called a fission-fusion-fission weapon; a weapon without this third step is called a fission-fusion bomb. The first thermonuclear weapon was called the superbomb; later versions are called the H-bomb (hydrogen bomb). H-bombs are much more difficult to design than atomic bombs. The problem is to prevent the A-bomb trigger from blowing the whole weapon apart before enough fusion material has been ignited to give the required explosive yield. In 1949, the Soviets tested their first atomic bomb. In 1951, President Harry S Truman responded by ordering the development of a hydrogen bomb. The key figure in the production of the H-bomb was Edward Teller, a nuclear scientist, who is known as the Father of the H-bomb. *See also* FISSION; FISSION-FUSION-FISSION WEAPON; NEUTRON BOMB; THERMONUCLEAR WEAPON.

Significance   The hydrogen bomb is much more destructive than the atomic bomb, which involves the initial fission reaction. A hydrogen bomb is the most powerful nuclear weapon; one medium-sized bomb can completely demolish a city the size of New York. The fusion reaction differs from a fission explosion in that it produces no residual radiation, since its by-product is mostly helium, a nonradioactive element. The United States exploded a hydrogen bomb in 1952; the Soviets achieved a comparable result in 1953. These tests made it clear that weapons 10 to 1,000 times as powerful as the Hiroshima bomb could be made. These powerful bombs make up the bulk of the world's nuclear arsenal today. Many critics believe that the development of the H-bomb has brought the possibility of the destruction of the world dangerously close.

I

Imaging Radar   A process of identifying an object by obtaining a high-quality image. An imaging radar is a hypothetical device for protecting against attacking nuclear missiles. It is part of a high-technology defense system that could distinguish between decoys (dummy warheads) and real warheads. Such radars would be based in space. The Reagan administration promoted research on the imaging radar under the Strategic Defense Initiative (SDI) program. It is too early to define precisely the structure of a strategic defense system. However, several technological options show great promise, and a scientific framework for creating such a system is now emerging. Research in imaging radar is designed to examine advanced technologies in order to build an effective defense against ballistic missiles. This research is being conducted within the government and with private-sector contractors in the United States and Western Europe. *See also* RADAR; STRATEGIC DEFENSE INITIATIVE (SDI).

Significance   An imaging radar would allow defensive systems to be selective in destroying their targets. An attacking missile approaching its target may release many decoys along with real nuclear warheads. These decoys are designed to protect the attacking warheads from enemy defenses by attracting the defense missile. In distinguishing a real warhead from a decoy, imaging radar would enable a missile defense system to operate more effectively. In March 1987, the Raytheon Company received a $174.2 million contract from the United States Army to develop a terminal imaging radar. That was part of the Reagan administration's plans for building a ballistic missile defensive system.

Impulse Kill   Destroying or disabling an attacking nuclear warhead by striking its surface with a powerful impact. An impulse kill involves a tremendous amount of energy transmitted in the form of a shock wave. Directed-energy weapons are based on futuristic technologies that can be used in an impulse kill. The directed energy can destroy a nuclear warhead or disable the sensitive electronics located inside the missile's outer shell. Directed-energy weapons under examination by Strategic Defense Initiative (SDI) program include laser beams, the X-ray laser, and the neutral particle beam. In the late 1970s General George J. Keegan, former director of Air Force Intelligence, tried to redirect research efforts toward directed-energy weapons. Lieutenant General Daniel O. Graham, former chief of the Defense Intelligence Agency, has developed a specific research agenda leading to defense against attacking missiles, which includes the use of directed-energy beams. *See also* HIGH FRONTIER; STRATEGIC DEFENSE INITIATIVE (SDI).

Significance   An impulse kill process uses kinetic energy, or the energy of a fast-moving body, to damage its target. It is relatively simple and can be accomplished with present-level technology. Also, it does not involve using nuclear warheads and is relatively less hazardous to human life. President Ronald Reagan, under the influence of Edward Teller, a nuclear scientist, and the conservative High Frontier group, expressed the dream that directed-energy weapons might someday comprise a complete defense against nuclear weapons. The president asked for a study in the style of the World War II Manhattan Project—one which would develop the research objectives leading to impulse kill and other defenses against enemy missiles. Today, perfect defense against nuclear weapons appears possible. Even if directed-energy weapons become a reality, they would not seem an alternative to MAD (mutual assured destruction) as the Soviets would surely not be lagging behind the United States for long.

Independent Deterrent   A nuclear weapons system that creates a deterrence on its own, without being part of a superpower's weapons program. Since France withdrew from the North Atlantic Treaty Organization (NATO) integrated military command in 1966, its nuclear arsenal has been characterized as an independent deterrent. But because Great Britain's nuclear weapons are regarded as part of the NATO forces, it is not considered to have an independent deterrent capability. China, however, has developed an independent nuclear deterrent similar to France's. France developed the policy of independent deterrence because it felt that all NATO allies need not share the same sense, at every stage, that security of their territory was inviolable. A policy of independent deterrence has worked for France, and it may continue to work. It may even be enhanced by an active defense strategy for the prevention of nuclear war. *See also* NORTH ATLANTIC TREATY ORGANIZATION (NATO); SECOND STRIKE.

Significance An independent deterrent allows a country to respond to a nuclear threat without the umbrella protection of a superpower. France's independent deterrent capability allows it to impress upon the Kremlin leadership that any possible invasion of France will be costly for the Soviet Union. Even though France does not have a re-taliatory second-strike capability, it can threaten to destroy only a few major cities in case of a Soviet nuclear threat. Thus an independent deterrent allows France to deter a Soviet attack, independently, by making such an attack costly for the Soviet Union. This strategy is feasible if the damage from such wars is small enough to distinguish them from a full-scale nuclear war and if escalation is not inevitable. In spite of its limitations, independent deterrence indicates the presence of stability in French strategy. This policy requires not only sufficient forces and weapons but also the adequate survivability of them.

Inertial Guidance A system designed to propel a missile over a preplanned path toward its target. Inertial guidance involves adjustments after a missile is launched by programmed instruments—three gyroscopes and three accelerators. These instruments determine the appropriate speed, position, and acceleration in detecting and correcting deviations from the intended speed and direction. Because inertial guidance has control over a missile's flight, inertial guidance is also known as the "computer brain" of a missile. In 1988 General Dynamics and McDonnell Douglas won a $4.38 billion contract from the United States Navy to build the Advanced Tactical Aircraft, designated A-12. These models will replace the current A-6 medium attack planes on aircraft carriers by the early 1990s. In March 1988 Litton Industries received a subcontract from the same two companies to develop the integrated inertial navigation system for the A-12 aircraft. *See also* GUIDANCE SYSTEM.

Significance An inertial guidance program is a self-contained system that functions independently of outside information. Thus it is immune to atmospheric conditions or jamming of electronic signals. The inertial guidance system safeguards against enemy tampering with a missile's flight path. Despite tremendous technological advances, doubts are still raised about the targeting accuracy of ballistic missiles. Areas of improvement in missile guidance systems are closely guarded military secrets, but it is known that mid-flight correction could be made. The past guidance improvements in the missile accuracy by both the Untied States and the Soviet Union suggest that, while there is not likely to be a sudden breakthrough by either side in the future, the gap will continue. If computers continue to improve they will produce future advances in weapons technologies that are highly dependent upon them—including any weapons guidance system.

Infrared Sensor   An instrument that detects heat. An infrared sensor identifies its target by picking up the heat given off. This is possible because missiles, like aircraft, emit heat in their engine exhaust. A missile equipped with an infrared sensor can discern this heat and guide itself toward its target. Infrared sensors can help guide an attacking missile to its target. The correlating pictures are obtained by visual, infrared, or radar microwave sensors, or a combination of two or more of these sensors, to provide accurate navigation to the target. A single detector is not enough for an infrared system. Coupling a single detector to a telescope allows the light from one narrow core in front of the telescope to be focused on the element; covering a wide area of view requires the telescope to be swept back and forth across the scene. Infrared sensors are also known as thermal or heat sensors. *See also* HOMING; IMPULSE KILL.

Significance   Infrared sensors detect the trail of hot rocket exhaust left in the aftermath of a ballistic missile launch. Both the United States and the Soviet Union use space-based infrared sensors to detect ballistic missile launchers. Such sensors can detect a ballistic missile in its boost-phase. Infrared sensors can be used to detect warheads in their mid- or space phase, as they fly in outer space. This is possible because they give out heat against the cold background of outer space. Very hot engines and exhausts emit much infrared radiation, which infrared terminal guidance systems can then detect. The current space-based system for detecting missile launches has satellites stationed in synchronous orbits and uses scanning infrared sensors.

Interactive Discrimination   A hypothetical method for distinguishing attacking nuclear warheads from decoys. An interactive discrimination involves transmitting neutral particle beams that can penetrate the outer shell of warheads and decoys. While both have the same appearance, warheads are much heavier than decoys because they are filled with electronic equipment and nuclear material. A warhead struck by a neutral particle beam emits gamma rays, while an empty decoy does not. A nuclear warhead could be exploded by the defense that can discriminate among the decoys and real reentry vehicles (RVs). The heavier and stronger RVs would survive this blast; the radar could pick them out and guide the antiballistic missiles to them. These tactics probably could be negated by using more solid decoys. *See also* BALLISTIC MISSILE DEFENSE (BMD) SYSTEM; IMAGING RADAR; STRATEGIC DEFENSE INITIATIVE (SDI).

Significance   An interactive discrimination can be a revolutionary component in a high-technology defense system against nuclear attack. Such a process will allow antiballistic missiles to concentrate on incoming enemy warheads rather than decoys. This will make the missile defense system more cost-effective. The United States is conducting research on interactive discrimination as part of the Strategic Defense Initiative. Most decoys can be distinguished from warheads if a terminal defense can be carried out inside the atmosphere. In the atmosphere, light balloons and chaff would be slowed by air resistance, and any chaff or decoys during launch would cause discriminating problems for the station's tracking and discrimination system.

Interceptor Missile   A missile that intercepts and deactivates or destroys an attacking nuclear warhead. An interceptor missile can be programmed to follow a definite trajectory or to change its flight path with a changing course of the attacking warhead. It may be designated to home in on a missile by identifying and tracking noise, heat, or light. In the 1950s and early 1960s, the United States had a high priority in the development and deployment of several thousand unguided Genies (air-to-air missiles). In 1964 the Soviet Union began to work on its Galosh interceptor system around Moscow. Interceptor missiles are ground-based. The United States deploys the Genie and the Soviet Union has Galosh. These ground-based missiles are designed to intercept an enemy missile in its terminal phase. The United States decided to incorporate the multiple independently targetable reentry vehicle (MIRV) into its intercontinental ballistic missiles (ICBMs) and to deploy the more advanced electronically steered NIKE-X antiballistic missile (ABM). *See also* BALLISTIC MISSILE DEFENSE (BMD) SYSTEM; HOMING.

Significance   Interceptor missiles are capable of intercepting an enemy missile at the boost or post-boost phase. The proposed space-based defensive system under the Strategic Defense Initiative (SDI) does not plan to use missiles in the traditional sense—the exception being the U.S. Army's kinetic weapons. The superpowers are limited to 100 interceptor missiles under the 1972 ABM treaty. Both the quantitative ceilings on offensive weapons and the concern for an ABM system were but two sides of the same coin: they reflect the need to stabilize mutual deterrence. However, enormous costs, and the fact that large nuclear explosions inside the atmosphere would be necessary to knock out MIRVs, has served to restrain both superpowers from going further with ABMs.

Intercontinental Ballistic Missile (ICBM)   A land-based rocket-propelled vehicle capable of delivering a nuclear warhead at a range in excess of 3,000 nautical miles (5,500 kilometers). An intercontinental ballistic missile is a small space rocket, similar to those used to launch men into space. It is composed of three parts that are related to the three phases of the missile's trajectory: a booster for take-off, a post-boost vehicle (the bus) for the intercontinental journey, and a re-entry vehicle (with its warhead and individual motor and guidance system) for the descent onto its target. Missile guidance is based on inertial navigation. After the rockets burn out, the missile falls down through the atmosphere, pulled by gravity to its target. In addition, precision mapping measures can assume missile accuracy within a radius of 30 to 100 meters. The Titan II, Minuteman II, Minuteman III, and Minuteman III (MK 12A) are examples of U.S. ICBMs. The Soviet examples are: SS-11, SS-13, SS-17, SS-18, SS-19, SS-24, and SS-25. The CSS-3 and CSS-4 are examples of Chinese ICBMs. *See also* GUIDANCE SYSTEM; INERTIAL GUIDANCE; TRIAD.

Significance   Intercontinental ballistic missiles were developed by the superpowers in the late 1950s. Recently China added a small number of ICBMs. Kept in underground missile silos, ICBMs are the most powerful and accurate nuclear weapons. Their intercontinental range makes them a keystone of a country's survival. Their travel time of about 30 minutes illustrates the limited reaction time to verify a nuclear strike, and to defend and retaliate. They are an essential component of the strategic triad—the other two being the submarine-launched ballistic missiles (SLBMs) and strategic bombers. While U.S. strategy places an emphasis on its SLBMs, ICBMs dominate the Soviet nuclear panoply.

Intermediate-Range Ballistic Missile (IRBM)   A land-based, rocket-propelled vehicle capable of delivering a nuclear warhead at a range of 1,500 to 3,000 nautical miles (2,750 to 5,500 kilometers). Intermediate-range ballistic missiles are propelled into the upper atmosphere by booster rockets. After the rockets burn out, earth's gravitational pull brings them down through the atmosphere onto their targets. The IRBMs have a range less than that of the intercontinental ballistic missile (ICBM) but greater than the medium-range and short-range ballistic missiles. The term intermediate-range ballistic missile is most commonly used to describe a ballistic missile. Ballistic missiles are weapons that fly a ballistic trajectory after being thrown into the air by rocket power. First introduced in 1961, the Soviet Union replaced its SS-5 Skean with the more sophisticated SS-20, originally deployed in 1977. This missile is solid-fueled and consists of the lower two stages of the SS-16 ICBM. The CSS-2 is China's IRBM and the S-3 is France's. *See also* INTERMEDIATE-RANGE BOMBER; INTERMEDIATE-RANGE NUCLEAR FORCES TREATY.

Significance   Intermediate-range ballistic missiles were incorporated into the December 1987 Intermediate-range Nuclear Forces (INF) Treaty between the superpowers. Accordingly, an entire generation of U.S. and Soviet IRBMs is being dismantled. Soviet SS-20s are unlike the other IRBMs: they can carry three 150-kiloton weapons and have a range of 5,000 kilometers. They are one of the most modern and accurate of Soviet missiles. It was the deployment of Soviet SS-20s that led to the North Atlantic Treaty Organization's introduction of Tomahawk cruise missiles and Pershing II missiles in Western Europe in the mid-1980s. This effort serves to remind the Western Europeans of their vulnerability, and to make it clear that it was by no means certain that it would benefit NATO, even militarily, to resort to using nuclear weapons. Deployment of IRBMs within range of key command targets, such as the United States has established in Europe and which the Soviet Union could establish in Central America, enables the superpowers to deliver a nuclear attack on each other's command system targets.

Intermediate-Range Bomber   Any aircraft capable of delivering nuclear or conventional weapons over a range of 3,680 to 9,200 kilometers. Intermediate-range bombers are capable of flying a broad geographical region, such as Europe or Africa. They have less range than long-range bombers, but more range than medium-range bombers. With a range of 8,000 kilometers, the Soviet Union deploys the Tu-22m/26 Backfire. One of the most advanced Soviet bombers, it was first introduced in 1974. Since 1969 the United States has deployed the FB-111, which is very effective in penetrating enemy defenses. Its range can be increased from 5,500 to 8,650 kilometers with midair refueling. These aircraft have variable geometric wings to adapt their shape to the particular operating speed. At low speed, the wings are spread to provide maximum lift; at high speed they are swept back to minimize air resistance. *See also* LONG-RANGE BOMBER; MEDIUM-RANGE BOMBER.

Significance   Intermediate-range bombers fly for a long period of time with in-flight refueling or if sent on a one-way mission. They can carry up to six short-range attack missiles, six nuclear free-fall bombs or combinations of the two, but which, in theory at least, cannot reach the Soviet Union from their U.S. bases without refueling. Because the Soviet Backfire bomber can reach the U.S. mainland with in-flight refueling, the United States holds that this is a strategic bomber and should be counted as one in arms control negotiations. The Soviets disagree, claiming that it is only intended for use in the European theater. There are 1,700 nuclear gravity bombs and 1,000 nuclear-capable aircraft, including F-111s and allied aircraft, scattered across Europe. At 17 air bases in Europe, U.S. and North Atlantic Treaty Organization (NATO) aircraft are maintained on quick-reaction alert, with bombs loaded and ready for takeoff on short notice.

Intermediate-Range Nuclear Forces (INF) Treaty (1987)   An agreement between the superpowers to eliminate all intermediate-range nuclear missiles, short-range missiles, associated launchers, equipment, support facilities, and operating bases worldwide. The INF treaty, signed by U.S. President Ronald Reagan and Soviet President Mikhail S. Gorbachev on December 8, 1987, includes all ground-launched missiles with ranges between 1,000 and 5,500 kilometers and SRMs—including all those with ranges between 500 and 1,000 kilometers. The treaty bans flight-testing and production of these missiles as well as production of their launchers. The 17-article treaty is supplemented by two protocols: one relating to elimination (dismantling and destruction) procedures and the other to on-site inspections. As of November 1, 1987, an accompanying Memorandum of Understanding provides detailed accounting of the number and location of all U.S. and Soviet missiles, launchers, equipment, and facilities subject to the terms of the treaty. The verification provisions of the treaty include an exchange of data on the systems limited by the treaty, including numbers, locations, and technical characteristics of all INF missiles and launchers; inspections of INF sites to confirm the validity of the data exchanged, to help verify elimination of these weapons and related infrastructure, and to help verify that INF activity has ceased; short-notice on-site inspection at INF-related sites during the three-year reductions period and for 10 years afterward; resident inspectors at key missile final assembly facilities; and prohibition on interference with verification by national technical means, which includes satellite imagery. The treaty has been ratified by both the signatories. *See also* NUCLEAR DISARMAMENT; STRATEGIC ARMS REDUCTION TALKS (START).

Significance The Intermediate-range Nuclear Forces (INF) Treaty is the first nuclear arms reduction agreement. The debate before and during the U.S. Senate hearing for treaty ratification centered on the question of whether the Soviets would comply with its provisions. The treaty's proponents, most notably President Reagan, maintained that the Soviets would comply with its provisions because the treaty's verification provision guaranteed that the United States could quickly detect any Soviet noncompliance. The treaty's supporters also noted that its verification provisions were adequate—enabling the open U.S. society to verify the closed Soviet society's compliance. In addition, permanent monitoring teams would also be stationed around the perimeters of plants where the destroyed missiles had been manufactured to ensure that production was not resumed. Opponents of the treaty argued that verification problems would be compounded by the inherent limitations of on-site inspections. The arguments made by both supporters and critics of the treaty clarified its implications for future arms control negotiations. During the Washington summit the two leaders of the superpowers agreed to instruct their Strategic Arms Reduction Talks (START) negotiators in Geneva to resolve outstanding issues, especially those related to verification.

International Atomic Energy Agency (IAEA) An agency of the United Nations that fosters cooperation and provides control among countries in their development of peaceful uses of atomic energy. The International Atomic Energy Agency was first proposed in 1953 by U.S. President Dwight D. Eisenhower; it was established by the United Nations as an autonomous institution in 1957. The agency is headquartered in Vienna, Austria. The IAEA safeguards nuclear activities in three ways. First, it conducts on-site inspections of nuclear power reactors and other nuclear facilities to detect diversion of atomic materials to make nuclear bombs. Second, it maintains detailed accounts and records of location, quantities, form, and movement of nuclear materials. Third, the agency reviews designs of nuclear facilities to ensure provisions for surveillance and for independent measuring devices. *See also* FISSION; FUSION; NUCLEAR NONPROLIFERATION; NUCLEAR PROLIFERATION.

Significance   The International Atomic Energy Agency is charged with three major activities. One involves controls over the supplying of nuclear materials to other countries for research purposes. It is also responsible for safeguarding against military use of atomic materials by nonnuclear nations that signed the Nonproliferation Treaty (1968). Initially, the IAEA sponsors research and conducts studies on health and safety hazards of atomic energy production. All major nuclear suppliers now require IAEA safeguards on their export of nuclear materials to nonnuclear nations. Some, including the United States, require recipient countries to have all peaceful nuclear facilities under IAEA safeguards prior to providing them with any atomic component. The agency conducts about 1,800 on-site inspections annually at 520 different locations in the world. The IAEA plays a pivotal role in dissuading horizontal nuclear proliferation—spread of nuclear weapons to current nonnuclear nations.

Ionizing Radiation   Any electromagnetic or particulate radiation capable of producing ions as it passes throughout matter. Ionizing radiation creates charged particles. This kind of radiation is harmful to living beings because it changes their charged state and, therefore, their chemical composition. Ionizing radiation emits a unit of radiation that produces certain changes, called ionization, in other atoms. It is different from thermal radiation, which damages cells by heat. Inside body tissue, radiation yields its effects through the ionization of molecules. The growth of nuclear power has led to a slight increase in the natural background radiation because of minute quantities of radioisotopes released from nuclear power plants and the fallout injected into the atmosphere by nuclear tests and accidents. People who work regularly with radioactive materials, such as nuclear reactor engineers, wear a radiation-sensitive badge. When they have absorbed what is considered a safe limit, they are temporarily taken off the job. *See also* RADIOACTIVE DECAY; RADIOISOTOPE; THERMAL RADIATION.

Significance   Ionizing radiation is extremely damaging to living cells, and it is created in massive amounts in a nuclear explosion. It is particularly harmful to cells in the digestive tract and bone marrow. This radiation attacks genetic molecules, interferes with cell reproduction, and may cause severe mutations. If the DNA molecules in human egg or sperm cells were damaged by radiation, a completely different gene, a mutation, could be formed. No amount of ionizing radiation, however small, can be said to be harmless. People are continuously exposed to ionizing radiation throughout their lives, even in peacetime. This exposure comes from cosmic rays (high-speed nuclear particles coming from the stars and other bodies in space), radioactive elements in the ground, and from medical X-rays. Nuclear warfare could lead to increased genetic diseases, cancer, and mass deaths.

Isotope   A variant of a single element. An isotope contains a different number of neutrons in its nucleus. While the nucleus of an element has a fixed number of protons, it can have different numbers of neutrons. Nuclei that have the same number of protons but a different number of neutrons are called isotopes. Uranium 235 and uranium 238 are isotopes of uranium. Uranium 238 contains three more neutrons than uranium 235. The heaviest element found in natural uranium has 92 protons within the nucleus of every atom. More than 99 percent of the natural element consists of uranium 238, which has 146 neutrons in the nucleus together with the 92 protons. Almost all the remaining natural uranium consists of isotope 235, which has only 143 neutrons in each nucleus. The separation of uranium 235 from natural uranium is difficult and costly because isotopes are the same chemically, and differ only slightly in mass. *See also* FISSON; FUSION; PLUTONIUM.

Significance   An isotope implies a different physical property; this differential in the properties of isotopes in a nuclear context is essential for two reasons. First, only a few isotopes are suitable for use in a nuclear weapon. It is crucial to have the right isotope to make the weapon work. In order to produce bomb material, a fissionable isotope must be enriched by using one of a number of very difficult and expensive enrichment methods. Second, certain isotopes emit potentially deadly radiation. Many of these radioactive isotopes—usually known as radioisotopes—are created in a nuclear explosion. After the detonation of a nuclear weapon, the stable isotopes will group on the pulverized fragments of the weapon itself and on the dust and ash of a ground burst. While different radioactive species, known as nuclides or isotopes, lose their radioactivity at varying rates, each isotope may be characterized by a particular time known as its half-life. Different radioactive isotopes may have vastly different half-lives, ranging from less than a billionth of a second to more than a billion years.

J

Jamming   A measure to make an adversary's sensitive electronic equipment ineffective. Jamming is used against any equipment that transmits signals. It involves the transmission of a competing signal that drowns out a signal transmitted by an opponent's satellites or radars. Jamming works on the same principle as playing two different radio stations at the same time. Jamming a radio link means transmitting noise to the receiving antenna to drown out the meaningful signals from the friendly transmitter. The jamming transmitter must arrange to have a clear propagation path to the enemy receiver, which implies some geographic constraints on jamming. Besides making clever use of geographic constraints and relays, the communicator has several options for dealing with jamming. One is to have friendly forces use the same frequencies as enemy forces, thus jamming their operations. Another is to attack and destroy the jammer. Still another is to increase transmitter power. *See also* RADAR.

Significance   Jamming can drown out radar signals that detect attacking warheads. It can render a country's antiballistic missile defense system ineffective against a surprise attack. The chief way military communicators defeat jamming is by lowering the data rate, essentially by repeating the message enough times to be sure of intelligible reception despite the jammer's noise. Jamming can be used to disrupt communications signals broadcast from a satellite. The United States and the Soviet Union often jam each other's communications and frequencies of similar wavelengths. The Eastern European countries prevent reception of broadcasts from Radio Liberty, Radio Free Europe, and The Voice of America. The Soviet Union has stopped jamming these radio broadcasts for the first time in 30 years. It is unclear how much U.S. strategic forces located on the continental United States would suffer from jamming of its wartime communications.

114

Joint Chiefs of Staff (JCS)   The principal advisers to the president, the National Security council, and the secretary of defense. The Joint Chiefs of Staff consists of the chairman of the JCS; the chief of staff, U.S. Army; the chief of naval operations; the chief of staff, U.S. Air Force; and the Commandant of the Marine Corps. They are appointed by the president, with Senate approval. The chairman has a tenure of two years, and the others serve four-year terms. The JCS is responsible for: (1) helping the president and the secretary of defense to provide for the strategic direction and planning of the armed forces; (2) allocating resources to implement strategic plans; (3) making recommendations for the assignment of responsibilities within the armed forces according to and in support of logistic and mobility plans; (4) comparing the capabilities of U.S. and allied armed forces with those of potential adversaries; (5) preparing and assessing contingency plans that conform to policy guidance from the president and the secretary of defense; (6) preparing joint logistic and mobility plans to back up contingency plans. The basic procedures for alerting nuclear forces were created by the JCS during the 1950s. The procedure is to permit central authorities to direct in discrete and clearly understood stages any change in readiness status of conventional and nuclear forces. *See also* COMMAND, CONTROL, COMMUNICATIONS, AND INTELLIGENCE (C3I); PRESIDENT; SECRETARY OF DEFENSE.

Significance   The Joint Chiefs of Staff is responsible for the conducting of military operations; the chain of command runs from the president to the secretary of defense and through the JCS to the commanders of combined and strategic commands. Orders moving forces to a different alert status would run through that sequence. The orders would follow defense condition (DEFCON) levels in five stages: DEFCON 5 and 4 (normal peacetime position), DEFCON 3 (troops on standby, awaiting further orders), DEFCON 2 (troops ready for combat), and DEFCON 1 (troops deployed for combat).[17] In peacetime, U.S. troops, except for the Strategic Air Command (SAC), are kept at DEFCON 5, the lowest level of readiness. Orders to the unified and specific commands are issued by the president, the secretary of defense, or the JCS. The commanders have operational control over all forces assigned to them.

K

Kill Radius   The surrounding area of a nuclear explosion in which all people are killed. The kill radius can vary, depending on four factors: weapon size, type of weapon, where it is used, and how it is used. The kill radius is determined by a combination of a missile's accuracy and its yield (destructive power), although it is the former that needs to be given greater consideration. The reason accuracy is taken into account is that even in a countervalue strategy, the closer a missile lands near a densely populated area, the more people it will kill. Soviet emphasis on lethal radius, which is similar to kill radius, gives their missiles greater kill radius than U.S. missiles, which stress greater accuracy. The Soviet Union has attempted to improve the accuracy of its SS-18 and SS-19 missiles while increasing their yield. This provides the latest Soviet nuclear missiles with a relatively greater kill radius. *See also* LETHALITY; OVERPRESSURE.

Significance   A kill radius is a measure of the destructive power of a nuclear missile. Most of the modeling of nuclear war scenarios to date has been done by the U.S. Department of Defense. These models tend to show very low death and damage estimates. The lethality is typically estimated by assuming that all persons within a 5 psi (pounds per square inch) exposure area will be killed, and those outside will survive. Nuclear war scenarios and their models do not consider the long-term effects on the environment. The nuclear weapons exploded on Hiroshima and Nagasaki were small, and their effects were localized to the immediate radius. But the effects of the detonation of 5,000 megatons of nuclear weapons in the northern hemisphere undoubtedly would be severe enough to cause the extinction of life in the hemisphere.

116

Kiloton Weapon   A nuclear fission weapon with a destructive capacity equivalent to 1,000 tons of trinitrotoluene (TNT). A kiloton weapon is less powerful than a megaton (one million tons of TNT) weapon, but more powerful than a nominal (20 kilotons of TNT) nuclear weapon. Kiloton weapons are usually tactical or theater nuclear weapons. Tactical nuclear weapons are short-range (up to 200 kilometers), and include bombs, short-range missiles, nuclear artillery, and atomic demolition munitions. These comprise the United States Army's Lance MGM-52c, Lance II, and Nike-Hercules MIM-14 artillery missiles, and a number of artillery-fired atomic projectiles and the small and medium atomic demolition munitions. The U.S. Air Force has one type of air-to-air nuclear armed missile—the Genie Air-2A. The U.S. Navy holds a number of ship-to-ship and ship-to-air missiles—the Terrier Rim-20, the Standard 2 Rim-67B. The Soviet Union generally avoids nuclear-capable artillery, with the single exception of the SS-23 180mm towed gun. The Soviet Navy carries a large range of submarine-launched cruise missiles in a ship-to-ship use. *See also* SHORT-RANGE BALLISTIC MISSILE (SRBM); TACTICAL NUCLEAR WEAPON (TNW); THEATER NUCLEAR WEAPON (TNW).

Significance   Kiloton weapons are more accurate and easier to deploy than the megaton weapons. They are intended to be used on the battlefield or within a specific geographical region. The bomb detonated on Hiroshima in 1945 had a yield of 12–15 kilotons. Most of the weapons built since the early 1970s have been kiloton weapons. These weapons are an essential component of a warfighting or counterforce strategy in Europe. Today, aircraft are the chief means of delivering theater nuclear weapons. There are 1,700 nuclear gravity bombs and 1,000 nuclear-capable aircraft scattered across Europe. At 17 air bases in Europe, U.S. and North Atlantic Treaty Organization (NATO) aircraft are routinely maintained on quick-reaction alert with bombs loaded and ready to take off on short notice.

Kinetic Energy Weapon (KEW)   A potential new weapon that is part of a high-technology antiballistic missile defense system. A kinetic energy weapon involves shooting nonnuclear projectiles against incoming enemy warheads. These projectiles, called kinetic kill vehicles, would disable a warhead by impact. A KEW could be placed on the ground or in space. At the center of the kinetic energy research is the "smart bullet." This small projectile, containing an elaborate miniaturized computer system, can be launched either from a satellite or from ground-based interceptors. The Reagan administration started research on kinetic energy technology under the Strategic Defense Initiative (SDI) program. SDI researchers are working on kinetic energy systems capable of destroying attacking weapons in all flight phases. This system would disarm the intended target through the sheer physical force of high-speed collision. No explosive is necessary; at such high velocity, mere impact causes destruction. *See also* ANTIBALLISTIC MISSILE TREATY; HIGH FRONTIER; KINETIC KILL VEHICLE (KKV); STRATEGIC DEFENSE INITIATIVE (SDI).

Significance   The kinetic energy weapon would not carry nuclear explosives—consequently it would not be a nuclear weapon. Instead, it would use the current level of technological knowledge. The kinetic energy of motion would be used to create an impact on the incoming enemy warhead. The destructive force would come from this collision. The main problem with the KEW is not so much getting enough energy to the enemy missile to destroy it as being able to make the projectile travel fast enough to reach the target during its boost phase. Despite this problem, kinetic energy weapons are actively being considered for attacking Soviet missiles in the post-boost and midcourse phases of the flight. While much work remains to be done, KEW research and development shows considerable progress. In recent tests it has exhibited a tremendous increase in the rate of fire of smart bullets.

Kinetic Kill Vehicle (KKV)   A small, high-speed rocket that could, in theory, destroy an attacking nuclear weapon or satellite. A kinetic kill vehicle could be projected from a kinetic energy weapon. Kinetic kill vehicles would destroy incoming enemy missiles on impact; they could be launched either from the ground or from space. A defense would use ground-, air-, and satellite-based sensors to detect, launch, and track offensive weapons. In the near future terminal defense would rely on interceptor missiles for kill; ground-based lasers might be adopted later. The three main layers in a defense would be boost-phase, midcourse, and terminal reentry interception. Terminal defenses are close to useful deployment; boost-phase interception could be practicable in the early 1990s; and the midcourse phase is the least advanced. *See also* HIGH FRONTIER; KINETIC ENERGY WEAPON (KEW); STRATEGIC DEFENSE INITIATIVE (SDI).

Significance   A kinetic vehicle would not carry nuclear warheads; consequently it would not be considered a nuclear weapon. Instead, it would use state-of-the-art technology on kinetic motion. The destructive force would come from the tremendous speed of the kill vehicle. The United States is conducting research on the kinetic kill vehicle as part of the Strategic Defense Initiative program. The problem of getting the necessary laser energy into space, whether on board satellites or by way of satellite-borne mirror detection, is far from solved, and some even believe it is insoluble in principle. A proposed scheme for KKVs in the early 1990s would use four surveillance satellites, ten tracking satellites, and a KKV force ranging from 500 to 1,500 small satellites. If this project succeeds, it will be a major element in the strategic defense of the United States.

L

Laser   A light amplification by stimulated emission of radiation (LASER). A laser is an intense beam of light produced by raising the energy level of certain substances with large amounts of electrical energy. For many years both the United States and the Soviet Union have been working to develop ever more intense beams of laser light. Several types of lasers are prospective strategic weapons. These include chemical lasers, excimer lasers, free-electron lasers, and X-ray lasers. The difference between each type is the wavelength of the radiation. Laser beams are, essentially, beams of radiation, such as light. When we switch on an electric light bulb, the light streams out of the bulb in all directions, illuminating the entire room. But radiation from a laser goes in only one direction. Laser weapons would thus function like superconcentrated spotlights; they would focus enormous energy on targets in order to destroy them. The beam moves at the speed of light, 300,000 kilometers (186,300 miles) per second. *See also* CHEMICAL LASER WEAPON (CLW); GROUND-BASED LASER WEAPON (GBLW); X-RAY LASER WEAPON.

Significance   Laser beams travel at the speed of light and can retain their intensity over thousands of miles in space. They would be capable of burning a hole through the skin (outer covering) of an incoming nuclear missile. Thus they could deactivate the sensitive electronic guidance system encapsulated inside the missile. When they are perfected they will revolutionize warfare. The Reagan administration encouraged further research on laser weapons under the Strategic Defense Initiative program. For the United States, one of the motives for such research has been an interest in using strongly focused energy beams to trigger the fusion of small quantities of deuterium and tritium. Much effort has gone into using lasers for conventional warfare, in which targets are marked for smart bombs that can detect the reflected laser beam. The critical problems in beam production are the available light intensities, the wavelengths of the light, and diffraction broadening. Critics believe that the use of lasers for endo-atmospheric defenses of intercontinental ballistic missile (ICBM) silos would be difficult because of atmospheric problems of cloud cover or particulates in the air. On balance, space-based weapons do not seem to be an effective near-term weapons system.

Launch Control Center (LCC)   An underground command post that coordinates the launching of land-based nuclear missiles. A launch control center always has two officers in charge. The safeguard system prevents any one officer from launching a nuclear attack individually: the two officers must cooperate to fire a missile. When an encoded launch order (called an emergency action message) is transmitted to an LCC, the officers must decode and validate the order. The methods for interpreting and authenticating the code are kept in a double-locked safe to which each officer has a key. A cruise missile flight consists, among other components, of two launch control centers. In peacetime each cruise missile flight is located on a Main Operating Base such as Greenham Common, and the LCCs are housed in specially constructed protective bunkers, which are resistant to surprise attack by conventional weapons delivered by aircraft or missiles. The bunkers themselves are partly concealed by earth, which provides additional blast protection. *See also* ACCIDENTAL NUCLEAR WAR; EMERGENCY ACTION MESSAGE (EAM); PRESIDENT.

Significance   A launch control center is ultimately responsible for pushing the button that releases the nuclear missile. Once the LCC unleashes a nuclear missile, the missile cannot be recalled. For this reason every possible precaution is taken to prevent any accidental nuclear war. That is why the launch procedures are not left in the hands of a single person. The system and the procedure, for example, work like this: the request to fire a ground-based cruise missile from Great Britain at a target in Eastern Europe would come from the Supreme Allied Commander in Europe. In the launch control center two officers are seated at computer keyboards and in radio contact (via the satellite network) with the highest-level officials in the United States. The European Command, which can send a prerecorded emergency action message to the LCC, uses a radio link. The European Command communicates with the National Command Authorities in the United States, and the airborne command posts that would carry the president and the military commanders in wartime communicate directly with each cruise missile launch control center.

Launcher   A structure that supports and holds a nuclear missile in position for firing. A launcher may be deployed on land, at sea, or in the air; it may be fixed or mobile. A launcher may fire many different types of nuclear weapons: from small battlefield artillery shells to giant ballistic missiles with an intercontinental range and capable of devastating an entire city. International ballistic missile launchers are land-based; submarine-launched ballistic missile launchers are the tubes on a submarine. An aircraft itself is a launcher for air-launched ballistic missiles. Launchers for cruise missiles can be mounted on aircraft, ships, submarines, or vehicles. To reduce the threat to U.S. intercontinental ballistic missiles (ICBMs) posed by Soviet forces, many new basing schemes, designed to improve the missiles' survivability, have been considered and rejected. Concealment and deception could contribute to the survivability of ICBMs, since the Soviets do not know where the U.S. ICBM launchers are and thus could not target them. The United States has other features built into its command and control system to give it some prospects of surviving attack. It has separated nuclear weapon launchers from populated urban centers. U.S. ICBMs and bomber bases are located in the sparsely populated western part of the country. *See also* HOT LAUNCH; LAUNCH CONTROL CENTER (LCC).

Significance   Launcher was a key word during both SALT I and SALT II (Strategic Arms Limitation Talks) negotiations. The SALT I agreement (1972) placed a ceiling on the number of launchers that each superpower may have. The SALT II treaty (1979) was the first nuclear arms reduction treaty, and it proposed a one-third reduction in the number of missile launchers by both sides. Irrespective of the number of warheads or the explosive yield of a missile, it is the launcher that is crucial in firing a missile. For this reason both SALT I and SALT II placed emphasis on bringing about a superpower nuclear parity by focusing on the number of their nuclear missile launchers.

Launch-on-Impact (LOI)   An order to fire nuclear weapons after enemy nuclear warheads have hit their targets. A launch-on-impact is undertaken in response to a confirmed enemy nuclear strike. It is distinct from both launch-on-warning and launch-under-attack in that a retaliation is not undertaken with a mere indication of a nuclear attack from the adversary. A launch-on-impact is also known as a launch-through-attack. Inside the launch control center the first warning of an attack would be an oscillating note on the loudspeaker, at the sound of which the crew would immediately close the center's blast doors and activate the emergency air supply. If it is a real attack, a voice over the speaker will announce, "Gentlemen, you have received an authorized launch instruction from the National Command Authorities," and, simultaneously, a printed code of letters and numbers would come through a telex machine. The crew would then open a strongbox on the wall and check the code contained within against the code just received. If the codes match, the launch command would be considered valid. *See also* LAUNCH CONTROL CENTER (LCC); LAUNCH-ON-WARNING (LOW); LAUNCH-UNDER-ATTACK (LUA); NATIONAL COMMAND AUTHORITIES (NCA).

Significance   A launch-on-impact strategy implies waiting for definite confirmation of an enemy attack before firing a retaliatory strike. It is used to assess the intent and extent of an enemy attack in order to determine appropriate countermeasures. The launch-on-impact strategy is designed to avoid an accidental nuclear war. Although the technical capability to launch-on-impact exists, the combined political and military processes of making and communicating a decision would normally take a considerable length of time, especially if Soviet missiles came without any prior buildup of tension between the superpowers. Some military observers believe that U.S. nuclear forces are on a far higher degree of alert than Soviet forces, presumably because the United States fears a surprise Soviet attack, whereas the Soviet Union does not share the same apprehension of a surprise U.S. attack.

Launch-on-Warning (LOW)   A strategy calling for a nuclear attack in response to an indication of incoming enemy missiles. A launch-on-warning is distinct from launch-under-attack, in which only land-based nuclear missiles are fired. It is also different from launch-on-impact, in which a retaliatory strike is launched after enemy missiles have struck their targets. The LOW strategy means that a nation plans to launch its counterstrike when its radars and computers indicate that an enemy attack is on its way. If a satellite detects evidence of a hostile launch, a computer signal triggers the firing of the recipient's weapons to protect them from incoming missiles. The LOW is also known as launch-on-tactical warning. Neither the United States nor the Soviet Union has ever adopted a launch-on-warning policy. *See also* ACCIDENTAL NUCLEAR WAR; FIRST STRIKE; LAUNCH-ON-IMPACT (LOI); LAUNCH-UNDER-ATTACK (LUA).

Significance   A launch-on-warning strategy is designed to ensure the emptying of missile silos if it is suspected that they have been targeted. In that way, the missiles can be used before they can be destroyed. Even though the launch-on-warning strategy increases the speed of a country's response to hostile nuclear attack, possible computer malfunction raises the specter of an accidental nuclear war. The ultimate uncertainty facing the attacker is whether the victim might choose to launch his missiles upon warning of an attack, or while an attack is under way. It is unclear how much deterrent value the launch-on-warning has if the attacker concludes that the potential victim is unlikely to be able to carry it out. A nuclear attack without enemy military preparation is not ruled out; it is recognized as an unlikely but distinct possibility. The U.S. policy has been to wait out a Soviet strike until it is confirmed by actual attack; this is because the LOW procedure is risky. In the past, flocks of birds have been interpreted on radar as possible incoming Soviet missiles; and computers have accidentally simulated a Soviet attack.

Launch-under-Attack (LUA)   A nuclear retaliatory strike in response to an indication of enemy attack. A launch-under-attack strategy, unlike a launch-on-warning, involves firing only land-based nuclear missiles. This policy implies waiting a little longer than launch-on-warning strategy before retaliating. A launch-under-attack is also distinct from launch-on-impact, in which the retaliatory strike is launched after the enemy missiles have hit their targets. The ideal sequence in which sensor data would appear at U.S. command centers is the following: intercontinental ballistic missile (ICBM) and submarine-launched ballistic missile (SLBM) launches detected by infrared satellites; close-in SLBMs detected by coastal (PAVE PAWS) radars; high-altitude SLBM bursts detected by terrestrial Electromagnetic Pulse (EMP) sensors and satellite-borne burst detectors; further coastal radar detections of SLBMs launched from far away places; detection of ICBMs by Ballistic Missile Early Warning System (BMEWS) radars; detection of ICBMs by the Perimeter Acquisition Radar Attack Characterization System (PARCS) in North Dakota if SLBMs have not already destroyed it; detection of ICBM bursts by satellite burst detectors. *See also* ACCIDENTAL NUCLEAR WAR; FIRST STRIKE; LAUNCH-ON-IMPACT (LOI); LAUNCH-ON WARNING (LOW).

Significance   A launch-under-attack strategy is a way of ensuring against a successful first strike by the enemy. The policy allows for using one's own missiles before they are destroyed by the enemy in the silos like "sitting ducks." Although a launch-under-attack strategy increases the speed of a country's response to hostile nuclear attack, a possible computer malfunction raises the danger of an accidental nuclear war. Nevertheless, in waiting a little longer, launch-under-attack is a slightly better strategy than a launch-on-warning in avoiding a nuclear war through misperception or faulty communication. A launch-under-attack in military usage means a launch after it has been definitely confirmed that enemy missiles are on their way. The LUA has a better chance of succeeding if the aggressor excludes the Command, Control, Communication, and Intelligence (C3I) system from its attack and, instead, targets missile silos, bomber bases and certain key nodes.

Layered Defense   A hypothetical missile defense system designed to deactivate or destroy enemy ballistic missiles during any of the four stages of their flight path. A layered defense includes the following four phases: boost phase, post-boost phase, midcourse phase, and terminal phase. During each phase an antiballistic missile defense system would attempt to destroy an enemy missile. A layered defense is also known as multilayered or multitiered defense. The strategy of layered defense assumes that there is always a 50 percent probability of missing or destroying an enemy missile. In a massive nuclear strike by an adversary, the first layer would destroy an estimated 50 percent of the enemy missiles. The second layer would destroy 50 percent of the surviving missiles; this would amount to destroying 75 percent of the enemy's original number of missiles fired. By this account, the third layer would destroy about 87 percent, and the fourth layer would destroy roughly 94 percent of the original missiles fired. *See also* BALLISTIC MISSILE DEFENSE (BMD) SYSTEM; DISTANT EARLY WARNING (DEW); GROUND-BASED ELECTRO-OPTICAL DEEP SPACE SURVEILLANCE (GEODSS); GROUND-BASED LASER WEAPON (GBLW).

Significance   A layered defense envisages that each layer would act as a backup to the previous layer. The first layer would attempt to destroy an attacking ballistic missile almost immediately after it is launched, in order to lessen the pressure on succeeding defense layers. Although a layered defense does not guarantee a foolproof defense, it increases the prospects for effectively blocking a greater number of enemy missiles from reaching their targets. This defense system is an attempt to meet the eventuality that, for various reasons, any one defensive layer may inevitably be inefficient. In a layered system, the latter layers in the sequence will normally be designed on the assumption that the earlier layers operate as planned. If for any reasons—malfunctions or enemy countermeasures—the first layer failed to achieve its planned efficiency, the later layers would function less effectively. Placing heavy emphasis on destroying enemy missiles during the first, or boost, phase would also greatly increase the danger of accidental war because of the short time period in which to make the decision to attack them.

Lethality   The ability of a weapon to locate, hit, and destroy its target. The lethality factor is more specifically evaluated when released against a reinforced target, such as a missile silo. It is assessed by a complex formula comprising a missile's accuracy and its yield (destructive power). A lethality is directly proportional to the two-thirds power of a missile's yield; it is inversely proportional to a square of a missile's accuracy. Helen Caldicott, a leading defense analyst, defines lethality as "a function of yield in megatons (EMT) to accuracy (CEP) and is expressed as L = EMT/CEP."[18] A rather complicated estimate can be made of the chance factor: that a weapon of specified yield with a prescribed expected error in aim—the radius of the circle within which half the shots at a target point are expected to fall, which is called the Circular Error Probable (CEP)—will destroy a strongpoint; these are called lethality estimates. A lethality is also known as countermilitary potential, hard-target kill capability, silo-busting potential, and warhead lethality. *See also* DECAPITATION ATTACK; MEGATON WEAPON; OVERKILL; YIELD.

Significance   Lethality is not of much concern against a soft target, such as a city, which is very likely in any event to be destroyed by a missile attack. Instead, it is a crucial factor against hard targets, such as hardened missile silos, which are designed to withstand the effects of a nuclear blast. Caldicott believes that "in practice, the area of blast destruction is enlarged by increasing the number of bombs and lowering their individual yield—that is, several small bombs with the same aggregate yield are much more effective spread out over the target than one large warhead."[19] In trying to achieve lethality, the Soviets have generally stressed yield, and the Americans have emphasized accuracy. In recent years each superpower is paying greater attention to both sides of the lethality coin, making present and future generations of nuclear missiles more accurate and more powerful.

Limited Nuclear War (LNW)   A strategy to use a small number of nuclear weapons in a conflict to achieve specific, limited objectives. Limited nuclear war had its root in the 1950s in the dissatisfaction with the massive retaliation doctrine. Limited nuclear war was made a part of U.S. nuclear policy in 1974 by Secretary of Defense James M. Schlesinger. Although challenged by President Ronald Reagan's 1983 proposal for a defensive nuclear strategy, it remains part of U.S.

nuclear doctrine. A limited nuclear war is limited by the types and the number of weapons employed—for example, tactical nuclear weapons only—or limited according to targets or to specific regions or countries. Any nuclear war short of a general or all-out nuclear war will be considered a limited one. The LNW strategy involves restriction on the kind of use of the strategic weapons. *See also* NUCLEAR WAR.

Significance   A limited nuclear war envisages a voluntary restraint not to escalate beyond a certain range and yield of nuclear weapons; there is also the assumption that such a war will be confined to a specific geographical region. The LNW doctrine has three essential components. First, it assumes that the use of nuclear weapons would be coupled with diplomatic and conventional military efforts in a conflict. Second, it implies that an all-out general nuclear war is not inevitable if some nuclear weapons are introduced in the battlefield. The LNW strategy introduces another option of using certain nuclear weapons against specific targets. Third, it gives nuclear weapons a legitimate role, without having to surrender or launch a massive, suicidal nuclear attack. Critics respond that this is a risky line of thought. They contend that creating plans and hardware for limited nuclear options might make it all too easy for those options to be used in a serious crisis. The notion that such warfare could remain limited is questionable.

Limited Test Ban Treaty (LTBT)   A multilateral agreement that prohibits nuclear weapons tests or any other nuclear explosion in the atmosphere, in outer space, and under water. The limited test ban treaty is "limited" in that it allows restricted nuclear tests underground, as long as any resultant radioactive debris does not go beyond the territorial limits of the country where the test is being conducted. Efforts to achieve an "all-inclusive" test ban agreement began in the early 1950s and continued for about a decade. The LTBT was the culmination of that effort. However, among the nuclear weapons countries, France, China, and India have declined so far to sign the treaty and conduct their nuclear weapons tests above-ground. The treaty was signed in Moscow in July 1963 and took effect in October of that year. Although Soviet and U.S. signatures were the primary prize, Article III of the treaty opens it to all the countries of the world. More than 110 countries have signed the treaty. The LTBT is also known as the Partial Test Ban Treaty. *See also* ANTARCTIC TREATY; THRESHOLD TEST BAN TREATY (TTBT); TREATY OF RAROTONGA; TREATY OF TLATELOLCO; UNDERGROUND NUCLEAR TESTS.

Significance   The Limited Test Ban Treaty was a milestone. For the first time nations placed some restraints on the nuclear arms race. The LTBT does not drastically hinder the development of new weapons systems but it does reduce the amount of dangerous radioactive material present in the atmosphere. Since the signing of this treaty, arms control advocacy has been more or less a permanent part of the context within which nuclear matters are decided. Subsequent efforts by the superpowers to ban weapons tests altogether have not borne fruit. The Threshold Test Ban Treaty (TTBT), which limits underground tests of weapons with yields of 150 kilotons, was signed by the superpowers in 1974. The TTBT has not been ratified by the U.S. Senate, but both superpowers claim to be abiding by its provisions. Up until the signing of the LTBT there had been 380 nuclear explosions in the world, which released radioactive materials into the atmosphere. It is apparent that worldwide environmental effects have been felt from those tests and from those conducted by several non-signatory nations, namely, France and China. In the 1980s the Soviet Union adopted a voluntary unilateral ban on all testing, but when other states refused to join in the ban the Soviets resumed underground testing in 1988.

Linkage   A process of relating two or more issues in negotiating and using one or several as trade-off bargaining chips. Linkage is especially associated with superpower relations in the field of arms control negotiations. It is basically a U.S. strategy that is employed to make progress in military, economic, and diplomatic fields. The idea is extended to incorporate Soviet foreign policy behavior regarding domestic human rights, economic issues, and the Third World. U.S. diplomatic initiatives, including arms agreements, have variously linked Soviet activities in Afghanistan, Angola, Cuba, Ethiopia, and Poland as well as the shooting down of a Korean passenger airliner in 1983, to progress in arms talks. The U.S. Senate rejected the Strategic Arms Limitation Talks (SALT II) agreement because of Soviet adventurism in Ethiopia, Cuba, and its invasion of Afghanistan. *See also* COUPLING; DÉTENTE; STRATEGIC ARMS LIMITATION TALKS (SALT II).

Significance   A linkage policy has been consistently opposed by the Soviet Union. U.S. opponents of linkage believe the nuclear arms race is too critical a priority to be mixed up with secondary concerns. Proponents of the strategy within U.S. leadership view linkage as a bargaining chip to get the Soviets to agree to a favorable package deal. Henry Kissinger, a former secretary of state, envisaged coupling the SALT I agreement and moderation of Soviet behavior in the Third

World. Kissinger hoped the Soviets would not try to disrupt the status quo in the Third World under the guise of supporting national liberation movements. The Carter administration attempted to relate better superpower relations with improved human rights conditions in the Soviet Union, something that Kissinger did not view favorably. While Kissinger's linkage focused in the external sphere, Carter's notion concentrated on the internal realm. When the U.S. Senate refused to ratify SALT II, its linkage strategy incorporated both external and internal demands for Soviet behavioral changes.

Liquid-Fueled Engine   A type of booster rocket that propels a ballistic missile and directs it toward its target. Liquid-fueled engine is run by a mixture of kerosense and oxidizers. Generally, liquid-fueled rockets operate by mixing two liquids within the engine itself during the firing process. Oxidizers such as liquified oxygen or liquid nitrogen pentoxide combine with a hydrogen-based fuel to give high exhaust velocities. Both the U.S. Army and Air Force developed intermediate-range liquid-fuel rockets—the Jupiter and the Thor. The Titan II is the last liquid-fueled intercontinental ballistic missile still deployed by the United States, although in limited numbers. Except for Titan II, all U.S. missiles use solid propellants, which are more stable and less vulnerable to enemy attack, and their smaller size makes it easier to build silos with high levels of blast resistance. *See also* INTERCONTINENTAL BALLISTIC MISSILE (ICBM); INTERMEDIATE-RANGE BALLISTIC MISSILE (IRBM); MEDIUM-RANGE BALLISTIC MISSILE (MRBM).

Significance   The liquid-fueled engine is very much like an automobile: one can increase or decrease the speed by pressing down or releasing the accelerator (gas pedal). It is possible to maneuver a liquid-fueled engine by turning the entire engine. Despite the above advantages, it has some major disadvantages. Preparing a liquid-fueled engine for use as a weapon, for example, requires a considerable time period, unlike solid-fueled missiles, which can be fired by pressing buttons. Also, missiles incorporating such an engine are less sophisticated and more prone to accidents than are solid-fueled missiles. Most of the missiles in the U.S. nuclear arsenal have been replaced by solid-fueled missiles. The Soviet Union still deploys some liquid-fueled missiles, although it has an impressive number of solid-fueled missiles. Solid fuels are cheaper and do not present storage or toxicity problems. However, firing solid-fueled rockets presents some difficulty because the magnitude of their thrust cannot be varied, as it can be with liquid fuels.

Little Boy   The first atomic weapon dropped by the United States on Hiroshima, Japan, on August 6, 1945, at 8:15 A.M., Little Boy measured about 10 feet long and weighed about 8,000 pounds, with an explosive yield of a minimum of 12,000 tons (12 kilotons) of TNT. It was exploded in an air burst 600 yards above the city. Little Boy was designed at Los Alamos, New Mexico, by a team of atomic scientists headed by J. Robert Oppenheimer. Code-named "Little Boy," it used uranium 235 and was slimmer and lighter than Fat Man (the bomb that razed Nagasaki). This first use of atomic weapons in a war killed about 75,000 people immediately, and many perished during the ensuing days. Little Boy, dropped by a B-29 bomber, also generated a shock wave, which shot outward from the blast center at roughly the speed of sound. *See also* FAT MAN; HIROSHIMA; MANHATTAN PROJECT; PLUTONIUM WEAPON.

Significance   Little Boy was a product of the Manhattan Project, the U.S. effort during World War II that built the first atomic bomb. It was the only U.S. weapon to be fueled by uranium, the highly radioactive substance that presently fuels most nuclear reactors. Today's nuclear weapons use plutonium as the basic raw material. The use of Little Boy gave mankind its first actual glimpse of the destructive power of atomic weapons. It revolutionized man's thinking about warfare, and introduced the notion of devaluation of power: having a nuclear weapon constrains a superpower from using its panoply. The power of a nuclear weapon was no longer in its utility in a war, but in preventing superpower wars in the first place.

Long-Range Bomber   An aircraft that can carry nuclear and conventional weapons from the home-base of one superpower to the military and civilian targets of the other superpower. A long-range bomber has a range greater than 9,200 kilometers (a tactical operating radius of over 2,500 nautical miles). It can travel farther than an intermediate-range and a medium-range bomber. Both the United States and the Soviet Union deploy three types of long-range bombers. The United States deploys the B-52G, B-52H, and B-1B and will soon deploy the B-2 (Stealth); the Soviet Union deploys the Bear, Bison, and Blackjack. Both the B-52G and the B-52H are modernized versions of the original B-52D. These two aircraft, like the B-1B, are equipped to deliver gravity bombs, short-range attack missiles, and air-launched cruise missiles. The Soviet counterparts to the above two U.S. aircraft are the Tu-95 Bear and the Mya-4 Bison. The Bear-H, the newest version of the Tu-95 Bear, is capable of carrying the AS-15, the most modern Soviet air-launched cruise missile. The U.S. B-1B is the counterpart of the Soviet Blackjack RAM-P, the most modern Soviet long-range bomber. Long-range bombers are also known as strategic bombers. *See also* AIR-LAUNCHED CRUISE MISSILE (ALCM); HEAVY BOMBER; STEALTH BOMBER.

Significance   The long-range bomber has gone through various stages of modernization in both the United States and the Soviet Union. The B-52G, first deployed in 1959, has a range of 12,000 kilometers; the B-52H, introduced in 1962, has a range of 16,000 kilometers. The B-1B has a relatively shorter range (9,600 kilometers) but can carry 48 weapons compared to 24 carried by the other two bombers. In addition, the B-1B can fly much farther than the other two aircraft; this is also true for Soviets' Blackjack RAM-P in comparison with their Bear and Bison bombers. In terms of range, there is not much difference among the Soviet variety. The Mya-4 Bison has a range of 11,200 kilometers; Tu-95 Bear 12,300 kilometers, and both the Bear-H and Blackjack RAM-P a range of 12,800 kilometers. The Bear-H entered production in 1983. Since 1987, Blackjack RAM-P has been replacing both the Tu-95 Bear and Mya-4 Bison, introduced in 1956. President Jimmy Carter cancelled the B-1 in 1977; its variant, the B-1B, was revived by President Ronald Reagan and is now deployed. Long-range bombers comprise one leg of the strategic triad, and both superpowers are striving to make it an independent and effective second-strike retaliatory force.

Low-Altitude Defense System (LOADS)   A hypothetical defense system that would destroy attacking nuclear warheads in the last seconds of their flight. A low-altitude defense system would allow interception of enemy warheads at altitudes ranging between 50,000 and 200,000 feet. The system is expected to undergo vigorous testing toward the end of 1980s in the United States. Several Ballistic Missile Defense (BMD) systems are being considered for development by the United States; one of them is LOADS. An initial BMD system capability is in the form of a low-altitude defense system called "Sentry," which has, for several years, been undergoing advanced development for potential use. *See also* ANTIBALLISTIC MISSILE TREATY; BALLISTIC MISSILE DEFENSE (BMD) SYSTEM; GROUND-BASED LASER WEAPON (GBLW).

Significance   A low-altitude defense system could be considered a subsystem of terminal phase interception of the enemy's ballistic missiles. It would allow for much shorter reaction-time, thereby intercepting the enemy warhead just before it hits its target. The LOADS received attention in the early 1970s as a possible way of protecting ballistic-missile sites. However, such a last-minute interception—whose practicality is in itself a debatable issue—may still allow for nuclear debris in the target country. In legal terms, the deployment of LOADS could be a violation of the Antiballistic Missile Treaty (1972). Both superpowers, however, conduct research programs in BMD and may go on to build LOADS to help protect land-based missiles, whether stationary or mobile. This type of program carries the arms race into space and hypothesizes the creation of exotic systems using missile-borne radars, satellites, lasers, and beams to detect, identify, and destroy an enemy's warheads and missiles.

M

Magnetic Contour Matching (MAGCOM)   An advanced guidance system that directs cruise missiles toward their targets. Magnetic contour matching uses the earth's magnetic field as a reference guide to keep a cruise missile on course. The on-board computer compares the actual ground reading with an altitude map stored in the computer memory. MAGCOM compares the actual magnetic field around the missile with the predicted one in the missile's computer. Any deviations are used to make in-flight adjustments of the missile's flight path to direct it toward its target. Cruise missiles are guided by an inertial-guidance platform, which is supplemented in turn by a sensor system called terrain contour matching (TERCOM). On quoted test performance, the technique enables the guidance system to fix a navigational position with the probability of an error less than one part in 10 million. *See also* CRUISE MISSILE; INERTIAL GUIDANCE; TERRAIN CONTOUR MATCHING (TERCOM).

Significance   Magnetic contour matching is specifically useful for a cruise missile that flies over water. The MAGCOM makes the cruise missile operate like a pilotless aircraft. It also gives the missile its high accuracy for target killing capacity; low-altitude flying makes the missile very difficult to detect on a radar screen. Thus radar evasion and the high accuracy of the MAGCOM technique make the cruise missile an extremely potent nuclear weapon. A cruise missile, however, destabilizes the arms control process: it is quite small and can be hidden from satellite detection, and thus the Soviets have no way to determine U.S. deployment of cruise missiles in the European theater or on surface ships and submarines.

Maneuverable Reentry Vehicle (MARV)   A ballistic missile re-entry vehicle equipped with its own navigation and control systems

133

that adjust its trajectory during reentry into the atmosphere. The maneuverable reentry vehicle is one of several types of nuclear warheads carried by a single ballistic missile that can be individually aimed and maneuvered, enabling a single missile to strike more than one target. The original MARV, named the Special Reentry Body (SRB), was equipped with an aerodynamic design that enabled it to fly like an aircraft on entering the atmosphere. MARVs are a more technologically advanced version of the multiple independently targetable reentry vehicle (MIRV). MARVs are not only well-aimed and multiple, but each has some degree of terminal, or final, homing guidance built in so that as it approaches the target, it can make a last-minute maneuver to avoid a defensive interceptor and improve its final aim. *See also* BALLISTIC MISSILE DEFENSE (BMD) SYSTEM; GUIDANCE SYSTEM; MULTIPLE INDEPENDENTLY TARGETABLE REENTRY VEHICLE (MIRV).

Significance   A maneuverable reentry vehicle has twofold advantages. First, the on-board guidance and control systems give MARV a greater probability for accuracy because of adjustment options in the midcourse and terminal phases. The guidance options include television, imaging infrared laser, and distance-measuring equipment (DME). Such accuracy may be crucial in a counterforce strategy, where the objective is to strike key targets while minimizing collateral damage. Second, the high maneuverability of MARVs enables them to evade an enemy's antiballistic missile defense. Integrated with the highly accurate NAVASTAR (Navigation System Using Timing and Ranging) global positioning guidance system, an advanced version of the MARV is scheduled for use on the Trident II submarine-launched ballistic missile (SLBM). Such an arrangement could give MARV an accuracy within a radius of 30 feet. The potential for an assured second-strike capability and a more consolidated deterrence is enormous, especially when each Trident II SLBM can carry as many as seventeen 75-kiloton MARVed warheads.

Manhattan Project   The highly classified U.S. program during World War II that produced the first atomic bombs. The Manhattan Project derived its name from the scheme's code name, "Manhattan Engineering District," which was used to conceal the nature of the secret work under way. Headed by General Leslie Groves, and at a cost of about $2 billion, the project spanned the years 1942 to 1945. It was conceived and executed in total secrecy at Los Alamos, a privately owned boys' school, in the mountains of New Mexico. Many prominent scientists, including Enrico Fermi, J. Robert Oppenheimer, and Niels Bohr were involved in the project. The project drew upon the work of specially built laboratories all over the country. Construction of a plant using the Lawrence electromagnetic method was started at Oak Ridge, Tennessee, in 1943. The plant provided weapons-grade uranium 235 by 1945. Research leading to the successful building and operation of a gaseous diffusion plant was conducted principally at Columbia University in New York. During the four-year wartime Manhattan Project, the United States produced enough fissionable uranium and plutonium to make three bombs. One of them was tested in the isolated desert of New Mexico in a place called Jornada del Muerto, "Journey of the Dead," and the other two were dropped on Japan. *See also* ATOMIC WEAPON; HIROSHIMA; NAGASAKI; PLUTONIUM WEAPON.

Significance   The Manhattan Project produced the world's first atomic weapons, revolutionized science, ushered in the nuclear age, and developed a new concept of warfare in which deterrence replaced defense as a military strategy among the major powers. Code-named "The Trinity Test," the first bomb exploded on July 16, 1945, in Alamogordo, New Mexico. The project developed the bombs that were dropped on the Japanese cities of Hiroshima and Nagasaki in August 1945, and the resultant devastation vividly demonstrated the destructive power of nuclear weapons. The Manhattan Project was successful not only because of its large funding but also because it involved the tremendous scientific and technological competence of thousands of brilliant scientists and technicians, and the dedication of large industrial concerns, such as the Dupont Company, in turning scientific concepts into industrial production.

Massive Retaliation   The U.S. military doctrine that called for countering any aggression against its interest anywhere in the world with an all-out nuclear retaliation. Massive retaliation relied on a credible commitment to launch a devastating nuclear response to deter any unfriendly provocation by an adversary. On January 12, 1954, Secretary of State John Foster Dulles incorporated the doctrine as a part of U.S. foreign policy. Domestic factors meant that the United States must oppose communism, and the international setting suggested that U.S. nuclear superiority was crucial in this regard. The result was an overall policy known as the "New Look," and its centerpiece became the nuclear strategy of massive retaliation. This strategy had both a conventional and nuclear component. In the early 1960s, the Kennedy administration replaced the idea of massive retaliation with the doctrine of Flexible Response (ranging from limited defense with conventional military forces to all-out nuclear war). *See also* COUNTERVALUE STRIKE; MUTUAL ASSURED DESTRUCTION (MAD); NUCLEAR DETERRENCE; NUCLEAR UMBRELLA.

Significance   Massive retaliation was the first major doctrine of the United States on the role of nuclear weapons in its foreign policy. It reflected the Eisenhower administration's "New Look" approach to defense. It was a cost-cutting measure that promised tax payers more "bang for the buck." Under this doctrine the United States relied on its nuclear umbrella to protect its allies, especially those in Western Europe. In cutting down massive investment in conventional weapons, U.S. leadership found investment in nuclear weapons more cost-effective. Dulles presented massive retaliation as a way of countering perceived Communist threats in Europe and Asia, especially in the aftermath of the Korean War. However, in 1957 the Soviet Union not only sent Sputnik-1 into space but also developed the capability to deliver a nuclear warhead from its Arctic region to anywhere in the continental United States. With the loss of U.S. invincibility, massive retaliation lost its credibility in view of the danger of a Communist nuclear confrontation with the United States.

Medium-Range Ballistic Missile (MRBM)   A ballistic missile designed to be used in a broad geographical region, such as Europe. A medium-range ballistic missile has a range of 1,100 to 2,750 kilometers. Its range is less than that of intercontinental and intermediate-range ballistic missiles, but greater than that of short-range ballistic missiles. The Soviet Union first deployed the SS-4 Sandal in 1959. It has a range of 2,000 kilometers, and carries a single one-megaton warhead. Beginning in the mid-1980s, these were replaced by the more advanced SS-20 missiles. The United States developed the Pershing I and Pershing II missiles. The latter has a range of 1,790 kilometers and delivers one warhead with a yield of 0.3 to 80 kilotons of TNT. In 1966 China deployed the CSS-I, which has a range of 1,100 kilometers and carries a single 20 kiloton warhead. MRBMs are also known as theater nuclear weapons. *See also* EUROMISSILES; INTERMEDIATE-RANGE BALLISTIC MISSILE (IRBM); SHORT-RANGE BALLISTIC MISSILE (SRBM).

Significance   Medium-range ballistic missiles, along with intermediate-range ballistic missiles, were negotiated to be destroyed in the Intermediate-range Nuclear Forces (INF) Treaty (1987), signed by the United States and the Soviet Union. This treaty has its roots in the Soviet replacement of SS-4 missiles with SS-20s in the early 1980s. In response, the North Atlantic Treaty Organization threatened to, and later in 1983, did deploy U.S. Pershing II missiles in West Germany. The Pershing IIs are ten times more accurate than Pershing Ia missiles, and thus threatened the western Soviet Union. It was a major factor in bringing the Soviets to the negotiating table. Removal of the

MRBMs, along with the IRBMs, took away the escalation ladder between the ICBMs and SRBMs. In view of the conventional superiority of the Warsaw Pact forces, the 1987 treaty has made Western Europeans very nervous. They fear the United States will not risk an all-out war in using the ICBMs if the SRBMs fail to stop the advancing Warsaw Pact forces, which means the decoupling of Western European security under the U.S. nuclear umbrella. The SS-4 Sandal missiles are well remembered because it was the secret introduction of these missiles into Cuba by the Soviet Union that led to the October 1962 Cuban missile crisis. As the first Chinese ballistic missile, the CSS-I will always have a crucial role in the evolution of Chinese nuclear strategy.

Medium-Range Bomber   Any aircraft that can carry nuclear and conventional weapons over a broad geographical region, such as Europe. A medium-range bomber has a range of less than 3,680 kilometers, which is less than either the long-range or intermediate-range bomber. The medium-range and intermediate-range bombers are also known as medium bombers. The Soviet Union deploys the Tu-16 Badger and Tu-22 Blinder. France developed the Mirage IV-A and Mirage 2000N. A consortium of British, Italian, and West German manufacturers developed the Tornado strike aircraft. First deployed in 1955, the Tu-16 Badger has a range of 4,800 kilometers and is designed to carry air-to-surface missiles. The Tu-22 Blinder, introduced in 1962, has a range of 4,000 kilometers and can carry both gravity bombs and air-to-surface missiles. Developed in 1964, Mirage IV-A has a range of 1,500 kilometers and carries two 70 kiloton gravity bombs. Mirage 2000N began test flights in 1983 and was to be deployed in 1988; it has a range of 1,400 kilometers. Introduced in 1982, the Tornado has a range of 2,600 kilometers and can deliver two gravity bombs. *See also* INTERMEDIATE-RANGE BOMBER; LONG-RANGE BOMBER.

Significance   Medium-range bombers are not deployed by the United States. This is probably because of the geographical distance of its major adversaries, which would necessitate their being stationed in forward bases in Western Europe. The Tu-22 Blinder can take off from both land bases and aircraft carriers. Mirage 2000N is the most technologically sophisticated French fighter bomber, and it will replace the Mirage IV-A. Tornado weapons carrying nuclear weapons are deployed by Britain; the nonnuclear version is in the service of the Italian and West German air forces. The plane is specially equipped for all-weather operations. The FB-111A is a swing-wing medium-range bomber. Because of its relatively short-range, this aircraft is not considered to be an intercontinental bomber and is not counted under the SALT agreements. Some of these planes are stationed in England and could be used, to some extent, in attacks on parts of the Soviet Union.

Megaton Weapon   A nuclear weapon that yields the energy equivalent of one million tons of TNT (trinitrotoluene). A megaton weapon would equal 1,000 one-kiloton weapons exploded together. Thermonuclear hydrogen weapons are measured not in terms of kilotons but of megatons. Today's one megaton bomb, a fairly standard size in arsenals, has the explosive power of one million tons of TNT. A one-megaton hydrogen bomb has the blast equivalence of one-third of all the munitions used in World War II. The Soviet Union has generally produced bigger hydrogen bombs than those of the United States. The Soviet weapons range from submegaton to 20 megatons in size. However, the military imperative has been to make nuclear weapons smaller, providing explosive yields appropriate to a given requirement. When a weapon is compact, reliable, and deadly, the delivery system becomes highly critical. *See also* HEAVY MISSILE; HYDROGEN BOMB; LIMITED TEST BAN TREATY (LTBT); THERMONUCLEAR WEAPON.

Significance   Megaton weapons are usually classified as strategic weapons. The world's thermonuclear and hydrogen weapons arsenals include an estimated 13,000 megatons. Robert Ehrlich, a physicist, in his book *Waging Nuclear Peace*, estimates that "the likely casualties that would result from the use of these arsenals [is] equivalent in total yield to one million Hiroshima bombs."[20] Megaton weapons are intended to be used in a countervalue strategy, deep inside the homeland of the adversary. In recent years, the superpowers have moved away from such weapons because of their lesser accuracy and a greater difficulty in deploying them. The trend now has shifted toward kiloton weapons, although many megaton weapons are still deployed. Despite the continuing growth in the world's nuclear arsenals, it appears that the potential threat, resulting from atmospheric nuclear tests prior to the Limited Test Ban Treaty (1963), actually declined.[21] The depletion of the ozone layer to a 50 percent of normal would have a serious effect on living beings.

Midgetman   A new, single warhead intercontinental ballistic missile (ICBM). The Midgetman is a small ICBM with a range of 10,000 kilometers and a yield of about 350 kilotons. A commission headed by

Brent Scowcroft, National Security Council Adviser, and reporting to President Ronald Reagan, urged the United States pursue a small single-warhead Midgetman missile and, for the short term, deploy the ten-warhead MX missile in fixed Minuteman silos. About 1,000 Midgetman missiles will be deployed by the early 1990s in the southwestern part of the United States. The commission's case for a small weapon with a throw-weight of 1,000 pounds, compared to the Minuteman III's 2,500-pound and the MX's 8,300-pound throw-weights, turns on the idea that a single-warhead ICBM denies an enemy the chance to destroy more than one warhead with one attacking warhead. The Scowcroft Commission concluded that such a small missile could be hardened against the effects of a nuclear explosion using available technology. Countering the U.S. Midgetman, the Soviets produced a parallel missile, initially called the PL-5, then SS-X-25. The Midgetman introduced a new classification of nuclear weapons: the small intercontinental ballistic missile (SICBM). The U.S. arms control negotiator, Paul Nitze, calls these new missiles the "little guys," and they have come to be known as Midgetman. *See also* MINUTEMAN MISSILE; MX MISSILE; SCOWCROFT COMMISSION; STRATEGIC WEAPON.

Significance   The Midgetman represents a new departure in U.S. land-based strategic forces—a light, mobile ICBM that would derive its protection from Soviet attack primarily by movement. Unlike currently deployed ICBMs, the Midgetman would eschew hardened sites and move around the country as and when required (the Midgetman can be moved in an armored vehicle, called "armadillo"). A new debate raged throughout 1982 over the MX missiles' survivability against a Soviet attack. President Reagan then appointed the high-level Scowcroft Commission to review the situation with MXs. The commission itself represented a device to achieve a compromise that would be acceptable to different elements in the U.S. Congress: providing funds for MX missiles and the new ICBM, popularly dubbed "Midgetman." While the Midgetman remains a subject of congressional debate, the Soviets are undertaking tests of the SS-X-25. The United States attempted to link the Soviet missile with the SS-16, a discarded prototype of a mobile missile, the further development of which was banned under the Strategic Arms Limitation Talks (SALT II), but such accusations were rebuffed.

Mike Shot   The first true explosion of a high-yield thermonuclear test. The Mike shot was conducted by the United States on November 1, 1952, at Elugelab Island in the South Pacific and had a yield of 10.4 megatons. It was much more powerful than the George shot, the first thermonuclear explosion. The Mike device had a reported weight of 62 tons, due in part to the cryogenic equipment needed to maintain its thermonuclear fuel, deuterium, at liquid temperatures. The Mike shot dug a hole almost a kilometer in radius into the test atoll, completely obliterating Elugelab Island on which it was detonated. The hole for this explosion was larger than a 10 megaton bomb because coral is very soft and is easier to crater than is typical soil. *See also* MEGATON WEAPON; NUCLEAR WEAPON; THERMONUCLEAR WEAPON.

Significance   The Mike shot was an unwieldly experimental contraption; it could not be used as a weapon. It spite of its inadaptability as a weapon, Mike shot is commonly referred to as the first successful superbomb. The Mike test was not yet a practical bomb since it also required refrigeration equipment and weighed 62 tons. The day before the Mike shot, England became a nuclear power by exploding a fission device installed in the frigate HMS *Plym*. This explosion, code-named "Hurricane," was in the kiloton range and took place in the Monte Bello Islands, west of Australia. Within a year of the Mike explosion, the Soviet Union announced that it had produced a dry hydrogen bomb. This weapon used lithium as a source of tritium and therefore did not require the bulky cryogenic equipment used in the Mike shot test. The United States responded by developing the intercontinental ballistic missile. Thus the present "superarms" race was ushered in during the 1950s.

Military-Industrial Complex   The driving force of militaristic ideology and policy. The military-industrial complex refers to the collusive relationship that is alleged to exist between the leading members of the military establishment and those industrialists involved in the production of military technology. The phrase "military-industrial complex" was first used by President Dwight D. Eisenhower in his farewell address to the nation in January 1961. He noted that until World War II there had been no permanent armaments industry in the United States; but because of the war and the Cold War, the nation was compelled to create a permanent armaments industry. President Eisenhower said "Now this conjunction of an immense military establishment and a large arms industry is new in the American experience. The total influence—economic, political, even spiritual—is felt in every city, every State House, every office of the Federal Government. . . . " Many powerful domestic groups within major states that have vested interests in military spending use their influence to promote productions of arms and development of new technology. These groups include: (1) military officers, (2) owners and managers of defense-related industries, (3) top government officials, and (4) legislators whose districts benefit from defense contracts. *See also* DEPARTMENT OF DEFENSE (DOD); STRATEGIC DEFENSE INITIATIVE (SDI).

Significance The military-industrial complex rationalizes high levels of military expenditure with an ideology of Cold War. In the heyday of the Cold War, defense was good business, and the military-industrial complex prefers to keep it that way. By the late 1980s the U.S. government expended over $300 billion annually in total defense spending. Many new defense projects—such as expanded naval construction, the MX missile system, the cruise missile, and the Strategic Defense Initiative—require enormous budgetary outlays, and millions of Americans benefit from the development of these new defense-related industries. The recent global trends toward gigantic military-industrial complexes have increased the rewards for those involved in the production and sale of armaments. Crucial to the understanding of this complex is the question of whether all citizens and lobbyist groups advocating a strong national defense are to be included in this rubric or whether it is comprised only of profit-seeking corporations, political and military groups, and certain individuals (scientists, engineers, managers, financiers, politicians, and military officers). To be sure, the social basis of the makeup of such a complex has always been the privileged role of the military-industrial establishment within a given society. The Soviets have also developed a military-industrial complex of immense proportions, and somewhat lesser complexes are typical of most industrialized states and a few of the Third World countries.

Milstar Satellite A planned U.S. military satellite designed to provide better communications between the various units of the armed forces during a war. The acronym "Milstar" stands for Military Strategic and Tactical Relay, and it is a very sophisticated military satellite. It was one of the top-priority defense projects of the Reagan administration, proposed in the early 1980s. The satellite would be positioned three times deeper in space than existing satellites to make it less vulnerable to enemy attack. It would be a high-frequency satellite communications system, highly resistant to jamming, with secure voice and data transmission capability. In addition, the Milstar satellite will enhance the reliability of links between intelligence sources and users. As the name implies, the Milstar satellite is also intended for communications to nonstrategic forces having suitable receivers and transmitters. Current plans call for 4,000 Milstar terminals for all three services, and they are expected to be deployed in the late 1980s. *See* *also* COMMAND, CONTROL, COMMUNICATIONS, AND INTELLIGENCE (C3I); MINIMUM ESSENTIAL EMERGENCY COMMUNICATIONS NETWORK (MEECN); NATIONAL EMERGENCY AIRBORNE COMMAND POST (NEACP).

Significance   The Milstar satellite is designed to allow maximum communications technology to be combined in one vehicle. It would be used for worldwide two-way communications, to coordinate efforts of the army, navy, and air force at all levels of conflicts. Its durability, survivability, and warfighting utility would make it valuable for a counterforce strategy and intrawar deterrence. More long-term plans include having a number of "silent" (dormant) partners stored in high orbits. If a functioning Milstar satellite is deactivated or destroyed, one of the silent satellites could be activated to take its place. The Milstar satellite is expected to replace the navy's Fleet Satellite Communications (FLTSATCOM) and the air force's AFSATCOM, which are judged to be relatively open to attack. Milstar is intended as a new-generation service Comsat system.

Miniature Homing Vehicle (MHV)   A small, highly advanced, hypothetical antisatellite weapon. A miniature homing vehicle is designed to destroy an enemy satellite by impact. It would be launched from a high-flying fighter plane. Traveling at 7,200 miles per hour, it is expected to destroy a target satellite flying at 10,000 miles per hour. Central to this high-speed collision is the presence of eight small telescopes that can detect infrared emissions from the target satellite. The sensors are cooled to an extremely low temperature in order to capture this very faint ray. Once the target has been detected, the MHV would move toward it by 56 small rocket tubes. These tubes form the outer shell of the cylinder, and they release their exhausts at right angles to the flight path. The MHV would be guided toward its target by a ring-laser gyro, which regulates the firing of the rockets and keeps the MHV spinning twenty times per second. Nicknamed the "Flying Tomato Can," the MHV has been under development by the United States since 1978. *See also* ANTIBALLISTIC WEAPON; HOMING.

Significance   A miniature homing vehicle would be a nonnuclear, antisatellite weapon. While using very high-technology instruments, it would still rely on the basic laws of motion of a moving body. In 1985, the U.S. Air Force carried out a test against a satellite using a miniature homing vehicle. The vehicle had an infrared sensor on board. The test MHV was launched from an F-15 aircraft, rose up out of the atmosphere into space, detected the target, and, steering itself into the target, made a direct impact. When fully developed, the

MHV would be a highly accurate weapon and could be used to play havoc on an adversary's satellite-based laser defense system. This makes the MHV an offensive weapon, and critics fear that such a weapon may further threaten to destabilize the already precarious superpower nuclear deterrence.

Minimum Deterrence   A strategy based on a small and limited nuclear arsenal. A minimum deterrence system would retain the ability to launch an unacceptable retaliatory nuclear strike, and require that each side deploy a nuclear arsenal powerful enough to ensure that the threat of destructive retaliation remain credible. A minimum deterrence could be achieved in two ways. First, in terms of the number of weapons a figure as low as 500 warheads has been suggested for the United States. Second, in terms of the kind of weapons, some suggest keeping only the submarine-launched ballistic missiles (SLBMs), that is, one leg of the strategic triad. The number of nuclear weapons needed in a minimum deterrence varies; an overall cutback of 50 percent in the U.S. arsenal seems generally acceptable to its supporters. A minimum deterrence is also known as "pure" deterrence or "finite" deterrence. *See also* COUPLING; DETERRENCE; EUROMISSILES.

Significance   A minimum deterrence relies on a countervalue retaliatory strategy against the major populated cities of the potential aggressor. It is a cost-effective strategy for a major power that cannot afford to be involved in the superpowers' arms race, but also cannot rely wholly on the nuclear protection of its superpower ally. Nicknamed the *force de frappe,* France undertook such a strategy of minimum deterrence in 1963 under Charles de Gaulle. Great Britain also has a similar strategy. But minimum deterrence can complicate arms control talks. That was demonstrated in the Intermediate-range Nuclear Forces (INF) Talks in 1987, when the Soviets at first insisted on counting the British and French nuclear missiles as part of the U.S. arsenal but later relented. The concept of a minimum deterrence appeals to many because it would move the superpowers away from considerations of war-fighting strategies and back to the notion of mutual assured destruction (MAD). Unless it is a credible policy, a minimum deterrence may not deter. But because of the entrenched vested interests of the military-industrial complex in the United States and the Soviet Union, a minimum deterrence policy would be hard for any U.S. and Soviet leader to accomplish.

Minimum Energy Trajectory   The missile flight path that reaches a given range with the least expenditure of propellant energy. A minimum energy trajectory involves propelling a ballistic missile into the atmosphere by booster rockets and then letting it be pulled down by gravity to its target. For launch angles of 6° and 51°, the rocket travels 7,360 kilometers in 17.5 and 49 minutes, respectively. For a launching angle of 19.3°, the rocket lands 11,300 kilometers away from the launch point after a flight of 35 minutes. This latter range is the longest that can be achieved for that ballistic velocity, and hence it is called the maximum range. The flight path is called the minimum trajectory, as it demands less fuel to reach 11,300 kilometers than any other trajectory. It is distinct from a depressed trajectory (the path that a ballistic missile could follow as it streaks toward its target), in which a ballistic missile flies closer in order to reach its target faster. *See also* BALLISTIC MISSILE DEFENSE (BMD) SYSTEM; GROUND-BASED ELEC-TRO-OPTICAL DEEP SPACE SURVEILLANCE (GEODSS).

Significance   A minimum energy trajectory missile takes longer to reach its target than a depressed trajectory missile. This longer time gives the enemy's ballistic missile defense system more reaction time after detecting the incoming missile. Further, it is more difficult to evade radar with a minimum energy trajectory. Such early detection gives the enemy missile defense system an additional reaction time to track and intercept the incoming missile farther away from its target. However, if the missiles were on a depressed trajectory (the path that a ballistic missile could follow as it streaks towards its target), interception would be more difficult.

Minimum Essential Emergency Communications Network (MEECN)
A system designed to provide communication ability during a nuclear war. The minimum essential emergency communications network consists of the National Military Command Center, the Alternate National Military Command Center, and the National Airborne Command Post. Established in 1970, the MEECN (pronounced meekin) is subject to constant updating and improvements to ensure the survival of communications with the missiles, submarines, and aircraft of the Single Integrated Operational Plan (SIOP), which is the highly secret contingency plan that details the use of the nuclear forces. The minimum requirement is that the MEECN be capable of one-way dissemination of emergency action messages (EAMs) ordering execution of one of the options of the SIOP. *See also* COMMAND, CONTROL, COMMUNICA-TIONS, AND INTELLIGENCE (C3I); NATIONAL COMMAND AUTHORITIES (NCA); NATIONAL MILITARY COMMAND CENTER (NMCC); WORLDWIDE MILITARY COMMAND AND CONTROL SYSTEM (WWMCCS).

Significance   The minimum essential emergency communications network is especially developed to allow U.S. military leaders to send uninterrupted messages in a nuclear war. Thus it forms an essential component of the command, control, communications, and intelligence system for a nuclear scenario. The MEECN is an integral part of nuclear forces management. The communications needs of the strategic forces are easy to identify because their basic operations are pre-planned and highly structured. But communications that are needed in order to operate bombers and cruise missile carriers, submarine-launched ballistic missiles (SLBMs), and intercontinental ballistic missiles (ICBMs) must also be exceptionally reliable in uniquely difficult circumstances. The United States dedicates a special, segregated portion of the Worldwide Military Command and Control System (WWMCCS) and the MEECN to this task. The aircraft also need communications in order to rendezvous with tankers en route to their targets. If the EAM dissemination system to the ICBMs is to permit them to operate at the survival level it has the demanding task of working within the 30-minute flight time of a Soviet ICBM, and possibly in the midst of detonations of Soviet SLBMs.

Minuteman Missile   A three-stage, solid-fueled, second-generation intercontinental ballistic missile (ICBM) equipped with nuclear warheads. A Minuteman missile series comprises the following: Minuteman II, Minuteman III, and Minuteman III (Mk-12A); all are equipped with nuclear warheads. The Minuteman I, first deployed in 1961, was succeeded by Minuteman II, which delivers a two-megaton warhead at a speed of 15,000 miles per hour and has a range of 12,500 kilometers (8,000 miles). Minuteman III was first introduced in 1970. Its LGM-30G version, Minuteman III (LGM-30G), first deployed in 1975, is 60 feet long, 6 feet at its widest point, and weighs 78,000 pounds. It has a range of 14,000 kilometers (9,000 miles), and delivers three MIRVed warheads with a yield of 170 to 220 kilotons of TNT each within a circular error probability (accuracy) of one nautical mile. In 1979 the United States placed the highly accurate Mk-12A warhead on 300 Minuteman III missiles, reducing the circular error probability even further to 0.12 nautical mile. This modified version is known as Minuteman III (Mk-12A). Like Minuteman III, it also has a range of 14,000 kilometers and carries three warheads, but each warhead has a yield of 335 kilotons of TNT. So named because it is fired on about one minute's warning, the Minuteman was produced in large numbers by the Kennedy and Johnson administrations. *See also* INTERCONTINENTAL BALLISTIC MISSILE (ICBM); MIDGETMAN; MISSILE.

Significance   A Minuteman missile is simpler, smaller, and lighter —designed for highly automated remote operation. It can be deployed either in a fixed or a mobile mode. Minuteman missiles can be deployed over a large area; they can also be placed on railroad cars and moved in order to create greater uncertainty for an enemy missile strike against them. Minuteman missiles are now the backbone of U.S. land-based intercontinental ballistic missiles; their increasing accuracy makes them all the more useful for a credible nuclear deterrence. Minuteman III missiles, which replaced Minuteman II in the period of SALT I (1972), carry three MIRVed warheads. Minuteman II carried only one. Despite the SALT I agreement, a new arms race ensued, not so much in numbers of missiles (which were limited) but in numbers of warheads on MIRVed missiles.

Missile   A self-propelled unmanned weapon thrown to its target by booster rockets or jet engines, and pulled down by gravity. A missile can carry either conventional or nuclear warheads. It is the warheads that account for the destructive potential, while the rockets or engines provide the driving force to carry the warheads toward their targets. There are two types of missiles: ballistic and cruise. A ballistic missile is propelled into the upper atmosphere by booster rockets. After the rockets burn out, the missile falls through the atmosphere and is pulled by gravity to its target. In contrast, a cruise missile is powered by jet engines. Missiles can be fired from aircraft, submarines, and land-based silos. Also, they can be deployed in a fixed silo or in a mobile mode. The missiles can carry a single warhead or many warheads. In the latter case, the warheads may be independently targeted under gravitational pull or they can be individually maneuvered to avoid an enemy's missile defense systems. In the former case they are inertially guided; in the latter, they operate under command guidance—much like a remote-control plane. They can be relatively fast (the ballistic missiles) or slow (the cruise missiles). In addition, land-based ballistic missiles can be further categorized according to their range: intercontinental ballistic missile (over 5,500 kilometers), intermediate-range ballistic missile (2,750 to 5,500 kilometers), medium-range ballistic missile (1,100 to less than 2,750 kilometers), and short-range ballistic missile (less than 1,100 kilometers). *See also* BALLISTIC MISSILE DEFENSE (BMD) SYSTEM; CRUISE MISSILE; GUIDED MISSILE; INTERCONTINENTAL BALLISTIC MISSILE (ICBM).

Significance   Missiles have ushered in a new era of warfare. It is no longer necessary to have piloted planes to carry nuclear bombs. Mounted on a missile, a nuclear warhead can be delivered against an enemy target without personnel ever leaving the home territory. As the range of missiles increases, it is no longer necessary to locate them farther away from home-base, close to the adversary. Such a measure cuts down both the required range and flight time of a missile. Apart from the number of warheads that a missile carries, its size and throw-weight are not of crucial concern—indeed sheer size is not a very good measure of anything. Although the two are not completely unrelated, warhead yield is a more critical factor than throw-weight.

Missile Gap   A situation in which one superpower falls behind the other in one phase of the nuclear arms race. A missile gap can be an account of a major disparity in terms of number, range, speed, yield and accuracy, basing mode, and the number and type of nuclear warheads. The term "missile gap" originated in the 1959 Gaither Committee report to President Dwight D. Eisenhower. According to this report, the Soviet Union was capable, at that time, of launching 100 intercontinental ballistic missiles at targets anywhere in the continental United States. Reports from various intelligence agencies warned that Soviet capabilities would rise to 1,000 to 1,500 missiles in the early 1960s, whereas the United States would have only 130. Acknowledgement of this gap caused the United States to commit itself to building 1,000 Minuteman missiles. However, by 1962 the Soviets had in fact produced fewer than 100 intercontinental ballistic missiles (ICBMs). *See also* BALANCE OF POWER; CUBAN MISSILE CRISIS; HAIR TRIGGER; NUCLEAR DETERRENCE.

Significance   The missile gap was made a major campaign issue by presidential candidate John F. Kennedy. The Soviet Union, Kennedy charged, had invested heavily in nuclear missile development while the Eisenhower administration had sat back and allowed the Soviets to gain the advantage. The U.S. public, fearful of a decade of U.S. nuclear superiority sliding away, believed the Kennedy line. The Pentagon was happy to produce more ballistic missiles. In 1961 the Polaris system was deployed, and it took the Soviets until 1969 to equal this achievement. In 1964 the United States had 834 ICBMs, a stockpile the Soviets equaled by 1968. In addition, the Kennedy administration placed missiles in the country's forward areas—with the North Atlantic Treaty Organization (NATO) allies and on U.S. aircraft carriers. It was the Soviet attempt to create its own forward base in Cuba that led to the October 1962 Cuban missile crisis. Although the missile gap was as fictitious as the bomber gap of the early 1950s, the Kennedy administration continued to boost missile production.

Mobile Missile   Missiles that can be moved around and fired from various locations. A mobile missile is usually launched from truck-like vehicles. The newest U.S. intercontinental ballistic missile (ICBM) is the MX or missile experimental, designed to be a mobile, invulnerable, and accurate system. Throughout its history, beginning in 1963, many methods of basing the MX have been considered, including placing missile pods in the bottom of ponds or in truck or railborne capsules, carrying the missile around on highways, hiding it in a submarine, and flying it around in an airplane. None of these options is particularly appealing, and all are expensive. Because the position of a mobile missile is not fixed, it would be less vulnerable to enemy attack. A mobile missile is distinct from a fixed missile, which cannot be moved around and thus would be more vulnerable in an enemy attack. *See also* MISSILE; STRATEGIC ARMS LIMITATION TALKS (SALT II).

Significance   A mobile missile is easier to hide, and hence harder to verify in policing any arms limitation agreements. Under the unratified SALT II treaty, the Soviet Union agreed not to deploy its mobile SS-16 solid-fuel rocket. Because of ICBM vulnerability, the United States prefers to deploy mobile missiles, even if these are not verifiable within the Strategic Arms Limitation Talks agreements. SALT II does not prevent the ultimate vulnerability of the ICBM forces of both sides through superaccurate multiple-independently targetable reentry vehicle (MIRV) warheads. The Soviet Union has an intermediate-range mobile missile, the SS-20, made up of the two upper stages of the SS-16 solid-fuel ICBM. For the United States, the issue of mobile missiles has aired in the debate about the MX deployment. The MX is to be located not in silos but, rather, is to be hidden. How to hide the MX has remained a matter of controversy during the 1980s.

Monad   A single leg of the strategic triad. A monad may be comprised of nuclear missiles based in underground silos, on submarines, or on long-range bombers with nuclear weapons. It must be distinguished from a triad that incorporates the following: land-based intercontinental ballistic missiles (ICBMs), submarine-launched ballistic missiles (SLBMs), and strategic bombers. While both superpowers maintain the triad of land-, sea-, and air-launched weapons, the mix is different—reflecting different geopolitical circumstances and strategic philosophies. Each triad leg of the United States has the capacity to deliver a crushing retaliatory blow against the Soviet Union in response to an attack, regardless of whether the other legs function. *See also* FIRST STRIKE; NUCLEAR DETERRENCE; SECOND STRIKE; TRIAD.

Significance   A monad is the essential building block of a triad. Taking a systemic perspective, a monad is a subsystem of a triadic system. The strength and effectiveness of a triad is enhanced by the independent deterrence capability of each of the monads. If each monad can independently deter an enemy surprise attack by a second strike, the second-strike retaliatory capability of the triad is enhanced as a whole. Each leg of the three-legged stool has its strengths and weaknesses. The manned bomber force is slow and is vulnerable on the ground as well. It is, more recently, supplemented by the air-launched cruise missile. Certainly it is impractical to build hard shelters for a fleet of big aircraft; they also need very long runways for take-off. Another leg of the triad is the land-based missile; the only real disadvantage here is that its position is fixed; everyone knows exactly where the missile is at all times. ICBMs, however, are the most accurate missiles. The primary advantage of the third leg of the triad, the SLBM, is that the delivering submarines are virtually undetectable. The SLBMs, as one monad, give the United States strategic force survivability, even though SLBMs are less accurate.

Monitoring Satellite   A satellite used for observing nuclear facilities and explosions. Monitoring satellites collect data through cameras, heat sensors, and radio receivers. They operate at a wide variety of altitudes. The United States first used monitoring satellites in 1960; the Soviet Union followed in 1962. Monitoring satellites are called surveillance satellites, and they include photo reconnaissance satellites. They are programmed to detect nuclear weapons tests in the atmosphere by recognizing such signals as a fireball (burning gas that forms immediately after a nuclear weapon explosion). Of the more than one dozen nuclear explosion-monitoring satellites that have been launched by the United States, three were operational in 1980. A variety of other techniques exist for detecting nuclear explosions, including detection of electromagnetic pulse (EMP), detection of characteristic double flash, detection of ionospheric disturbances of various frequencies, and the scattering of sunlight from debris. Some of these means are used by earth satellites to detect nuclear detonation. *See also* DISTANT EARLY WARNING (DEW); GROUND-BASED ELECTRO-OPTICAL DEEP SPACE SURVEILLANCE (GEODSS); ON-SITE INSPECTION.

Significance   Monitoring satellites are capable of producing very detailed images. They are even said to be capable of taking pictures of individual human faces. Monitoring satellites are an essential component of arms control negotiations. They allow the superpowers to learn about each other's weapons testing and deployment, which information-gathering might indicate a change in the level of threat or in the strategic balance between the two nations. Monitoring satellites are crucial in the process of arms control verification, which, in turn, is the central plank of any progress in ongoing negotiations. The Limited Test Ban Treaty (LTBT) of 1963 prohibits nuclear testing above the ground, under water, and in outer space by its signatories. Since then virtually all nuclear tests have been conducted underground. To avoid concern that clandestine testing might be performed, many nations have surveillance systems for the detection of nuclear detonations.

Multilateral Nuclear Force   A military arrangement proposed by the United States in the 1950s by which nuclear weapons systems of different countries would be combined into a single institutional structure. A multilateral nuclear force, more specifically, refers to a proposal for a fleet of 25 surface ships to be deployed in the Mediterranean and North Seas. Armed with Polaris nuclear missiles, on ships committed to the defense of the North Atlantic Treaty Organization (NATO), the missiles would be launched only after unanimous approval of the participating states. The primary objectives of the United States in proposing the creation of the multilateral nuclear force were threefold: to assuage European doubts about the willingness of the United States to use strategic nuclear weapons; to maintain credibility vis-à-vis the U.S. defense of Europe; and to create the appearance of a more equitable distribution of decision-making powers within NATO and a more compelling rationale for other members to pursue their own independent nuclear forces. *See also* COUPLING; HORIZONTAL PROLIFERATION; NORTH ATLANTIC TREATY ORGANIZATION (NATO); NUCLEAR CLUB.

Significance   A multilateral nuclear force was proposed as a way of giving the NATO countries a role in the use of nuclear weapons in the defense of the North Atlantic community. Essentially, it was a U.S. plan to give West Germany a role in the defense of NATO without permitting West Germany to possess nuclear weapons of its own. By this arrangement the United States hoped to soften French and British concern over a West German nuclear role; it was an abortive effort to reassure Europeans that their interests would be taken into account and safeguarded. The weapons, on the other hand, would still be subject to U.S. control under a two-key system. The idea failed to win support because of the cost and the European belief that it did not add very much to their strategic leverage. While it might not have done so physically, management of the force would inevitably have compelled the United States to share more nuclear knowledge with its allies. Finally, the plan failed because it was too complex, the control aspects too vague, and the approach too naive.

Multiple Independently Targetable Reentry Vehicle (MIRV)   A mechanism whereby separate targets can be hit by one missile. A multiple independently targetable reentry vehicle enables a single missile to strike different targets along its flight trajectory. The warheads are released by the bus (launch vehicle) and delivered by computerized internal and stellar inertial guidance (for desired position and velocity) at different points along a missile's flight path. They are then pulled to their respective targets by gravity, over an area of up to 20,000 square miles, known as "MIRVed missiles' footprints." The exact size of the footprint depends on a number of factors, including the amount of propellant in the bus and the time interval over which individual reentry vehicles are released. The superpowers introduced MIRV technology in the early 1960s, and it was fully developed by the early 1970s. The earliest MIRV was mounted on the Polaris A-3 submarine-launched ballistic missile (SLBM) in 1964; it delivered three 200-kiloton warheads at a range of 2,500 nautical miles. The first MIRVed intercontinental ballistic missile (ICBM) was tested in 1968; three warheads were placed on a Minuteman III. In 1970 the Polaris C-3 SLBM was designed to carry up to fourteen 50-kiloton warheads. Current Minuteman missiles still have three warheads, the majority delivering 335 kilotons per reentry vehicle. The newest RV (reentry vehicle), the Mk-12A, has been retrofitted on 300 Minuteman III missiles, replacing the Mk-12. *See also* BALLISTIC MISSILE DEFENSE (BMD) SYSTEM; DEMIRVING; INTERCONTINENTAL BALLISTIC MISSILE (ICBM); MANEUVERABLE REENTRY VEHICLE (MARV); MULTIPLE REENTRY VEHICLE (MRV).

Significance   The multiple independently targetable reentry vehicle has complicated arms control negotiations. It is no longer enough to reduce the number of missile vehicles, as was proposed under the 1979 Strategic Arms Limitation Talks (SALT II). For that reason the Reagan administration deflected its attention to reducing the number of warheads themselves. Moreover, multiple warheads make such missiles more inviting to a surprise attack, because each strike would destroy many retaliatory threats in one stroke. In recent years, the superpowers have been moving away from MIRVs. Instead they are developing smaller, single-warhead missiles, which are easier to deploy and are less inviting targets for an enemy nuclear attack. The proponents of de-MIRVing put forward a concept that returns to a pre-MIRV world in which all launchers have but one warhead. They acknowledged that the price for this was delimiting the number of launchers a country could contain. Military reality soon defeated de-MIRVing; the fine-tuning of technology could no more be discarded than could nuclear technology itself.

Multiple Protective Shelters (MPS)   A hypothetical method for deceptively deploying nuclear missiles. Multiple protective shelters would involve building several shelters for each missile, with missiles being shuttled between different shelters. In 1979, President Jimmy Carter announced the selection of a "race track" basing mode, involving 200 tracks of about 25 miles circumference, each equipped with 23 shelters and one MX missile. It was a constrained-mobile scheme wherein 200 MX missiles would have roamed randomly between 4,600 shelters in Utah and Nevada on roads specially constructed at a cost of about $50 billion. The scheme was defeated for economic reasons and because of ecological objections. The Reagan administration considered several alternatives. These included placing MX missiles in deep caves and mine shafts, or simply placing the MX in silos as an interim step until a permanent mode could be devised. The plan for MPS was abandoned, however, and the United States eventually decided to deploy the MX in existing underground missile silos. The multiple protective shelters system is also referred to as the shell game. *See also* BALLISTIC MISSILE DEFENSE (BMD) SYSTEM; SECOND STRIKE.

Significance   The multiple protective shelters idea was aimed at keeping the potential aggressor guessing as to the exact location of missiles. An enemy would have to strike each shelter in order to be certain of destroying all the missiles. This would induce a greater uncertainty for the potential aggressor. It is designed to act as a restraint against a surprise attack by reducing the vulnerability of the land-based intercontinental ballistic missile (ICBM). This would strengthen the second-strike capability of those land-based nuclear missiles, which, in turn, would further promote superpower nuclear deterrence. In the absence of some version of MPS, the most sensible solution may well be to replace some Minuteman missiles either with MX missiles or with a version of the Trident II (D-5) missile. The choice depends on such factors as relative costs and value of earlier deployment; this was an ongoing fight between Congress and the Reagan administration. Congressional critics consistently refused to appropriate funds for a MX construction until agreement could be reached on a satisfactory basing mode.

Multiple Reentry Vehicle (MRV)   Several warheads on a single missile that are not independently targetable. A multiple reentry vehicle enables a single missile to bombard a target with many warheads. If the missile system carries several RVs (reentry vehicles) that are not independently targetable, it is referred to simply as a multiple reentry vehicle system. The acronym MRV represents the use of several smaller warheads by one missile, such as a shotgun spreading the charge into small pellets instead of one bullet. The MRV system was developed to penetrate antiballistic missile (ABM) defenses by flooding them with too many targets to be intercepted. The MRVs cannot strike at more than one target, because the warheads cannot be directed at separate targets or maneuvered independently. When the United States deployed the Polaris A-3 submarine-launched ballistic missile (SLBM) in the late 1960s, it became the first operational ballistic missile to employ the concept of multiple reentry vehicles. The Soviet Union has also deployed MRV warheads. *See also* INTERCONTINENTAL BALLISTIC MISSILE (ICBM); MANEUVERABLE REENTRY VEHICLE (MARV); MULTIPLE INDEPENDENTLY TARGETABLE REENTRY VEHICLE (MIRV).

Significance   A multiple reentry vehicle system has two major goals. First, it works to distribute more efficiently the warhead's nuclear effects over a large target area. Second, it aims to assail an antiballistic missile defense with multiple targets. Both superpowers have moved away from MRV technology to the more sophisticated multiple independently targetable reentry vehicle and the maneuverable reentry vehicle. However, Great Britain still has some MRVs in use on its Polaris submarines; in comparison with the superpowers', this force is small, but capable of inflicting serious damage on an enemy. The independent deterrent components of this force consists of four Polaris submarines—each with 16 missiles (individually armed with three MRVs). Although only one submarine can be guaranteed to be on station at any time, the destructive power of a single warhead now far exceeds those unleashed against Hiroshima and Nagasaki in 1945.

Mushroom Cloud   The gas, dust, and other debris that form in the aftermath of a nuclear explosion. The mushroom cloud is composed of everything that is pulverized in a nuclear blast. It may measure ten miles wide and eight to ten miles high. Its name is derived from the destructive cloud's shape. The fireball of a surface burst rises in the shape of a mushroom cloud, with the stem bearing dust from the ground and carrying the bomb debris itself. The fireball from the explosion of a one-megaton nuclear weapon grows to more than a mile in diameter in seconds and rises into the atmosphere, forming a mushroom cloud ten miles across and extending to an altitude of 70,000 feet. The larger explosive yield of the fusion, as contrasted with fission, bombs ensures that the quantitative effect of their fallout will also be felt over a much larger area as the mushroom from the fireball penetrates higher into the stratosphere. *See also* AIR BURST; DUST DEFENSE; GROUND BURST; HIROSHIMA.

Significance   A mushroom cloud of smoke 10,000 feet in diameter covered a part of Hiroshima after the first atomic bomb strike by the U.S. Air Force on August 6, 1945. In 1952, a cloud phenomenon rose ten miles high after the first thermonuclear test at Elugelab Island in the South Pacific. The mushroom cloud has become a symbol of the nuclear age. It facilitates the spread of deadly radioactive by-products developed in a nuclear explosion. The contamination spreads over a very large area, beyond the frontiers of the country where it is detonated. According to scientists, these radioactive materials are harmful for living beings, and the resultant suffering may continue for generations.

Mutual and Balanced Force Reduction (MBFR)   Negotiations aimed at reducing the massive confrontation of conventional forces in Europe. The MBFR negotiations were initiated in 1973 between the North Atlantic Treaty Organization (NATO) allies and the Warsaw Pact nations. There are several central issues in the negotiations. There is disagreement on the size of the respective NATO and Warsaw Pact ground forces in Europe. The United States claims that there is a disparity of ground forces (790,000 allied troops versus 960,000 Warsaw Pact forces); the Soviet Union claims that a rough parity exists. In NATO's view, any agreement must be based on agreed manpower data. Geography gives the Soviet Union greater reinforcement capability in Europe. At issue are Soviet forces stationed in the western part of the Soviet Union, which is outside the territory identified in an eventual MBFR agreement. NATO insists on a program of confidence-building and verification measures.

The NATO and Warsaw Pact positions are embodied in draft treaties of 1982. Basically they provide that U.S.-Soviet force reductions should be by mutual example, an agreed-upon freeze on all forces and armaments in the MBFR area, and subsequent negotiation of a treaty. *See also* NORTH ATLANTIC TREATY ORGANIZATION (NATO); WARSAW PACT.

Significance   The Mutual and Balanced Force Reduction negotiations have had useful political results within NATO and have favorably influenced decisions for some unilateral reductions on each side. However, they have not produced any agreements between NATO and the Warsaw Pact nations. This arms control negotiation has been under way in Vienna since 1973. In the beginning the United States insisted on the MBFR negotiations in order to balance the Helsinki Conference on Security and Cooperation in Europe—in which the Soviets sought to legitimize post–World War II European boundaries. The Soviet Union achieved its objectives in the Helsinki negotiations, but it also had to agree on economic provisions and human rights principles that have subsequently embarrassed its national agenda. Both sides in the MBFR negotiations have agreed upon the objectives of a common collective ceiling for conventional forces, and a first-phase reduction in U.S. and Soviet troops. But the negotiations have stalled on the issues of whether to establish separate ceilings on individual Western forces. As a result of the Intermediate-range Nuclear Forces (INF) Treaty (1987), which eliminated an entire generation of intermediate- and medium-range nuclear forces from Europe, and the 1988 Gorbachev proposal to cut, unilaterally, Soviet conventional forces worldwide, there is likely to be an impact on conventional balance needs in Europe, thereby creating a link with the so far unsuccessful negotiations in that area under the umbrella of the MBFR.

Mutual Assured Destruction (MAD)   A condition in which an overwhelming destructive capability is possessed by opposing sides. Mutual assured destruction (MAD) makes nuclear war by either of the superpowers a suicidal move; each side is deterred from attacking the other by the realization that its own destruction would be assured through a second-strike retaliation. The acronym MAD stems from an occasion in 1964 when Secretary of Defense Robert S. McNamara coined the phrase "assured destruction." Defense analyst Donald Brennan added the word "mutual" to create the well-publicized acronym, "MAD." The Soviet Union does not officially accept MAD as a military doctrine. For that reason MAD is now understood to stand for "mutual assured deterrence." According to the MAD doctrine, it does not matter which side has more nuclear weapons, so long as each has enough to assure the destruction of the other in retaliation. This strategy is based on the realization that both the United States and the Soviet Union possess the ability to inflict an unacceptable degree of damage on each other by means of a second strike, even after absorbing a first strike. Thus MAD has a "hostage effect"—Americans are Soviet hostages as Soviets are of Americans. *See also* BALLISTIC MISSILE DEFENSE (BMD) SYSTEM; COUNTERVALUE STRIKE; MASSIVE RETALIATION.

Significance   The mutual assured destruction policy is based on the key notion of a second-strike capability by both the superpowers. Thus, any nuclear confrontation will wreak havoc on both. Mutual assured destruction is a grim reminder of that reality, which is thought to be instrumental in preventing a global nuclear war. In the past, when there had been unacceptable discontent by some of the principal powers, major wars broke out, which eventually decided the future distribution of power. World War I and World War II demonstrated that military superiority can be the final arbiter of the global balance of power. However, the destructiveness of nuclear weapons changed that notion of settling disputes between the United States and the Soviet Union. The MAD doctrine is thought to be at the heart of superpower nuclear deterrence, which has so far managed to prevent World War III. Despite preparation by both superpowers to fight a war using only conventional weapons, it is unlikely that either side would accept defeat without resorting to the use of its nuclear arsenal with its MAD potentials.

MX Missile   A third generation of U.S. intercontinental ballistic missile (ICBM). The MX missile, which derives its acronym from "missile experimental", has a range of 13,000 kilometers and carries ten 300-kiloton warheads. This missile is a four-stage ICBM: it combines three stages of solid fuel and one of liquid fuel. It is 72 feet long, 92 inches in diameter, and weighs 190,000 pounds. The MX missile uses the highly accurate Advanced Inertial Reference Sphere (AIRS) guidance system to deliver its Mk-21 warheads. The warheads are MIRVed (multiple independently targetable reentry vehicle). Using AIRS will give a circular error probability (CEP) of 400 to 600 feet; using the NAVSTAR (navigation system using timing and ranging) global positioning will reduce CEP to 300 feet; adding MARV (maneuverable reentry vehicle) will further reduce CEP to 100 feet. MX missile development began in 1972, but it was President Jimmy Carter who authorized full-scale development in 1979. While he desired 200 MX missiles, the Reagan administration cut the number to 100. The MX missile's submarine-launched counterpart is the Trident missile. The Reagan administration referred to the MX missile as the "Peacekeeper." *See also* HARD-SITE DEFENSE; MINUTEMAN; MISSILE.

Significance   The MX missile has four times greater throw-weight, noticeably greater accuracy, and higher yield warheads than Minuteman III. The MX is designed to combine two crucial factors necessary for an effective ICBM: accuracy and survivability. Without sacrificing payload and yield, this missile is more accurate, and its basing mode is designed to ensure survivability against a potential surprise attack. In inducing greater uncertainty, it is aimed not only at enhancing a second-strike capability but also at discouraging a potential first strike. Even though there was eventual agreement on the survivability goal, there is less of an agreement on the means (the basing mode) to acquire the mobility needed to achieve survivability.

N

Nagasaki   A Japanese port city of the northwest coast of Kyushu where the second atomic bomb was dropped by the United States in World War II. Nagasaki was destroyed on August 9, 1945, killing 50,000 persons instantly and injuring 25,000. The 10,000-pound bomb—known as "Fat Man" (because of its size)—was dropped by a B-29 at 11:02 A.M., and exploded 52 seconds later, producing an upward explosion. This plutonium bomb missed its target point by a mile and a half. The city burned for over twenty-four hours. Forty percent of Nagasaki's buildings were obliterated in the explosion. The primary target was Kokura, the site of one of the largest war plants. Nagasaki, the secondary target, was one of Japan's largest shipbuilding and repair centers. When the plane carrying the atomic bomb reached Kokura, thick clouds obscured the city. The aircraft circled repeatedly, searching for a break in the cloud cover that would enable a visual drop of the bomb. During the third circle over the city, the U.S. mission commander noticed antiaircraft fire and approaching Japanese fighter planes. At this point he proceeded to Nagasaki, which was shrouded in bad weather. As the B-29 completed its pass over the city, a slight opening appeared, and the atomic bomb was exploded 1,640 feet over Nagasaki. *See also* ATOMIC WEAPON; FAT MAN; HIROSHIMA; PLUTONIUM WEAPON.

Significance   Nagasaki was the world's second city to feel the devastation inflicted by an atomic weapon. This was the signal that finally convinced the Japanese to surrender unconditionally on September 2, 1945. About 280,000 people were thought to have been in Nagasaki when the atomic bomb exploded. As many as 74,000, or 26 percent, of the people died by the end of 1945. There were many Koreans in Nagasaki, and their exact casualties are not known. The number of Nagasaki A-bomb victims who died after 1945 is also not known. Today survivors of Nagasaki suffer from genetic and other effects of the bombing. However, the bomb dropped on Nagasaki carried an insignificant nuclear payload compared to those thousands of times more powerful in the arsenals of the superpowers today.

National Command Authorities (NCA)   The top U.S. national security decision makers. The Congress has authorized the National Command Authorities, in agreement with the president, to make final decisions on national security matters. This hierarchy, which includes the president and the secretary of defense, is responsible for making final decisions about the use of nuclear weapons. An elaborate Command, Control, Communications, and Intelligence (C3I) system links the NCA to the military command system, and particularly to the nuclear forces, through ground, air, and seaborne links. A new Ground Wave Emergency Network (GWEN), initially in service in 1987, provides the only Electromagnetic Pulse (EMP) hardened system linking the NCA to both the warning system and the retaliatory forces. Once the NCA has made its decisions, the Pentagon command center and its backups, including the National Emergency Airborne Command Post (NEACP), will disseminate the required emergency action message to all nuclear combat commands. *See also* COMMAND, CONTROL, COMMUNICATIONS, AND INTELLIGENCE (C3I); NATIONAL EMERGENCY AIRBORNE COMMAND POST (NEACP); NATIONAL COMMAND SYSTEM (NMCS).

Significance   The National Command Authorities group consists of leaders who have many duties in addition to commanding nuclear operations, and who spend most of their time in unprotected locations. This is true of the president and his immediate delegates as well as their Soviet counterparts. Given an hour or so of warning, either set of leaders can probably be protected, but the possibility of a surprise still remains. Although the National Emergency Airborne Command Post is available to the NCA, its main limitation is the necessity to land periodically. The problem facing the nuclear decision makers, the NCA, encompasses these dilemmas and more. For example, there are formidable questions such as how to underline the peaceful intent of the nation while insisting that U.S. armed forces be ever on the ready. There is also the fear that leaders may not have sufficient confidence in their assessments to launch the ICBM (intercontinental ballistic missile) force, since it could not be recalled in case of error.

National Emergency Airborne Command Post (NEACP)   The aircraft designated to provide for the airborne removal and safety of the president and top leaders in case of nuclear war. The National

Emergency Airborne Command Post would allow the president to issue orders from this airborne center. It consists of four Boeing 747 aircraft that have been converted into flying command bunkers. The NEACP (pronounced kneecap) is kept on constant alert at Andrews Air Force Base, outside Washington, D.C.; code-named "Nightwatch," it became operational in 1975. The NEACP is also known as the Doomsday Plane. National command and control might be spread across three main ground facilities: the National Military Command Center (NMCC) in the Pentagon; the blast-resistant Alternate NMCC at Raven Rock, Pennsylvania; and the Alternate NMCC facility at Mount Weather, Virginia, which is a hardened special facility. A NEACP plane could evacuate the president if he chooses such a course. A helicopter (standing by at the White House) could transport him and his senior advisers to the NEACP in about 10 minutes. The NEACP has been modified for Electromagnetic Pulse (EMP) and thermal protection with multimedia communications and data processing, for support of a staff, advisers, and the NCA. *See also* ALTERNATE NATIONAL MILITARY COMMAND CENTER (ANMCC); MINIMUM ESSENTIAL EMERGENCY COMMUNICATIONS NETWORK (MEECN); NATIONAL COMMAND AUTHORITIES (NCA).

Significance   The National Emergency Airborne Command Post is designed to serve as a backup to command centers on the ground. It operates as if the Command, Control, Communications, and Intelligence (C3I) network has become airborne. The NEACP will be useful in a limited nuclear war. Such a command post may prevent decapitation of the decision-making authority. It will give political leaders a greater incentive to avoid launch-on-warning in order to confirm a potential nuclear threat in favor of launch-under-attack. Thus, it would prevent a preemptive strike from a misperceived threat. The leaders aboard a given command post might be just one cadre among many cadres of alternatives and successors distributed among several means of survival. For these reasons, the concern about the NEACP's vulnerability to a submarine-launched ballistic missile (SLBM) attack is likely to be crucial to the continuity of the national command during a crisis.

National Military Command Center (NMCC)   A top U.S. military command post where decisions could be made whether to launch a nuclear strike. The National Military Command Center is the war room of the Department of Defense in Washington, D.C. Originally known as the "Joint War Room Annex," the NMCC was established in 1959. Located on the second and third floors of the Pentagon, it is operated by the Joint Chiefs of Staff (JCS). It analyzes indications of enemy attack and makes recommendations to the National Command Authorities (NCA), which are headed by the president. The NMCC incorporates into its system the White House Hot Line, the direct teletype communications link between Washington and Moscow. It leans heavily on surveillance, damage assessment, and similar planning information relayed by the NORAD (North American Aerospace Defense Command) computers in Cheyenne Mountain in Colorado. The NMCC is backed up by the Alternate National Military Command Center, which has been hardened to withstand a nuclear attack. *See also* COMMAND, CONTROL, COMMUNICATIONS, AND INTELLIGENCE (C3I); JOINT CHIEFS OF STAFF (JCS); MINIMUM ESSENTIAL EMERGENCY COMMUNICATIONS NETWORK (MEECN); NATIONAL MILITARY COMMAND SYSTEM (NMCS).

Significance   The National Military Command Center serves as both a peacetime and wartime command post. It has direct military communications with the White House and with U.S. military installations worldwide. The NMCC was set up in the aftermath of the Soviets' launching of Sputnik I in 1957, which gave them the capability of launching the intercontinental ballistic missile. The military commanders report to the secretary of defense and the president through the JCS, using the NMCC. Each component of the nuclear command has forces that are committed to various options of the preplanned Single Integrated Operational Plan (SIOP). These planning options are reviewed periodically by the JCS in order to evaluate the extent to which they meet national objectives.

National Military Command System (NMCS)   The command organization for all U.S. nuclear forces. The National Military Command System gathers information, transmits communications, and orders the launching of U.S. putative nuclear weapons. It was established in 1962 by Secretary of Defense Robert S. McNamara. The NMCS involves a vast network of satellites, communications systems, and other technical equipment. It is the component of the Worldwide Military Command and Control System (WWMCCS), which supports the National Command Authorities (NCA) and the Joint Chiefs of Staff (JCS). The NMCS consists of the National Military Command Center (NMCC) in the Department of Defense, the Alternate National Military Command Center (ANMCC) near Ft. Ritchie, Maryland, and the National Emergency Airborne Command Post (NEACP). The NMCS facilities are connected to one another, to the united and specified commands, and to the services. *See also* COMMAND, CONTROL,

COMMUNICATIONS, AND INTELLIGENCE (C3I); NATIONAL COMMAND AU-
THORITIES (NCA); NATIONAL MILITARY COMMAND CENTER (NMCC).

Significance   The National Military Command System is designed
to coordinate previously independently developed branches of U.S.
defense. The NMCS joins the following systems: continental air defense (416L), traffic control and landing (413L), weather observation
(433L), intelligence handling (438L), ballistic missile warning (474L),
air communications (480L), and satellite surveillance (496L). During
the early 1960s the introduction of the Soviet intercontinental ballistic
missile led the U.S. defense planners to extend the command infrastructure to include an oceanic presence. The NMCS formed the
hierarchy of this command infrastructure. It was seen as an urgent
priority from the outset, and, consequently, an essential step to that
end—the deployment of an airborne command post for the NCA—
took place in 1962. NMCS is a network undergirded by the Department of Defense. It supports automatic data processing, computer
display, and display distribution systems necessary for its operation. It
also prepares and disseminates appraisals and analyzes attack hazards
and the vulnerability of forces worldwide.

National Security Agency (NSA)   The organization responsible
for centralized coordination, direction, and carrying out of specialized
technical functions in support of U.S. government efforts to protect
communications and produce foreign intelligence. The National
Security Agency is an arm of the Department of Defense (DOD),
created by President Harry S Truman in 1952. The agency was
charged with an additional mission—computer security—in a 1984
presidential directive. A Central Security Service (CSS) was formed in
1972 to provide a more unified cryptologic unit within the Department of Defense. The CSS operates under the director of the National
Security Agency. The NSA/CSS has three primary tasks: to act as a
communications security mission, a computer security mission, and a
foreign intelligence resource. The agency is located at Fort Meade, 20
miles northeast of Washington, D.C. *See also* CENTRAL INTELLIGENCE
AGENCY (CIA); DEFENSE INTELLIGENCE AGENCY (DIA); DEPARTMENT OF DE-
FENSE (DOD); NATIONAL SECURITY COUNCIL (NSC).

Significance   The National Security Agency operates a massive
bank of the largest and most advanced computers available to any
agency in the world—computers that code and decode, direct spy
satellites, intercept electronic messages, recognize target words in spoken communications, and store, organize and index this information.

To accomplish these missions the NSA has been given the following responsibilities: outlining certain principles, doctrines, and procedures; organizing, operating, and managing selected activities and facilities for the production of foreign intelligence information; regulating certain communications in support of the agency endeavors; operating Computer Security Center, telecommunication security, and automated information security. Because of the necessity for extreme secrecy in the work of this agency, and because it operates in a highly technical field, the NSA is free to define its own goals relating to national security; it is not subject to any congressional review.

It was an embarrassment for the Johnson administration when in January 1968 North Korea seized a NSA-manned intelligence ship, USS *Pueblo* with 83 crew members off the North Korean coast. The United States, insisting that the *Pueblo* had been in international waters, demanded the release of the ship and its men. North Korea maintained that the spy ship was captured legally because it had been inside the 12-mile territorial waters of North Korea. However, by the end of the year, North Korea freed the crew but kept possession of the ship. The seizure of the *Pueblo* in international waters came as an abrupt object lesson to the United States that the world's greatest power could be roundly and resoundingly put down by a miniscule power.

National Security Council (NSC)   The foreign policy advisory body of the president. The National Security Council is the agency that coordinates the foreign policy activities of other major U.S. agencies. The NSC is not under the secretary of state; it is run independently by the national security adviser to the president. This adviser reports directly to the president. The agency was created by the National Security Act of 1947, as amended by the NSC Amendments Act of 1949. Under the Reorganization Plan No. 4 of 1949, the National Security Council was placed in the Executive Office of the President. It is chaired by the president; the other statutory members are the vice president and the secretaries of state and defense. The chairman of the Joint Chiefs of Staff is the statutory military adviser to the NSC, and the director of the Central Intelligence Agency (CIA) is its intelligence adviser. The NSC is responsible for advising the president with respect to the integration of domestic, foreign, and military policies relating to national security. The NSC runs the White House Situation Room, the emergency headquarters equipped with advanced communications gear. In 1983 the Reagan administration created the Crisis Management Directorate within the NSC, which has introduced modern technology, built a new coordination center, created new data bases, and internetted a computers and warning system to coordinate crisis operation between agencies. *See also* DEPARTMENT OF DEFENSE (DOD); DEPARTMENT OF STATE; PRESIDENT.

Significance   The National Security Council has the task of sorting out conflicting bureaucratic interests in foreign policy matters. The agency is expected to advise the president on the best policy choice aimed at serving the interests of the United States. Unlike membership in the presidential cabinet the appointment of the head of the NSC is not confirmed by the U.S. Senate. Hence Congress cannot subpoena the NSC adviser to testify before a congressional hearing. This has led presidents to initiate some foreign policy moves from the office of the national security adviser. President Harry S Truman, who created the NSC, had no desire to see the kind of parochialism that has since developed between the Department of State and the NSC. Among the chief problems associated with its operation is the overlap of functions with other departments and agencies, especially the Department of State and the CIA. Conflicts between these interests are still prevalent.

National Technical Means of Verification (NTM)   This construct refers to a number of different devices and techniques used by the superpowers for monitoring compliance with the provisions of arms control agreements. The National Technical Means of Verification includes photo reconnaissance satellites, aircraft equipped with radars and other sensors, seismic stations, and ground- and sea-based systems for collecting telemetry (electronic signals transmitted by missiles to earth). Strategic arms control agreements have included provisions to facilitate the unilateral collection, by nationally available technical means, of information relevant to treaty verification. These measures are embodied in Article 14 of the SALT II treaty (1979) and Article 12 of the ABM treaty (1972). They prohibit interference with the operation of the National Technical Means of Verification and ban deliberate concealment which impedes verification by NTM. This is distinct from cooperative means of verification, such as on-site inspections, which rely on collaboration between nations. *See also* INTERMEDIATE-RANGE NUCLEAR FORCES TREATY; LIMITED TEST BAN TREATY (LTBT); OUTER SPACE TREATY; STRATEGIC ARMS LIMITATION TALKS (SALT II); THRESHOLD TEST BAN TREATY (TTBT).

Significance   The National Technical Means of Verification encompasses reconnaissance satellites and aircraft and ship-and-shore listening posts; they are designed to verify compliance, without direct cooperation from the state under surveillance. It does, however, depend upon an agreement not to hinder another country's monitoring activities, such as concealment of nuclear facilities. The NTM is the officially designated means of verification of the SALT I and SALT II treaties, and of several other international arms control agreements negotiated under the auspices of the United Nations. It provides an opportunity to verify compliance with treaty provisions without requiring access to the adversary's territory itself. Although these measures are usually viewed as cooperative measures assisting in the verification of treaty compliance, they are—in a broader sense—confidence-building measures, because the information received increases each party's knowledge about the characteristics and deployments of the other's forces.

NAVSTAR   The U.S. navigation system that uses timing and ranging. NAVSTAR is based on ultra-accurate time clocks that provide forces with a sophisticated global position from a network of 18 (eventually 24) satellites. It facilitates blind bombing, route navigation, artillery ranging, troop movements and rendezvous, and has particular effect on missile delivery. The NAVSTAR is based on the principle that if the velocity of two points and the time needed for a radio signal to travel between them are known, the distance between can be calculated and accurate navigational fixes can be taken. The essence of the system is an extremely accurate timer. The United States has added NAVSTAR terminals to its B-52, FB-111, and B-1 bomber and tanker aircraft. The latest generation of NAVSTAR satellites will also be fitted with NDDS (Nuclear Detonation Detection System) sensors. *See also* NUCLEAR DETONATION DETECTION SYSTEM (NDDS).

Significance   While NAVSTAR has many conventional uses, its potential in missile targeting is immense. First, it greatly increases the accuracy of U.S. nuclear missiles. NAVSTAR also provides highly accurate navigational information to a missile's on-board computer throughout the missile's flight. It is used to supplement a missile's existing guidance system. In the future, major improvements may come from guidance after the propulsion phase, as the payload and warheads become maneuverable during the ballistic and reentry phases. External information will be fed into the missile from a satellite navigation system (such as NAVSTAR), from star sightings or from radar mapping of the target. The system can be used as a threat if it can be shown to the enemy that NAVSTAR will give absolute accuracy to any strike, with missiles poised for action, in the hope of a diplomatic solution. Receivers for NAVSTAR signals might someday be installed in U.S. ships, aircraft, and tanks to determine their exact position.

Neutron Bomb   A nuclear weapon that kills chiefly through radiation; it is specifically modified to produce limited destructive effects. The development of the neutron bomb owes its beginning to Edward Teller, a physicist. In 1957 he created a "clean" nuclear weapon—one without the massive fallout associated with traditional nuclear bombs. This bomb was first tested successfully in 1962. Linus Pauling (and later Andrei Sakharov) pointed out that the millions of neutrons released by the bomb would combine with the nitrogen in the air to form carbon 14. This carbon isotope would emit a deadly and an almost never-ending form of radiation that would be likely to increase cancers and genetic defects for generations. The project was shelved until it was reopened in 1974. The new objective was to maximize radiation and minimize (compared to the force of an intercontinental ballistic missile) blast and heat damage in the development of a theater nuclear weapon. If detonated 300 feet above a battleground, for example, this bomb would kill tank crews. However, such a one kiloton bomb would create only minimum damage to material. The neutron bomb is known as an enhanced radiation weapon. *See also* CHEMICAL AND BIOLOGICAL WEAPONS (CBWS); ENHANCED RADIATION WEAPON (ERW); KILOTON WEAPON.

Significance   Neutron bomb radiation is capable of killing people while leaving buildings and the landscape intact. This inaccurate and misperceived notion caught public attention in the 1970s. The bomb became a controversial issue in 1977 and 1978 when President Jimmy Carter planned to deploy it in Western Europe. The Dutch Communist party, which is independent of Moscow's control but not of its influence, launched the first public campaign against the neutron bomb. Because the neutron bomb is designed to enhance radiation to kill combatants but to minimize blast effects, it was easy for propagandists to describe the enhanced radiation weapon as a warhead designed to kill people but to leave property intact. While proponents introduced it as an effective antitank weapon, opponents painted the bomb as immoral. In 1981, President Ronald Reagan added the bomb to the U.S. nuclear arsenal, but made no plan for future deployment. France made a successful neutron bomb test in 1980; the Soviet Union is also reported to have tested its version. The future role of enhanced radiation weapons is unknown but open to speculation.

Nevada Test Site (NTS)   The principal U.S. nuclear experimentation site. The Nevada test site is located about 70 miles northwest of Las Vegas; it covers about 800,000 acres of desert terrain, and was established in the early 1950s. Operation Ranger was the first series of tests conducted there on January 27, 1951. There are two categories of nuclear weapons tests: weapons-related and weapons effects. Weapons-related tests are tests of nuclear devices intended for specific types of weapons system. The weapons effects are conducted to verify a warhead's yields before or immediately after entry into the stockpile. About 79 percent of U.S. tests have been weapons-related. Depending upon its complexity, the cost of a test ranges between $6 million and $70 million. Since 1963, all tests at the site have been conducted underground because of the prohibition of atmospheric tests under the Limited Test Ban Treaty (1963). Britain also conducts its nuclear tests at the Nevada test site. See also LIMITED TEST BAN TREATY (LTBT); THRESHOLD TEST BAN TREATY (TTBT).

Significance   The Nevada test site was established to avoid nuclear testing in the South Pacific. The change of place was needed because of financial and logistical problems. However, thousands of sheep deaths, and high rates of leukemia and other cancers have been reported among local residents of the area contiguous to the Nevada test site. The need for a continental test site arose from national decisions to increase the size of the nuclear arsenal. Land-based testing also reduced the expense and logistical problems of testing in the South Pacific. The Nevada desert was selected because of its geology, favorable weather conditions, and safety. The U.S. government owns the Nevada test site, and several U.S. private corporations run it. Exxon, Phillips, Atlantic Richfield, and other energy companies mine uranium here. General Electric makes electrical components and neutron generators. The U.S. Department of Energy, which administers the site and conducts the testing, announces nuclear tests only when it considers such a disclosure to be appropriate.

Nonproliferation Treaty (NPT)   An international treaty that aims to control the spread of nuclear weapons. The Nonproliferation Treaty, officially known as the Treaty on the Nonproliferation of Nuclear Weapons, is the fundamental instrument of international nonproliferation policy. It has three basic provisions: first, an obligation on the part of those states possessing nuclear weapons not to transfer the technology or major ingredients to nonnuclear states; second, a commitment by nonnuclear weapons countries not to acquire or develop nuclear weapons; and, third, an undertaking by the original signatories—the United States, the Soviet Union, and the United Kingdom—to pursue serious talks on arms control and nuclear disarmament. To ensure commitment to its basic goals, a provision of the treaty calls for periodic conferences reviewing operations. The Nonproliferation Treaty was signed in Washington, Moscow, and London on July 1, 1968. It entered into force on March 5, 1970; over 140 countries have become party to the agreement. France, China, India, and more than half a dozen other nations have not acceded to the treaty. *See also* HORIZONTAL PROLIFERATION; LIMITED TEST BAN TREATY (LTBT); THRESHOLD TEST BAN TREATY (TTBT); VERTICAL PROLIFERATION.

Significance   The Nonproliferation Treaty is designed to prevent horizontal nuclear proliferation. At the same time, the nuclear weapons states pledge themselves to negotiate the containment and reduction of vertical proliferation. This is often referred to as an "unequal treaty" because it imposes heavier obligations on nonnuclear weapons states; it denies them any nuclear capabilities and access to the attendant great power status in international politics. However, the Nonproliferation Treaty does not deny countries the right to employ nuclear energy for peaceful purposes. The NPT is the linchpin of international efforts to slow or stop the spread of nuclear weapons.

Membership in the treaty compact gives a somewhat misleading impression, however, of the degree to which nations have come to rely on nuclear weapons for security. The belief that a truly nonproliferation regime actually exists may attribute too much meaning to a "marriage of convenience" between nuclear and nonnuclear states. Although there are limits to what the nuclear "haves" can do in slowing proliferation, their promise to negotiate in good faith toward ending their own arms race has not been given serious consideration, except in the 1987 INF treaty between the superpowers. The military disparity between the "haves" and most of the rest of the world's nations has grown in the years since the Nonproliferation Treaty came into force.

North American Aerospace Defense Command (NORAD)   A joint U.S.-Canadian military installation, designed to detect enemy nuclear attacks and coordinate efforts to determine an appropriate response. The North American Aerospace Defense Command (NORAD) is plugged into 19 radars and 9 telescopic cameras that can detect incoming missiles. It was originally established in the 1950s to locate and intercept Soviet bomber strikes. The headquarters of NORAD, embedded in Cheyenne Mountain in Colorado, was opened in 1966, and it is one of the three hardened U.S. military command posts. The headquarters facility is buried one-third of a mile underneath the granite of Cheyenne Mountain, and includes 15 reinforced steel structures that are mounted on shock-absorbing helical springs. The NORAD complex also includes the Aerospace Defense Command (ADCOM), the Space Defense Operations Center (SPADOC), the Ballistic Missile Early Warning System (BMEWS), two phased-array radars in Massachusetts (PAVE PAWS), Perimeter Acquisition Radar (PAR), a phased-array radar in Florida (FPS-85), the original Distant Warning line (SEEK FROST) and the Pinetree line (SEEK IGLOO) guarding the northern United States and Canada. It also receives reports from the Airborne Warning and Control System (AWACS) and two over-the-horizon backscatter radars (OTH-B) in Maine and Washington state as well as from the Regional Operations Control Centers (ROOC), which control about 46 radars in the United States and Canada. It also monitors the entire complex of civil and military air traffic over the continental United States. *See also* AIRBORNE WARNING AND CONTROL SYSTEM (AWACS); DISTANT EARLY WARNING (DEW); STRATEGIC AIR COMMAND (SAC).

Significance   The North American Aerospace Defense Command has a direct link to various radar and satellite monitoring installations. It is promptly alerted to any potential nuclear attack. New and more powerful computers were installed in 1978 to make the system more effective. Despite its satellite-sensitive complexity, NORAD is by no means perfect. Within 18 months following the installation of new computers, the system registered 147 false alarms of hostile attack, four of which raised the worldwide U.S. troop alert status by one level. Backup systems, verifiable with all sensors in one minute, ensured against any accidental nuclear war. Even then, the fear of other false alarms and resultant catastrophe, cannot be dismissed lightly.

North Atlantic Treaty Organization (NATO)   A military organization comprising countries of the North Atlantic region. The North Atlantic Treaty Organization (NATO) was created in 1949, and is based on a regional military alliance of democratic, capitalistic countries. Its arsenal includes both conventional and nuclear forces, and is made up of thousands of nuclear weapons, including intermediate-, medium-, and short-range ballistic missiles and small artillery shells. Its nuclear strategy is formulated by the Nuclear Planning Group, which meets twice a year and designs the Nuclear Operations Plan (NOP), NATO's blueprint for fighting a nuclear war. The 16 members of the organization are: Belgium, Britain, Canada, Denmark, France,

West Germany, Greece, Iceland, Italy, Luxembourg, the Netherlands, Norway, Portugal, Spain, Turkey, and the United States. *See also* EURO-GROUP; EUROMISSILES; SUPREME ALLIED COMMANDER EUROPE (SACEUR); WARSAW PACT.

Significance   The North Atlantic Treaty Organization is designed to protect its members against any aggression by the Warsaw Pact countries. NATO's strategy is often referred to as a "sword and shield." The alliance symbolizes the coupling (uniting) of West European and U.S. security interests. However, like any other alliance, NATO has had its problems. In 1966 France withdrew from its integrated military command in a protest over the leadership role of the United States. By 1974 war between Greece and Turkey over Cyprus weakened NATO's southern flank. These developments have given rise to debate about whether the Europeans are doing enough to ensure their own defense. Meanwhile there has been an improvement in the climate of East-West relations, which presents new opportunities and challenges for the North Atlantic Alliance. The Intermediate-range Nuclear Forces (INF) Treaty (1987) between the superpowers paved the way for removing intermediate- and medium-range ballistic missiles from Europe. That would leave only short-range ballistic missiles in the two Germanys, and West Germany is not very happy with this prospect. The INF treaty signifies to some Western Europeans an eroding of U.S. commitment to their defense, but support for the treaty in NATO member-countries is overwhelming.

Nuclear Accident   An unforeseen situation, incident, or happening involving nuclear weapons or reactors. A nuclear accident may involve any one of the following four incidents: (1) the firing of a nuclear missile; (2) the destruction of a nuclear weapon; (3) the radioactive contamination of a nuclear installation; and (4) the loss or theft of a nuclear weapon. Ultimately it refers to any event involving radioactive materials or a nuclear device that causes a public danger. There is distinction between a nuclear accident and nuclear incident. Whereas a nuclear incident may cause a long-term hazard, a nuclear accident poses an immediate danger to life and property. An incident in a nuclear power plant could release enough radiation to kill thousands of people and contaminate cities, land, and water for decades. Both nuclear incidents and accidents are commonly referred to as accidents. Equipment failures and human error caused an incident at Unit 2 of the Three Mile Island nuclear power plant near Harrisburg, Pennsylvania, in 1979. Runaway reactions during a test at Unit 4 of the Chernobyl nuclear power plant near Kiev in the Soviet Union in

1986 caused a series of explosions that ruptured the containment and sent massive amounts of radiation throughout the Northern Hemisphere. *See also* ACCIDENTAL NUCLEAR WAR; GROUND ALERT; GROUND-BASED ELECTRO-OPTICAL DEEP SPACE SURVEILLANCE (GEODSS).

Significance   A nuclear accident is always a possibility because of human error or mechanical failure. There have been numerous false nuclear attack alarms because of computer malfunction or other problems. In 1979 the United States experienced at the Three Mile Island nuclear power plant in Pennsylvania the most serious disaster in the history of the U.S. nuclear power plant industry. During a period of three days a combination of faulty information, poor communications, overlapping authority, and some sensationalism in the handling of the event by the media came close to creating a public panic. As it turned out, by the time the incident became publicly known there was no longer any danger of a core meltdown or hydrogen explosion. It was determined that the radioactivity that was released did not constitute a threat to the general public. The Chernobyl nuclear power plant disaster resulted from the combination of a reactor design with inherent control problems and the reckless and deliberate disregard of established safety procedures by plant operators. This was the first accident in an operating nuclear plant anywhere in the world that involved direct fatalities and a considerable amount of radioactivity leakage. The Chernobyl accident had an adverse effect on nuclear-power programs throughout the world. Several countries abandoned their nuclear power plant programs. In the 1980s, serious contamination problems were found to exist in several U.S. plants producing warhead materials, with cleanup costs estimated in the hundreds of billions of dollars.

Nuclear Arms Control   Measures that affect the numbers, types, characteristics, deployment, and use of nuclear weapons. Nuclear arms control encompasses a wide variety of activities intended to limit or reduce the number of nuclear weapons. It includes two major categories: arms limitation and arms reduction. General nuclear disarmament can be viewed as an extension of arms reduction. Arms limitation involves only restricting future deployment of nuclear weapons. President John F. Kennedy set up the United States Arms Control and Disarmament Agency (USACDA) in 1961. It is an independent agency of the executive branch, reporting directly to the president. Top agency officials head U.S. delegations to most arms control conferences and coordinate the country's negotiating positions. The 1972 Strategic Arms Limitation Talks (SALT I), an example of a negotiated arms limitation, is a case in point, since it placed a ceiling on the number of intercontinental ballistic missiles that each of the superpowers could possess. Arms reduction, on the other hand, entails the actual reduction of nuclear weapons. In the 1979 SALT II treaty, which is an example of arms reduction, the Carter administration took the first major step toward actually reducing the number of weapons. While President Jimmy Carter sought to reduce missile launchers—the "body"—President Ronald Reagan's Strategic Arms Reduction Treaty (START) proposal aimed at reducing the number of warheads—the "head"—by one-third. In the Intermediate-range Nuclear Forces (INF) Treaty (1987), the superpowers limited their European-based intermediate-range nuclear forces. *See also* ARMS CONTROL; DISARMAMENT; UNITED STATES ARMS CONTROL AND DISARMAMENT AGENCY (USACDA).

Significance   Nuclear arms control negotiations are central issues in the nuclear era. Various agreements reached during the 1950s, 1960s, and 1970s include many major steps toward providing some controls on the arms race. However, with each successful step in arms reduction, progress toward actual disarmament has become more difficult and time-consuming. A crucial factor in overcoming bottlenecks will likely result from an improvement in verification methods and technologies. Satellite monitoring has made a key contribution to arms control talks, and Soviet willingness to allow on-site inspection paved the way for the Intermediate-range Nuclear Forces (INF) Treaty, which provided for the elimination of all such missiles from Europe. Nuclear over-kill capacity by the superpowers implies that they have redundant weapons—in excess of what would be required for a second-strike capacity. Under such circumstances, arms control agreements would be a beneficial option in the attempt to reduce the level of nuclear weapons to mutually acceptable levels. Disarmament progress in the future will likely be a product of a strong base of arms control agreements that demonstrate the advantages of cooperation.

Nuclear Arms Race   A competitive relationship between the superpowers that inevitably results in their continuing nuclear weapons buildup. The nuclear arms race is a complex phenomenon involving different weapons systems and different types of improved capacity; its inception can be traced to the first atomic explosion in 1945 by the United States. The Soviet Union became competitive in 1949, and both countries went on to develop hydrogen bombs in the early 1950s. In 1957 the launching of Sputnik gave the Soviets the delivery potential of intercontinental range. Recent developments include multiple warheads and the cruise missile. A zero-sum game ensued: each side's security became the source of insecurity for the other. Not only were there vertical proliferations in terms of *numbers* of weapons but also horizontal proliferations in terms of the *types* of weapons systems. This action-reaction process continues in a vicious cycle. *See also* HORIZONTAL PROLIFERATION; NUCLEAR PROLIFERATION; VERTICAL PROLIFERATION.

Significance   The nuclear arms race is a manifestation of the difficulty of using nuclear weapons in an actual test of strength; the objective, consequently, is a psychological one of preventing the other superpower from attacking by providing a strong second-strike deterrence. Failure to keep up in the arms race may suggest a devastating first strike by the other party. It is easier to build weapons than to rely on the goodwill of another power. Increasingly sophisticated monitoring devices became necessary to ensure an acceptable balance of weapons; steps to reverse the trend toward such heavy development costs by reducing nuclear weapons, were therefore encouraged. The arms race has incurred substantial costs in terms of economic expenditures, although relative to the total world gross national product (GNP), they have been decreasing in recent years. Yet, both superpowers have accrued tremendous national debts in supporting the arms race over many years, and both appear to be locked into it by the power and prestige of their respective military-industrial complexes. New, more precise and more destructive weapons are less expensive, the popular key to deterring war. But even with the best safeguards and control procedures, mishaps can occur—whether they result from the misguided act of a terrorist or computer error, a major nuclear war might bring the world to an end.

Nuclear Artillery   Mobile cannons and tanks that can fire small, tactical nuclear weapons; they are mostly deployed in Europe. Nuclear artillery is composed of the most widely dispersed and numerous weapons; it is now undergoing major modernization, with guns and projectiles being upgraded. The United States uses, among others, M 110 (203 mm), M 109 (155 mm), and M 198 (155 mm). The Soviet Union is known to have S-23 (180 mm). First made operational in 1961, the M 110 is a tanklike vehicle that is capable of delivering nuclear warheads with a yield of five to ten kilotons. In contrast, the M 109 and M 198 can fire nuclear warheads with a yield of 0.1 kilotons. While the M 109 is also a tanklike vehicle, the M 198 is towed by a truck. The M 109 was first introduced in 1969, and the M 198 was ready in 1979. All three are deployed in the United States, Western Europe, South Korea, and Okinawa. The exception is the M 198, which is not deployed in Western Europe. Like the M 198, the Soviet S-23 is also towed by a truck. It is capable of delivering a one-kiloton (conventional) nuclear warhead. *See also* NUCLEAR WEAPON; SHORT-RANGE BALLISTIC MISSILE (SRBM).

Significance   Nuclear artillery would probably provide the first nuclear weapons used if a conventional war were to escalate beyond the firebreak (the barrier between conventional and nuclear weapons). These have less yield than short-range ballistic missiles. Nuclear artillery is considered to be in the lowest echelon of nuclear weapons, but the mobility of the weapons makes them practical in a theater nuclear war. The use of artillery is likely to provide a major instrument of coercion in intrawar deterrence. The United States deploys many types of nuclear artillery; the Soviet Union has only one type. The range and design of the nuclear artillery is beginning to reach practical limits, with restraints imposed by noise, target acquisition, accuracy, and reliability.

Nuclear Bomb   A weapon dropped over its target that derives its explosive force from atomic fission or fusion reactions. Nuclear bombs built so far have used the isotopes uranium 235 or plutonium 239 as the fissile material. Modern designs incorporate parachutes, slowing down the bombs and facilitating them in hitting their targets more precisely. The United States deploys five types of nuclear bombs; a sixth type is in the making. The yields of these bombs range from five kilotons to nine megatons. The basic nuclear weapon is the fission bomb, or atomic bomb as it was first called. A fission chain reaction is used to produce an incredible amount of energy in a very short time—roughly a millionth of a second. The fission occurs in a heavy material, uranium or plutonium. Fission must be distinguished from fusion; the latter is much more potent than fission. In a fission-fusion weapon, an atom-splitting (fission) reaction generates very high temperatures that trigger the combining of atoms (fusion). Fusion is the essential mechanism of thermonuclear weapons. *See also* FISSION; FUSION; NUCLEAR WEAPON; PLUTONIUM WEAPON.

Significance   A nuclear bomb can be dropped from tactical aircraft and strategic bombers. The fact that the bombs have to be carried by planes limits their size and payload. Nuclear bombs are quite different from any other form of weapon. Their explosive power can be millions of times greater than the largest conventional bombs, and they generate dangerous radiation. At present there are five identifiable nuclear powers: the United States, the Soviet Union, the United Kingdom, France, and China. Of these five, the two superpowers maintain nuclear bombs on a vastly greater scale than the other three. India exploded a nuclear device in 1974, but claims that it has not developed a nuclear weapons capability. Growth of the number of nuclear arsenals has been driven by the desire to have a counterforce capability against the enemy in order to limit damage to oneself.

Nuclear Chain Reaction   The process of self-sustaining nuclear reaction that makes a nuclear weapon and power generation work. A nuclear chain reaction may involve fission or fusion. In a fission chain reaction, energy is released in the process of splitting the atom. In a fusion chain reaction, energy is released in the process of joining together the split atoms to create a third atom. A nuclear chain reaction is triggered when a sufficient amount of nuclear material, known as the critical mass, is present. The possibility of a nuclear chain reaction was first theorized in the 1930s. To appreciate nuclear power plant design, one must understand the nature of nuclear fission and the maintenance and control of the chain reaction. Fission is the splitting of the nucleus of a heavy atom following absorption of an extra neutron. The chain is a series of fission reactions linked by neutrons—each neutron being generated by one fission event and inducing the next. *See also* ATOMIC WEAPON; ATOMS FOR PEACE PROGRAM; CRITICAL MASS; ENRICHED NUCLEAR FUEL; NUCLEAR REACTOR.

Significance   Toward the end of World War II, a nuclear chain reaction was adapted to nuclear weapons to produce the first atomic bomb. The chain reaction is the essential mechanism of atomic weapons. The rate of such a chain reaction can be controlled; this process is used to create a slower chain reaction in nuclear power plants. Thus the energy from the nuclear chain reaction can be used as nuclear energy for peaceful purposes. The first chain reaction occurred in a laboratory in 1942 at the University of Chicago by a research group headed by physicist Enrico Fermi. This experiment gave U.S. scientists the confidence to produce a fission bomb. After producing this chain reaction, these scientists became nuclear engineers. Once they were able to manufacture uranium 235, they needed to determine the smallest amount of fissionable material that could sustain a chain reaction—and this became known as the critical mass. Because weapons' grade fissionable material was so difficult to produce, only three atomic weapons were produced in 1945, two of which were dropped on the Japanese target cities of Hiroshima and Nagasaki.

Nuclear Club   A collective term for all countries possessing their own nuclear weapons or having demonstrated the potential to do so by successfully conducting a nuclear explosion. The Nuclear Club members and the dates when they detonated their first nuclear device are: the United States, 1945; the Soviet Union, 1949; the United Kingdom, 1952; France, 1960; China, 1964; and India, 1974. The United States, the first country to possess a nuclear weapon, was determined to prevent the spread of this arsenal, but failed to do so. To some extent, U.S. efforts to stop proliferation actually provoked expansion. By the early 1960s all the major powers that had won World War II had become nuclear nations. With the Indian nuclear tests, what has come to be known as the "Nuclear Club" was temporarily completed. Some evidence exists today that Israel and South Africa have secretly developed nuclear weapons, and other countries such as Pakistan and Brazil may soon do so. *See also* HORIZONTAL PROLIFERATION; NUCLEAR ARMS RACE; VERTICAL PROLIFERATION.

Significance   The Nuclear Club can be described as horizontal proliferation. In addition to security reasons, there is also a political reason for wishing to "join" the club: it enhances a country's status in the global power balance. Such status can establish a country as a leading regional power. This, in turn, can give the Nuclear Club member diplomatic leverage in regional politics. Thus, a conflict of interest has developed between the Nuclear Club members and nonnuclear weapons states. The club members would like to preserve their special status and attendant privileges. The nonmembers, on the other hand, especially those with the potential, would like to gain the status of nuclear power and enjoy the privileges that accompany that status. South Africa, Israel, Pakistan, and Brazil are considered potential members of the Nuclear Club. These countries may already have developed a nuclear bomb, but they are keeping the matter secret to avoid world political reaction.

Nuclear Delivery System   The totality of all components that are required to deliver a nuclear weapon from one country to the target country. A nuclear delivery system includes the container of nuclear explosives (warhead or bomb), the vehicle responsible for carrying the container from one place to another, the ground equipment that houses the construct from which point the journey begins, and those accessory instruments that facilitate the process. The whole delivery system can be categorized into two elements depending on the explosive container: bomb or warhead. For a nuclear bomb, the vehicle is the aircraft, and the starting point is the airfield. For a nuclear warhead, the delivery vehicle is the ballistic missile, cruise missile, or booster rockets, and the starting point is the launch pad. The launch pad may be a fixed missile silo or a mobile missile launcher. Radars that detect a threat and guide the missile, as well as the Command, Control, Communications, and Intelligence (C3I) network, are also part of a nuclear delivery system. *See also* LAUNCHER; SUBMARINE-LAUNCHED BALLISTIC MISSILE (SLBM).

Significance   The nuclear delivery system is evolving. Missiles are making slow-moving planes obsolete. Now a single missile can carry multiple warheads that can be maneuvered and directed independently at different targets. Warhead yields have increased and so has missile accuracy. *Strategic* delivery vehicles, such as intercontinental ballistic missiles, can cover the distance from the home territory of one superpower to that of the other. *Theater* delivery vehicles refer to shorter-range ballistic missiles and low-flying, slow-moving cruise missiles. *Tactical* delivery vehicles, such as nuclear artillery shells, are intended for use over battlefield distances. Thus the nature of the delivery vehicles determines both the speed and range covered; it also determines the payload that can be carried. While all these developments have better ensured the mutual hostage situation, they have also made arms control negotiations more complex.

Nuclear Deterrence   A strategy of preventing a nuclear attack by threatening the perceived enemy with unacceptable retaliatory damage. Nuclear deterrence literally means dissuasion by nuclear terror. It is fundamentally a psychological relationship that is based on mutual fear. Nuclear deterrence entails avoiding the actual use of nuclear weapons against each other, because that very act will mean the breakdown of deterrence. It can be traced back to the successful explosion of the Soviet Union's first atomic bomb in 1949. That event broke the U.S. nuclear monopoly. In the second half of the 1950s the mutual development of a capability to project nuclear warheads across intercontinental distances further promoted deterrence. For nearly 40 years U.S. strategic planners, government leaders, and military officials have sought to define the requirements for deterrence, to determine how much is enough. No generally agreed-upon answer has been reached, and the question continues to be controversial. Meanwhile, both superpowers continue to produce additional nuclear warheads and new delivery systems to increase their deterrence capacities. *See also* COUNTERFORCE STRATEGY; COUNTERVALUE STRIKE; MUTUAL ASSURED DESTRUCTION (MAD); SECOND STRIKE.

Significance   Nuclear deterrence, which is generally based on the second-strike capability of both superpowers, is considered to be the primary factor responsible for avoiding World War III. The essence of deterrence is not to use the nuclear weapons in the first place—at that point deterrence ceases to be an alternative, and no one can predict the consequences. Some hold that a breakdown of deterrence would lead to an all-out nuclear war between the superpowers. Others believe that there is a critical need to prepare for limited nuclear warfare, should deterrence fail to keep the peace. Deterrence of nuclear war is expected to remain the supreme military objective of both super-powers for the foreseeable future. Yet the possibility that deterrence might fail must be addressed. The vulnerabilities of the current U.S. command system indicate that it is likely to be severely degraded, if not destroyed, in the wake of a major nuclear attack. If deterrence fails, nothing will prevent the conflict from becoming a devastating one for all.

Nuclear Detonation Detection System (NDDS)   A U.S. satellite system designed to locate and report nuclear explosions during a nuclear war. A nuclear detonation detection system is made up of sensors placed atop satellites. These sensors can distinguish the size and location of nuclear detonations anywhere in the world. The program was formerly known as the Integrated Operational Nuclear Detection System (IONDS). The NDDS was first deployed by the United States in the mid-1980s. It places advanced technology detectors on the NAVSTAR global-positioning system satellites. The NDDS is planning to mount much more sophisticated nuclear detonation (nudet) sensors on satellites of the NAVSTAR network in IONDS—a system that is intended to provide detailed damage assessment both within the United States and within enemy territory during and after an attack. *See also* COMMAND, CONTROL, COMMUNICATIONS, AND INTELLIGENCE (C3I); GENERAL NUCLEAR RESPONSE; NAVSTAR.

Significance   A nuclear detonation detection system is not designed for use during peacetime. It would be used only in a nuclear war in order to help military leaders redirect their missiles away from targets that have already been destroyed. The NDDS would be useful in a general nuclear war, making nuclear war more efficient and effective and would be a major component of force management. A partially deployed NDDS could well be the only means of discerning the extent (and, by inference, the intent) of a large Soviet nuclear attack on the United States. The Soviet sensor systems are new, but they do not reveal a comparable capability. The United States, on the other hand, has maintained detectors aboard satellites for many years to verify the ban on atmospheric nuclear tests, and the system is receiving a major upgrade with the NDDS. The new nuclear detection system on NAVSTAR satellites not only determines the location and yield of nuclear explosions but also delivers preattack communications to deeply submerged submarines, provides low-frequency receivers for bombers, and upgrades existing space-based early warning sensors.

Nuclear Disarmament   The reduction or abolition of nuclear weapons. Nuclear disarmament is to be distinguished from nuclear arms control, with the former involved with actual reduction in weapons whereas the latter seeks to limit or control nuclear weapons or delivery systems. Nuclear disarmament can take place in three ways. First, unilateral disarmament occurs when a certain country reduces its nuclear arsenal level without a reciprocal move by any other country. Second, bilateral disarmament involves mutual reduction of nuclear weapons by the agreement of two countries. Finally, multilateral disarmament entails cutting down the number of nuclear weapons by more than two parties. Many bilateral and multilateral treaties have been signed by the two superpowers and other nations aimed at controlling nuclear arsenals throughout the world. Some of these treaties are: Antarctic Treaty (1959), Outer Space Treaty (1967), Treaty of Rarotonga (1985), Treaty of Tlatelolco (1967), Nonproliferation Treaty (1968), Sea-Bed Treaty (1971), Strategic Arms Limitation Talks (1972 and 1979), and Intermediate-range Nuclear Forces (INF) Treaty (1987). The last—the INF treaty—is the major disarmament agreement; the rest are mainly arms control or limitation agreements which do not provide for reduction in nuclear weapons systems. *See also* ARMS CONTROL; DISARMAMENT; NUCLEAR ARMS CONTROL.

Significance   Nuclear disarmament paves the road to a nuclear free world. A reciprocal and gradual process may be the best way to go about achieving this goal without sacrificing national security. However, with each step in arms reduction, additional steps may become more risky. When a stockpile is diminished each additional nuclear weapon that might be concealed provides a substantial advantage in the nuclear power balance; thus verification becomes increasingly more crucial. The most progress, so far, has been achieved in bilateral arms reduction agreements between the United States and the Soviet Union. Critics of nuclear disarmament proposals still contend that it will be necessary to spend more on stocking conventional arms if nuclear weapons are sharply reduced. Should nuclear arsenals be eliminated altogether, defenders of the status quo argue that the only foreseeable effect would be a return to the prenuclear world—a world that was dominated by conventional arms races and great world wars.

Nuclear Energy   The power released when an atom is split or combined with another atom. Nuclear energy is used to propel submarines, generate electricity, and fuel nuclear bombs. The vast amount of energy liberated in nuclear reactions results from the conversion of mass into energy. Of the two methods of releasing nuclear energy, the first is a process that involves the spontaneous splitting (fission) of a heavy nucleus into two or more less heavy nuclei. The second process involves the union (fusion) of two light nuclei to form a heavy nucleus. The nuclear energy presently and potentially available to the world results from the fact that some nuclei are bound more tightly than others. Much smaller amounts of nuclear energy are released by unstable or radioactive elements such as radium, whose nuclei spontaneously change, one by one, to a more stable form by an internal rearrangement called radioactive decay. *See also* ATOMS FOR PEACE PROGRAM; NUCLEAR POWER; NUCLEAR REACTOR; RADIOACTIVE DECAY.

Significance   Nuclear energy is emitted in a nuclear reaction or in a radioactive decay. It is extremely potent: a relatively small reaction can generate a tremendous amount of energy. This energy is the key to nuclear weapons and nuclear power, such as producing electricity in a nuclear power plant. Nuclear energy first received public attention on August 6, 1945, when an atomic bomb devastated Hiroshima, Japan. Since then great improvements have been made, not only in nuclear weapons but also in the controlled release of nuclear energy in devices known as nuclear reactors. Such reactors are now operated in many parts of the world, including the United States, to produce electricity. From an economic standpoint, the great potential of nuclear energy lies in the enormous amount of power released from a relatively small amount of fissionable material. However, accidents involving nuclear energy can be very harmful—whether they involve nuclear weapons or nuclear power plants—because of the deadly radiation that accompanies nuclear accidents. The Three Mile Island incident of 1979 in the United States and the Chernobyl episode of 1986 in the Soviet Union are cases in point.

Nuclear Football   The nickname of the briefcase in which the president's copy of the nuclear codes to launch an attack is carried. The Nuclear Football contains top-secret codes and the black book, which outlines the president's options in the event of a nuclear war.

The thirty-pound metal briefcase is carried by an aide to the president who accompanies the chief executive wherever he goes. The black book is kept in the locked satchel stuffed with nuclear codes (a random jumble of letters and numbers, changed daily and simultaneously delivered to nuclear command posts around the world). The book provides instructions on how to execute the central U.S. nuclear war plan, called the Single Integrated Operational Plan (SIOP). A National Military Command System (NMCS) was established in the late 1950s to coordinate the command system of U.S. nuclear forces. By 1959 the U.S. Air Force had capped them all under the NMCS, responsible ultimately to the president and charged with the task of waging putative nuclear war. The NMCS is backed up by its Support Center in the Department of Defense (DOD). *See also* NATIONAL MILITARY COMMAND SYSTEM (NMCS); SINGLE INTEGRATED OPERATIONAL PLAN (SIOP).

Significance   Nuclear Football contains the coded presidential message used for strategic nuclear communications, which tells the forces when to attack, when to hold fire, and when to cease fire. The military command codes must be transmitted in the event of launching a nuclear attack or responding to a preemptive first strike. Only upon receiving these codes, which have to be matched with relevant countercodes and a variety of allied security devices, can U.S. nuclear missiles be launched. In war, as well as in peace, the president is the commander in chief. The constant reminder of his role is the locked attaché case stuffed with nuclear codes. The ominous use of "football" is comparable with a football game plan. In a football game the head coach draws up an offensive and defensive game plan and executes it through the quarterback. Similarly, in a nuclear game plan, the chief executive (head coach) is responsible for the war and peace plan and carries it out through the Joint Chiefs of Staff (quarterback).

Nuclear-Free Zone (NFZ)   A geographical area where nuclear weapons are prohibited by international agreement. The nuclear-free zone countries, as a designated area, must agree to refrain from producing, acquiring, or possessing nuclear weapons. The signatories must not introduce nuclear weapons in that region, and must not use them against another country within the zone. A nuclear-free zone is also known as a denuclearized zone. There are treaties banning nuclear weapons from the Antarctic, Latin America, outer space, the seabed, and the South Pacific. Briefly, these treaties are: (1) the Antarctic Treaty (1959), which provides that the Antarctic shall be used exclusively for peaceful purposes; (2) the Treaty of Tlatelolco (1967), which makes Latin America a nuclear-free zone; (3) the Outer Space Treaty (1967), which prohibits placing in orbit, or upon the moon, or upon other celestial bodies, any weapons of mass destruction; (4) the Sea-Bed Treaty (1971), which bans emplacement of nuclear and other weapons of mass destruction on or under the ocean floor; and (5) the Treaty of Rarotonga (1985), which establishes a South Pacific nuclear-free zone. *See also* ANTARCTIC TREATY; OUTER SPACE TREATY; SEA-BED TREATY; TREATY OF RAROTONGA; TREATY OF TLATELOLCO.

Significance   A nuclear-free zone requires a system of verification and control to ensure compliance. In addition to political intent, there is also a technological qualification. Several geographical areas such as Latin America and the South Pacific have been declared nuclear-free zones. Other specific geographic areas have been proposed for such designation: for example, Central Europe, the Middle East, Africa, the Balkans, the Baltic, and Scandinavia. Proponents of nuclear-free zones argue that the establishment of them greatly enhances international peace and security by providing a powerful instrument to supplement the Treaty on the Nonproliferation of Nuclear Weapons. Opponents maintain that nuclear-free zones are merely ploys on the part of certain nations whose security interests require such designations. The establishment of NFZs has been supported in principle by both superpowers, and it is considered by them to be a partial disarmament measure, aimed at controlling nuclear weapons in designated zones.

Nuclear Freeze   An agreement to ban testing, production, and deployment of nuclear weapons. A nuclear freeze encompasses not only existing weapons systems but also new systems. However, it does not seek to reduce or destroy existing weapons. The weapons freeze campaign had its origin in late 1979. At that time a draft paper entitled "The Call to Halt the Nuclear Arms Race" was circulated to a number of well-known arms control experts, directors of national organizations, and peace groups throughout the United States. The paper called on the superpowers to stop the nuclear arms race. Specifically, it urged them to adopt a mutual freeze on the testing, production, and deployment of nuclear weapons, including missiles and aircraft designed to deliver nuclear weapons. Since March 1981, when the national campaign began, support for the freeze has broadened and deepened. A call for such a freeze was narrowly rejected in 1982 by the U.S. Congress. Many other efforts were defeated in the Senate. A resolution favoring a verifiable freeze passed in the

House of Representatives on May 4, 1983, but failed to receive Senate support. *See also* NONPROLIFERATION TREATY (NPT); NUCLEAR ARMS; NUCLEAR ARMS CONTROL; NUCLEAR DISARMAMENT.

Significance   The nuclear freeze proposal has both proponents and opponents arguing the case. Advocates contend that, first, it would halt the arms race, thereby giving the superpowers a breathing space to pursue further arms control and disarmament measures; second, that the arms race is dangerously increasing the risk of a nuclear holocaust; and third, that a nuclear war, whether by accident or design, is the greatest peril facing humankind. Critics argue, however, that it would be impossible to verify Soviet compliance with such a freeze, and that a freeze would deny the superpowers an opportunity to correct existing inequalities in their nuclear arsenals. The 1982 defeat of a nuclear freeze proposal in the Congress by a narrow margin only demonstrates a widespread support on both sides of the issue. Groups favoring arms control, such as the Council for a Livable World, SAVE, and the National Committee for an Effective Congress, began to cancel funding efforts to defeat freeze opponents, and to attempt instead to elect candidates favoring the measure; they did not succeed in these endeavors, however.

Nuclear Holocaust   The heavy toll of death and destruction resulting from a nuclear war. A nuclear holocaust would be much more destructive than both World War I and World War II, and is likely to occur if World War III were to develop, since both superpowers have nuclear overkill capacity. It implies that these nations have the panoply to destroy each other—and would—many times over. Under such circumstances, a nuclear holocaust is more than frightening. In World War II, the two atomic bombs dropped on Hiroshima and Nagasaki killed about 100,000 people and an untold number of wounded, many of whom perished afterward. By comparison, the devastation wrought by today's nuclear weapons would be incalculable. The United Nations has estimated that in a nuclear war the Northern Hemisphere would be attacked with a destructive force roughly equal to a thousand Hiroshima bombs. Such a war would quickly escalate into other areas of the world making the survival of civilization itself doubtful. *See also* ACCIDENTAL NUCLEAR WAR; GENERAL NUCLEAR WAR; NUCLEAR WINTER; OVERKILL.

Significance   Nuclear holocaust is a controversial issue in terms of whether or not it is inevitable. Proponents of limited nuclear war argue that it is possible to restrict the use of nuclear weapons in a conflict. Opponents hold that any use of nuclear weapons will rapidly escalate into a devastating nuclear holocaust. What effect an all-out nuclear war is likely to have on the world is still debated. Generally, persons nearest a nuclear explosion would be killed instantly or seriously injured by the blast, the heat, or the initial radiation. Those who are several miles away would be endangered by the fires caused by the explosion. People surviving the hazards of nuclear explosion would be at risk from radioactive fallout. Buildings and other structures would collapse instantly. The use of nuclear weapons threatens life—all life on earth; a holocaust will threaten civilization with extinction.

Nuclear Nonproliferation   Measures designed to prevent the acquisition of nuclear weapons by nonnuclear countries. Nuclear nonproliferation implies preventing the horizontal extension of nuclear weapons. This idea was documented in the Nonproliferation Treaty (1968). Under the terms of that treaty, nonnuclear weapons states agree to neither seek nor acquire the technology or materials for nuclear weapons production, while nuclear "have" nations pledge not to transfer the same to nuclear "have not" states. Today, most nations are signatories to this treaty and accept its terms as a limitation on their freedom of action in the nuclear weapons area—except for Argentina, Brazil, Chile, Cuba, France, China, India, Israel, Pakistan, Saudi Arabia, South Africa, and Spain. The treaty does not impinge on the right of nations to employ nuclear energy for the peaceful application of nuclear technology, and making that available to nonnuclear parties. *See also* NUCLEAR ARMS RACE; NUCLEAR PROLIFERATION.

Significance   Nuclear nonproliferation is essential in preventing what is known as a unit veto system. Under such a scenario, a number of major powers would have nuclear weapons capability. Each nuclear state would be able to use the threat of a nuclear war to protect its national interests. Many scholars believe such a power configuration to be highly unstable for global peace. China and India have successfully exploded nuclear weapons. Israel and South Africa are thought to have nuclear weapons. Pakistan and Brazil are potential nuclear powers. Nuclear nonproliferation has been threatened by these and more than a dozen other states who soon may have the scientific, technical, and industrial base for developing nuclear capability. Nuclear proliferation poses a serious threat to international peace and stability and to the security interests of all nations. Accordingly, a main objective of the world community is to prevent the spread of nuclear weapons to additional countries.

Nuclear Operations Plan (NOP)   A general nuclear strategy by the North Atlantic Treaty Organization (NATO). The nuclear operations plan was developed by the Supreme Allied Commander Europe (SACEUR) for nuclear confrontation with the Warsaw Pact countries. The official name for the NOP is the Supreme Allied Command Europe Supplementary Plan. The Nuclear Activities Branch of SHAPE (Supreme Headquarters Allied Powers Europe) was charged with developing targeting plans against military forces and support locations either in Eastern Europe or, during conflict, in invaded NATO territory. This planning is done in parallel with SACEUR's annual Nuclear Weapons Requirement Study. SHAPE has designated 18,500 short- and medium-range targets, with 10 percent being considered priority targets. At the top of NATO's military chain-of-command is the Supreme Allied Commander Europe—a post always held by a U.S. general. However, while the commander has the authority to call alerts, in practice he must gain the support of those governments affected. On the fundamentals of security policy there are no differences between the European and North American allies. The policies of NATO are agreed upon by all its members; this unity of purpose is maintained in all aspects of common security. *See also* FLEXIBLE RESPONSE; NORTH ATLANTIC TREATY ORGANIZATION (NATO); SINGLE INTEGRATED OPERATIONAL PLAN (SIOP);SUPREME ALLIED COMMANDER EUROPE (SACEUR); WARSAW PACT.

Significance   The nuclear operations plan is associated with NATO's policy of flexible response. This policy would enable NATO to respond to Warsaw Pact aggression with a variety of responses, including the use of limited nuclear and conventional weapons. Such a policy, it is hoped, would allow for intrawar negotiations, thereby avoiding the possibility of a general nuclear war over minor policy objectives. Today, Europe boasts the most powerful concentration of armed forces the world has ever seen, including the largest collection of nuclear weapons dedicated to regional use. This armed fortress is the consequence of the mobilization of an immense army in Central Europe at the end of World War II. A solution to this imbalance was the creation of NATO in 1949 by the Western powers and the introduction of U.S. military forces to the continent on a permanent basis. With the rise of Soviet nuclear power doubt has been cast on the prudence of sole reliance on nuclear weapons. Consequently, the United States has influenced its allies to adopt a strategy of flexible response, although this is at the base of the NATO nuclear strategy. This policy calls for aggression to be met initially on its own terms— that is, if the means of confrontation are conventional, then efforts will be made to conduct a direct defense using conventional weapons.

Nuclear Parity   A force structure that demands the nuclear capabilities of both superpowers be qualitatively similar, though not necessarily quantitatively the same. Nuclear parity exists when each of the two superpowers has a second-strike capability, enabling the intended victim to strike an unacceptable retaliatory blow against the aggressor. The nuclear era dawned in 1945 with the destruction of Hiroshima and Nagasaki in Japan. By 1949 the Soviet Union had built its own nuclear arsenal to become the second atomic nation after the United States. In the decades since then the superpowers have grown enormously powerful and are roughly equal to each other in destructive potential. The current situation is an outgrowth of the developments of past years, technological advances, the Soviet decision to catch up with the United States, and strategic choices made by the United States. The current U.S. stockpile of nuclear weapons is estimated to have the destructive power in TNT equivalents equal to several thousand megatons (millions of tons), distributed in 30,000 nuclear weapons. The Soviet nuclear arsenal is believed to be of somewhat smaller size—an estimated 20,000 weapons—but with roughly equal megatonage. *See also* BALANCE OF POWER; BALANCE OF TERROR; PARITY; STRATEGIC BALANCE.

Significance   Nuclear parity is a declared goal of the superpowers in arms control negotiations; it is affected by perceptions of parity on each side. One of the major practical problems of such a theoretical position is that of categorizing and evaluating various types of weapons systems. Another difficulty is that of actually counting and then verifying the respective nuclear arsenals. An additional obstacle is that of relating different kinds of weapons systems. Whereas the U.S. deterrence strategy places greater emphasis on submarine-launched ballistic missiles, the Soviet emphasis is on land-based intercontinental ballistic missiles. Soviet naval policy pays greater attention to building submarine forces; Americans have focused more on surface fleets. The United States views British and French nuclear forces outside the realm of superpower arms negotiations. In contrast, the Soviet Union feels that because of the proximity of these two countries to the Soviet Union's European borders, their arsenals must be included in the arms control talks between the superpowers.

Nuclear Planning Group (NPG)   An organization for planning North Atlantic Treaty Organization's (NATO) nuclear strategy. The Nuclear Planning Group gives nonnuclear members of NATO an opportunity to share information and participate in nuclear planning. The NPG consists of both permanent and rotating members. The four permanent members are the United States, Britain, Italy, and West Germany. The three to four nonpermanent members serve for a period of nine to eighteen months. The NPG meets twice a year and is chaired by the NATO secretary general. The meetings are attended by the defense secretaries of the NPG's member-countries, as well as by their permanent representatives. Since its establishment in 1966 the NPG has deliberated on the political guidelines for initial nuclear use. The option of predelegation has been rejected as politically unacceptable; reportedly the guidelines are still very general and contain such terms as "appropriate use." The NPG has proved a valuable forum for consultation among NATO members. *See also* EUROGROUP; EUROMISSILES; MULTILATERAL NUCLEAR FORCE; NORTH ATLANTIC TREATY ORGANIZATION (NATO).

Significance   The Nuclear Planning Group was created the same year that France withdrew from NATO's Integrated Military Command. France left because it resented U.S. political as well as military leadership of NATO. The NPG was designed to give each member-country a feeling of involvement in strategy making. However, the countries where NATO's nuclear weapons were actually deployed were given greater status by designating them permanent members. Despite this seeming fraternity, the ultimate decision to use a nuclear weapon remained with the country that owned it. Thus the United States was accorded the ultimate authority to use NATO's nuclear weapons and the Nuclear Planning Group kept intact the very factor that led to France's withdrawal from NATO's military decision making. Nevertheless, it is a mark of the maturity and solidarity of NATO that the decisions that have been made endured through periods of questioning and pressure.

Nuclear Power   The usable energy produced when atoms are split in a nuclear reaction. "Nuclear power" also refers to a country that possesses nuclear weapons. Such countries are more accurately known as nuclear weapons states. These countries are the United States, the Soviet Union, the United Kingdom, France, China, and India. The United States and many other nations have made a commitment to a large civilian nuclear power industry. By 1989, the United States had 200 nuclear power plants, and other nations had a total of 194 producing electricity. Although U.S. nuclear power plants have been surrounded by controversy, other industrialized nations, such as France, have actually made more commitment for nuclear power development. Some of the developing countries with the most advanced nuclear programs include South Korea, Taiwan, India, Pakistan, South

Africa, Argentina, and Brazil. Because of President Dwight D. Eisenhower's decision to exploit nuclear fission for peaceful purposes—used especially as a source of energy in the United States—other nations competed for this new source of power. *See also* FISSION; NUCLEAR ENERGY; NUCLEAR NONPROLIFERATION.

Significance   Nuclear power provides a portion of the world's total supply of electricity. The 1968 Nonproliferation Treaty allows for the spread of such peaceful use of nuclear energy. There remains considerable potential for supplying a much larger proportion of the world's energy from nuclear sources. With adequate safeguards against accidental radiation hazards, nuclear power can be a very cheap, long-term source of electricity. In contrast to power generation, it is the military use of nuclear power that threatens the destruction of the world. As more and more countries develop such weapons, the global situation may become increasingly unstable. While six countries already have nuclear weapons, a substantial number are potential nuclear powers.

The overreliance on cheap oil brought about the energy crisis of the 1970s. Since then many serious arguments have been made for stepping up the use of nuclear power for the generation of electricity. But what sets this resource development apart from all other alternate sources of energy is its inherent potential for nuclear weapons proliferation. Second, the effects, implications, and ramifications of the 1979 Three Mile Island (Pennsylvania) power plant incident, and the Chernobyl (Soviet Union) power plant accident of 1986, have been far-reaching. More serious accidents could occur, potentially causing thousands of short-term and delayed deaths and billions of dollars in property damage. However, supporters of nuclear power emphasize that, unlike coal and oil, it is a "clean" source, whereas its opponents point out the failure to deal with radioactive wastes produced in generating nuclear power.

Nuclear Proliferation   The spread of nuclear weapons to nonnuclear states. The 1968 Nonproliferation Treaty was designed to prevent the spread of nuclear weapons. The International Atomic Energy Agency (IAEA) and the supplier countries have adopted strict guidelines to prevent the spread of nuclear materials and technology for military purposes. Following the use against Japan of the only two nuclear bombs in its arsenal in 1945, the United States did not immediately begin a massive nuclear weapons development program. But the stage for competition between the two superpowers was set in 1949 when it was discovered that certain workers who developed the first nuclear weapons in the Manhattan Project were spies who helped the Soviet Union produce its first nuclear weapon. The arms race thus begun has continued unabated for four decades. Various nuclear agreements have been concluded, but they have added up to only a modest restraint on proliferation. *See also* HORIZONTAL PROLIFERATION; NUCLEAR NONPROLIFERATION; VERTICAL PROLIFERATION.

Significance   Many experts agree that nuclear proliferation is a very alarming prospect. It is difficult to prevent such a course if the gains in international status, strengthened regional negotiating positions, and deterrence capability outweigh the international political cost of acquiring such weapons. It is not morality, but political utility, access, and purchasing power that play the greater roles in deciding whether a nation becomes nuclear. It is for this reason that the Nonproliferation Treaty (1968) concentrated on reducing accessibility and raising the cost, such as limiting foreign aid or other facilities, to hinder nuclear proliferation. The IAEA has been trying to stem the tide of nuclear proliferation by rigorous inspections and monitoring of nuclear power plants in nations without nuclear weapons that are signatories to the Nonproliferation Treaty. The proliferation of nuclear weapons logically increases the likelihood of nuclear war merely by raising the statistical probability. What more precisely concerns those who worry about proliferation is that such a profusion of atomic installations might place nuclear weapons in the hands of terrorists and unstable nations.

Nuclear Radiation   Deadly material emitted from a nuclear explosion or accident. Nuclear radiation involves particulate and electromagnetic radiation from atomic nuclei in various nuclear processes. From a detonated weapon, alpha and beta particles, gamma rays, and neutrons are the substantial nuclear radiations. Nuclear weapons produce their biological effects through the direct or indirect effects of heat, burn, and radiation. These weapons inflict ionizing radiation on living beings in two different ways. Direct radiation is received at the time of a nuclear explosion; fallout radiation occurs from particles that are made radioactive by the effects of the explosion. A direct form of radiation is thermal radiation, most of which takes the form of visible light; fallout radiation is distributed at varying distances from the site of the blast. Radiation energy cannot be seen, and can be measured only with complicated instruments. It is an insidious and invisible killer that can penetrate biological tissue and cause cancers and genetic defects. *See also* IONIZING RADIATION; RADIOACTIVE DECAY; THERMAL RADIATION.

Significance   Nuclear radiation is ionizing radiation in proportions depending on the type of weapon and where it was exploded—in the air, underground, or underwater. Regarding nuclear weapons, there are two basic forms of transmitting radiation: direct and fallout. Direct, or prompt, radiation may be intense, affecting a limited area, and only for a short time. Fallout radiation may affect a major portion of the earth for months or years. The lethality of nuclear radiation stems primarily from its very harmful effects on human beings, including death and long-term, painful mutilation. It is not known whether the interaction of ionizing radiation with environmental agents produces a greater incidence of cancer in humans than would be expected from estimates of their separate effects.

Nuclear Reactor   A device in which a fission chain reaction can be initiated, maintained, and controlled. A nuclear reactor is the basic technology required either to produce nuclear weapons or to generate electricity. Its essential component is a core with fissionable fuel. Other components include a moderator, reflector, shielding, and coolant and control mechanisms. There are many different types of commercial reactors; the main one currently in use is the light-water reactor (LWR). The water in a LWR serves the dual purpose of carrying heat away from the reactor core and moderating, or slowing-up, the neutrons generated by fission reactions. Three other common types of nuclear reactors in commercial use are: (1) graphite-moderated, gas-cooled; (2) heavy-water; and (3) liquid-metal fast breeder. These four types of nuclear reactors account for 95 percent of total power output of commercial reactors in the West. *See also* ATOMS FOR PEACE PROGRAM; CRITICAL MASS; ENRICHED NUCLEAR FUEL; NUCLEAR ENERGY; NUCLEAR POWER.

Significance   The nuclear reactor produces energy that has three principal applications. First, it is used to produce plutonium, which can be used to fuel nuclear weapons. Second, the energy generated in the reaction process is a very cost-effective and pollution-free source of electricity. Third, it is used to power submarines, which solves their fueling problem over a long period of time. However, safeguards are essential to a nuclear reactor, in order to minimize hazards of an accident. There already have been several major accidents: Pennsylvania's Three Mile Island reactor, where there was equipment failure, and the Soviet Chernobyl nuclear power plant, where an explosion occurred. To try to prevent such catastrophic events, the technology and material needed to build and operate nuclear reactors are controlled under the Nonproliferation Treaty (1968) and IAEA (International

Atomic Energy Agency) guidelines. However, the potential for the proliferation of nuclear weapons lies in the expansion of nuclear installations, research, and commercial reactors, especially in Third World countries.

Nuclear Regulatory Commission (NRC)   An independent body established to carry on licensing and regulatory functions in the civilian and military use of nuclear power. The Nuclear Regulatory Commission was established under provisions of the Energy Reorganization Act of 1974. This five-member body was set up to replace the Atomic Energy Commission (AEC), which had been established in 1946. The AEC's research-and-development functions were transferred to a new Energy Research and Development Administration (ERDA), which became a part of the Department of Energy. The major programs making up the NRC are the Office of Nuclear Reactor Regulation, the Office of Nuclear Material Safety and Safeguards, and the Office of Nuclear Regulatory Research. The NRC issues licenses and regulations for the construction and operation of nuclear reactors and other nuclear facilities; and the possession, use, processing, handling, and disposal of nuclear materials. The NRC also contracts for the research deemed necessary for carrying out licensing and related regulatory functions. It makes rules and sets standards for activities of related companies and persons to ensure that they do no violate NRC safety rules. The NRC can order temporary or permanent closing of a power plant for violations of safety regulations. *See also* ATOMS FOR PEACE PROGRAM; DEPARTMENT OF ENERGY (DOE); NUCLEAR ENERGY; NUCLEAR POWER.

Significance   The Nuclear Regulatory Commission is responsible for protecting public health, safety, and the environment from nuclear hazards. The NRC is supervised by the Congressional Joint Committee on Atomic Energy. It ensures that civilian uses of nuclear materials and facilities conforms to the national security statute and antitrust laws. For this purpose, the NRC inspects licensed facilities and activities; investigates nuclear incidents and allegations of violation of rules; enforces license limitations and regulations by the issuance of orders and the impositions of civil penalties; conducts public hearings on nuclear and radiological safety, and defense and security matters; and develops a working relationship with the state governments regarding the nuclear materials. Although there has not been a catastrophic nuclear plant meltdown accident, there have been two close calls—too close for anybody's comfort. The Three Mile Island incident in Pennsylvania in 1979, and the Chernobyl accident in the Soviet Union in

1986, reinforced the public debate on the extent to which the people should depend on nuclear power for their energy needs.

Nuclear Risk Reduction Center (NRRC)   A step toward reducing the risks of a superpower nuclear conflict. The Nuclear Risk Reduction Center is a "hotline" between the U.S. Department of State and the Soviet Foreign Ministry. Born of a working group organized by two U.S. Senators, Sam Nunn (D.-Ga.) and John Warner (R.-Va.), the U.S.-Soviet NRRCs began operations on April 1, 1988 (the agreement was signed on September 15, 1987). Located on the seventh floor of the State Department, not far from the secretary of state's office, the U.S. NRRC works around the clock, 365 days a year, to maintain contact with its counterpart in Moscow. Russian-speaking foreign service officers use the latest computer technology to send and receive messages on a variety of arms control issues, such as advance warning of ballistic-missile test launches. In Moscow, the matching center is staffed by English-speaking Soviet watch officers. The centers exchange information needed to implement the elaborate verification and compliance procedures of the 1987 Intermediate-range Nuclear Forces (INF) Treaty. *See also* HOT LINE.

Significance   The Nuclear Risk Reduction Center is the first direct hookup established between the two superpowers since the hot line between Washington and Moscow was instituted in 1963. Speed and reliability are crucial for computers and watch officers alike. Transmitting at a rate of 6,400 words per minute, each NRRC sends messages using computer keyboard, screens, and datafax rather than voice communication. Simultaneous transmission via the Western Intelsat and the Soviet Statsionar satellites keeps the NRRCs on-line 24 hours a day. The NRRCs do not replace normal diplomatic channels, nor are they intended to be a crisis-management mechanism. They provide another useful communications link between the U.S. and Soviet nuclear systems to help reduce the risk of a superpower conflict. The role of these centers would be limited during a critical superpower crisis. Yet they could prove valuable in clarifying ambiguous circumstances caused by inadvertence or accident.

Nuclear Stockpile   Nuclear weapons that are in storage, but not actually deployed. A nuclear stockpile can contain many types of weapons systems: these may range from large, powerful intercontinental ballistic missiles to small, tactical artillery shells. The U.S. weapons stockpile contains 30,000 nuclear warheads, including eight strategic-

missile types; one strategic defensive warhead; eleven tactical warheads for missiles, artillery, and atomic demolition munitions; and
five nuclear-bomb types. Beginning in the 1960s, and continuing
throughout the 1970s and 1980s, the Soviet stockpile grew both in
quality and quantity, reaching an estimated 20,000 nuclear weapons
similar to those of the United States (although the U.S. qualitative
edge remains). While both superpowers maintain the triad of land-,
sea-, and air-launched weapons, Britain, France and China have a
mixture of different types of nuclear weapons, reflecting their technological, geographical, and economic circumstances. *See also* BALANCE
OF TERROR; NUCLEAR ARMS RACE; NUCLEAR WEAPON.

Significance   A nuclear stockpile involves weapons that are a few
steps away from deployment. They need to be assembled, transported
to launch facilities, or fitted on mobile launchers. The common notion
of a nuclear stockpile implies weapons that are in storage, but ready
for use whenever needed. Although such weapons are a large component of any nuclear stockpile, they also include weapons not yet ready
for actual deployment. The United States and the Soviet Union have
the world's largest nuclear stockpiles. Each has overkill capacity: the
ability to destroy one another, and the world, many times over. This
has transformed the nuclear balance of power into a nuclear balance
of terror. Many defense specialists disagree on the superpowers' nuclear balance, although they do agree that as long as nuclear peace is
maintained, it is impossible to measure with any certainty the complex
balance between the two nuclear stockpiles. Recent refinements of
superpower strategy had led to forced modernization resulting in a
decline in each nation's total stockpile. The needed number of weapons has not resulted in less destructive capacity, but is believed to be
more effective.

Nuclear Strategy   A planned development of objectives, procurement, deployment, and employment of nuclear weapons. A nuclear
strategy consists of the following four discrete but interrelated elements: (1) objectives: what goals nations attempt to achieve by the
possession of nuclear weapons; (2) procurement: how many and what
kinds of nuclear weapons would best serve those objectives; (3) deployment: how should the weapons be deployed to best achieve those
goals; and (4) employment: how should the weapons actually be used
in a conflict. The U.S. nuclear strategy has always been dominated by
the need to defend Western Europe and Japan, as well as the United
States. The Soviet Union stresses (more than the United States) that
nuclear weapons are embedded in the total matrix of military and

political power. A debate exists over the basic relationship between nuclear weapons and nuclear strategy. There are some who argue that the designers of weapons devise whatever man's inventiveness will allow, and strategy is then determined by the weapons' capabilities. On the other side are those who maintain that weapons are designed to suit a particular strategy. *See also* NUCLEAR ARMS RACE; NUCLEAR WEAPONS.

Significance   A nuclear strategy is shaped by the interaction of many factors, such as available technology and national strategy. One of the most difficult elements to analyze is that relationship between technology and policy. The military cannot afford to neglect any possibility that technology offers, for fear that an adversary will exploit it. In general, U.S. and Soviet strategists now appear to be on a more similar track than in the past, with both sides paying more attention to war-fighting strategies. A technological determinist might say that new destabilizing weapons have made war-fighting scenarios more feasible. A "dove" may suggest that the changes in the U.S. nuclear strategy have come about due to an overly militant administration in Washington. Finally, nuclear strategists generally assume that in the buildup of nuclear weapons, ends exist that would justify their threatened or actual use.

Nuclear Suppliers Group   An organization that aims to prevent horizontal proliferation of nuclear weapons by restricting exports of necessary technology and materials. The 15-member Nuclear Suppliers Group was created in 1974 to prevent states from transferring the sophisticated technology and materials that make up nuclear weapons to nonnuclear states. In May 1974, India exploded a small 150-kiloton bomb, using material obtained from its Canadian-supplied research reactor. Following this event, the Canadian government proposed to control the spread of nuclear technology. At a secret meeting in London, the United States, the Soviet Union, Britain, France, Canada, West Germany, and Japan drew up a list of sensitive technology that they agreed would not be exported unless proper restrictions on its use were assured by the recipients. The group was enlarged in 1975, and is known as the London or Nuclear Suppliers Group. Under President Jimmy Carter the United States sought to place an embargo on the export of reprocessing and enrichment plants, and to place tougher safeguards on the export of all materials and equipment supplied by the United States. During the Reagan administration, the United States also greatly restricted exports of enrichment and reprocessing technology to nonnuclear nations. *See also* ENRICHED NUCLEAR FUEL; HORIZONTAL PROLIFERATION; WEAPONS-GRADE NUCLEAR FUEL.

Significance   The Nuclear Suppliers Group was established partly in response to India's nuclear explosion which made her an additional member of the Nuclear Club. India defied existing guidelines by using U.S. and Canadian technology and materials to develop and detonate its first nuclear bomb. That nuclear test illustrated the danger of applying the Atoms for Peace Program without proper safeguards. Nuclear assistance had been obtained from Canada and the United States ostensibly to enable India to produce plutonium for "peaceful" nuclear devices. The facilities had not been safeguarded, and the Indian government made full use of a certain legal loophole under the Atoms for Peace agreements. The Nuclear Suppliers Group promotes the peaceful use of nuclear energy, such as in the generation of electricity. It supports the 1968 Nonproliferation Treaty and the guidelines of the International Atomic Energy Agency. Since the group is composed of members from both the East and the West, it attempts to stay above Cold War politics. However, its greatest challenge is to win support among potential Third World powers who may strongly desire nuclear weapons and believe they are in their national interests. Yet, the Nuclear Suppliers Group has consistently voted down proposals to make full-scale safeguards a condition for the sale of nuclear materials and technology.

Nuclear Terrorism   The threat of, or actual use of, nuclear weapons for coercive purposes. Nuclear terrorism is generally associated with the possibility of nuclear weapons falling into the hands of nongovernmental, subnational organizations. For example, terrorists penetrated the security of a West German nuclear station, accelerating international concern for the possibility of nuclear terrorism. There may be many objectives for the diversion of nuclear material besides physical assaults on nuclear power plants; most terrorists may not seek to seize the means of killing large numbers of people. Rather, they might be interested in holding a large number of people hostage in order to accomplish certain personal or national political objectives. Although the potential for nuclear terrorism must be taken seriously, there are ways that nations can greatly reduce the risks. They can, for example, follow the U.S. lead and forge commercial reprocessing so as to avoid sizable plutonium stockpiling. There are other precautions of a technical nature, such as spiking the reprocessed plutonium with various radioactive isotopes so as to make it unusable for weapons. *See*

also ACCIDENTAL NUCLEAR WAR; BALANCE OF TERROR; HORIZONTAL PRO-
LIFERATION.

Significance   Nuclear terrorism could be used by terrorist groups
for financial gains. It can also be resorted to in order to promote certain political interests. Theoretically, nuclear terrorism could be an
instrument of either a subnational group or a sovereign nation-state.
In the turmoil of international politics, it has become an ambiguous
concept. There is a fear in the West that groups such as the Palestine
Liberation Organization (PLO) and the Red Brigades would use the
threat of nuclear weapons to exploit political advantages, if such weapons were to fall into their hands. It is also feared that Libya would resort
to nuclear terrorism if it could acquire such weapons. A similar perception of China's behavior emerged in the 1950s, regarding the recovery
of its offshore islands from the Nationalists; there was fear on the part
of Taiwan that Chinese acquisition of nuclear weapons would dissuade
the United States from its protective involvement. Gunboat diplomacy—the use of vessels with nuclear weapons by major powers to
threaten smaller powers—is often interpreted by the latter as a form of
nuclear terrorism. The concept of nuclear terrorism is perceived in
different lights, for different reasons, by different people.

Nuclear Test Site   The location of nuclear tests. A nuclear test site
is a sophisticated installation; it is equipped to carefully analyze the
launching and explosion of experimental nuclear devices. Located 70
miles northwest of Las Vegas, the Nevada Test Site is the principal
U.S. test site. Developed in the early 1950s, it covers about 800,000
acres of desert terrain. The U.S. Defense Nuclear Agency (DNA)
conducts weapons effects tests for the Department of Defense at the
Nevada Test Site. The tests provide survivability, and sometimes lethality, information for analysis of the effectiveness of U.S. nuclear
weapons against enemy targets. The Soviet nuclear test site is located
in Kazakhstan, in the south-central part of the country. British nuclear
weapons are tested at the U.S. test site in Nevada. Since 1966 the
principal French testing ground has been the Mururoa atoll, in the
South Pacific. Situated in the west-central part of the country, Lop Nor
is the major Chinese test site. India's nuclear test site is in the Rajasthan
Desert, in the western part of the country. *See also* LIMITED TEST BAN
TREATY (LTBT); NEVADA TEST SITE (NTS); THRESHOLD TEST BAN TREATY
(TTBT).

Significance   A nuclear test site is a major component of a country's
nuclear panoply. It is needed to examine the efficiency and effective-

ness of a weapons system. A nuclear test site is an essential part of nuclear weapons research and development. It is one of the most visible indicators of a country's independent weapons' development capacity. The test sites are usually located in sparsely populated desert areas so that the effects of the explosions are minimal. After being forced to cease testing in the Sahara Desert in 1966, France made a South Pacific atoll its testing ground. Like France, Britain lacks a large, suitable desert area for testing its nuclear weapons. Testing of weapons in the United States does not bode well for the growth of an independent British nuclear force. The safety and reliability of the U.S. nuclear system is certified by laboratory tests and by the underground tests at the Nevada Test Site. Several nuclear tests are normally conducted on each weapons system to certify safety and yield reliability.

Nuclear Testing   An experiment to check the efficacy of a nuclear device or weapon. Nuclear testing is a vital stage in the development of nuclear weapons. It gives researchers confidence about the deployability of a new or changed weapon. Testing is the crucial intermediate stage between conceptualization and research on the one hand, and operationalization on the other. The first test of an atomic weapon was conducted at Alamogordo, New Mexico, on July 16, 1945. The purpose was to test whether an atomic bomb—code-named "Trinity"—would work as theoretically predicted. Almost at once, in the aftermath of the first atomic test, the terminology of the nuclear age entered the vocabulary. What we know of the physical effects of nuclear explosions comes from the series of above-ground tests, and from the experience of Hiroshima and Nagasaki. Since the Limited Test Ban Treaty of 1963, nuclear tests in the atmosphere, oceans, and space have been forbidden. Today's nuclear weapons are tested only by underground explosions; some models are never tested. Two nuclear powers, France and China, still continue to conduct above-ground nuclear tests. *See also* LIMITED TEST BAN TREATY (LTBT); NEVADA TEST SITE.

Significance   Nuclear testing is an essential component of the deployment of nuclear weapons, for two reasons. First, it is the only reliable way of ensuring that a particular type of weapons design is workable. Second, it is a cost-effective way of demonstrating a weapons system's capability to other countries. However, the dispersion of consequent deadly radioactive fallout in the environment led to drastic curtailment of nuclear testing. The 1963 Limited Test Ban Treaty prohibits nuclear testing above ground, underwater, and in outer space. The treaty allows underground nuclear testing as long as any resultant radiation does not spread beyond the testing country's territorial boundaries. The treaty was a major step toward protecting the environment from short-term and long-term consequences of radiation. The 1979 Test Ban Treaty between the two superpowers placed a further ceiling of 150 kilotons on all underground nuclear tests. There were extensive negotiations between the United States and the Soviet Union over a comprehensive test ban treaty, but no agreement has been reached; the U.S. position is opposed to a complete ban. The Soviets placed a unilateral moratorium on testing in 1980s (but resumed it in 1988), and attributed the failure to achieve a comprehensive test ban to a U.S. desire to build a new weapons system.

Nuclear Umbrella   The concept that refers to a country's nuclear arsenal when used to provide protection for another country. The U.S. nuclear umbrella defense system provides for the use of nuclear weapons in defense both of itself and its allies. It incorporates a second-strike capability not only to prevent a Soviet attack against the United States mainland but also to deter Warsaw Pact aggression in Western Europe. The Intermediate-range Nuclear Forces (INF) Treaty (1987), which provides for the removal of all U.S. and Soviet land-based intermediate-range nuclear missiles from Europe, will not by itself bring about any fundamental change in the security situation in that region. While the Europeans are ready to do what is necessary to defend their freedom, bringing their forces up to the Soviet level is hardly practical. That is why the U.S. commitment to the defense of Europe—made credible by the presence of U.S. nuclear forces in Europe—is so essential. *See also* COUPLING; NORTH ATLANTIC TREATY ORGANIZATION (NATO).

Significance   "Nuclear umbrella" protection implies that the threat of an unacceptable retaliatory blow prevents an adversary from undertaking either a limited nuclear war or a conventional war against a superpower or its allies. It is believed that it was the assurance of U.S. nuclear protection that allowed West Germany and Japan to concentrate on their respective economic recoveries. Rather than relying on expensive conventional means a threat of nuclear retaliation allows the United States to protect its allies in a more cost-effective manner. During the height of the Cold War in the 1950s, U.S. concern about the need to contain communism led the United States to reinforce the strength of the North Atlantic Treaty Organization (NATO). But once the Soviet Union began to amass a large nuclear arsenal in the 1970s, Western Europeans increasingly questioned the premise of the U.S. nuclear umbrella on which the defense of Western Europe rested. These uncertainties have led France and Britain to develop their own nuclear weapon capabilities, and Western European nations to accept intermediate-range nuclear missiles on their soil. Most, however, are ambivalent about the 1987 INF treaty, supporting the limited disarmament involved but also concerned over whether the U.S. nuclear umbrella will be maintained in the future.

Nuclear War   A confrontation that leads to the use of nuclear weapons. A nuclear war would characterize World War III. It would be very different from a conventional war, like World War I and World War II. In terms of destruction, nuclear war would result in far more deadly carnage than the world has ever witnessed, with suffering far worse than in both conventional world wars. How likely is a nuclear war? Some analysts maintain that nuclear war is becoming more likely. They point to the growth of nuclear stockpiles and to the development of more sophisticated arms and an accurate nuclear weapons delivery system. They hold that both sides are aware of the suicidal nature of nuclear war. Other analysts believe that nuclear war is unlikely. They also believe that precautions taken by both superpowers make accidental use of nuclear weapons unlikely. The sheer size and complexity of modern nuclear weapons, however, raises the risk of accidental nuclear war. It is possible that, if a conventional war broke out in Europe involving the North Atlantic Treaty Organization (NATO) an escalation would occur through the use of nuclear weapons to counter the Warsaw Pact's superiority in conventional forces. Accidental nuclear war, or one by design, remains the most critical concern for all people. *See also* BALANCE OF TERROR; GENERAL NUCLEAR RESPONSE; NUCLEAR WEAPON.

Significance   A nuclear war, in terms of destructiveness, represents a drastic departure from a conventional war. The radiation hazards from a nuclear war will plague its survivors, if any, for long after the war is over. Such a war may so affect the earth's environment that it could no longer support human life. Certainly civilization—as we know it—would cease to exist. Nuclear war would be mutually destructive for both superpowers, and a general nuclear war might destroy all societies. It is this very fear of mutual annihilation that, so far, has restrained the superpowers from engaging in a nuclear war. Since the dawn of the nuclear era the focus of U.S. strategic thought has been on deterring nuclear war by dissuading its adversary—the Soviet Union—from using nuclear weapons against the United States, or its allies, through a threat of retaliation. However, there is no historical experience in nuclear war upon which strategists can draw. Only in the unlikely situation of a prolonged, small-scale nuclear war might there be time to learn and adapt to events. The potential destructiveness of a general nuclear war has been the essential factor in postwar systemic (global) stability.

Nuclear Weapon   Any explosive device that uses the power of the atom. "Nuclear weapon" is a generic term that refers to any weapon derived from nuclear reaction. The key to such a reaction is the nucleus of the atom: the tiny compact core of the smallest particle. There are two types of nuclear weapons: atomic and thermonuclear. In the atomic weapon the reaction process involves splitting a nucleus (fission); in a thermonuclear weapon the reaction process involves splitting followed by combining nuclei (fusion). The first atomic weapon was developed in 1945, and the first thermonuclear weapon was created in 1952. The yield of a nuclear weapon may range from a fraction of a kiloton to many megatons (millions of tons) measured in TNT equivalents. Nuclear weapons are deployed in underground missile silos, in submarines, in artillery, and in aircraft. The basic nuclear weapon is the fission bomb, popularly known as the A-bomb. The three nuclides of interest are uranium 238, uranium 235, and plutonium 239, but only the last two are known to have been used in nuclear weapons. *See also* FISSION; FUSION; PLUTONIUM WEAPON; URANIUM.

Significance   In many ways a nuclear weapon is very different from all other weapons. First, the magnitude of explosion created by a nuclear weapon is a quantum jump from that of conventional weapons. Even small bombs, such as those dropped on Hiroshima and Nagasaki, have tremendous destructive power. In this light, one needs to realize that many nuclear weapons have a yield equivalent of millions of tons of TNT. Second, a nuclear weapon emits deadly radiation, which can cause genetic damage, cancer, radiation sickness, and death. Scientists suggest that the effects of radiation could continue for many—even thousands—of years.

Nuclear Weapons Authorization   The authority to plan, develop, acquire, deploy, and launch nuclear weapons. U.S. nuclear weapons authorization rests with the president and the secretary of defense, who may delegate some of the powers to the departments of Defense and Energy. The nuclear commanders in the field are asked by the Joint Chiefs of Staff (JCS) to describe the forces necessary to accomplish their missions. In so doing, they must consider the immediate and long-range threat, the international situation, and the U.S. security policies. The JCS provides the secretary of defense with a description of which U.S. forces they believe are necessary to satisfy national needs. The JCS has been requested to develop an eight-year program assessment covering defense capabilities and associated risks, and to submit their recommendations on action to improve the overall defense of the country. They are required to describe the nuclear weapons stockpile needed to support forces with strategic and tactical weapons for each of the eight-year planning periods. In doing so, the JCS must take into account research, development, and acquisition of the weapons system. The Nuclear Weapons Deployment Plan, prepared annually by the Department of Defense upon the advice of the Department of State, defines the levels of types of weapons to be deployed abroad. The president approves development, production, launching, and retirement of nuclear weapons. *See also* DEPARTMENT OF DEFENSE (DOD); DEPARTMENT OF ENERGY (DOE); JOINT CHIEFS OF STAFF (JCS); PRESIDENT.

Significance   The release of nuclear weapons can only be authorized by the National Command Authorities (NCA), which consists of the president as commander in chief, and the secretary of defense— or their duly constituted successors. The decision involves a legal and universally acknowledged prerogative of the president with respect to an action that only the president is empowered to perform. The NCA is connected to the commanders of the nuclear forces in the field by a highly streamlined chain of command.

War plans for all U.S. strategic forces are prepared under the guidelines set by the president, the National Security Council (NSC), the secretary of defense, and the JCS. The superpowers do not have identical attitudes toward military planning and preparedness. The Soviets, however, like the Americans, prefer the primacy of political control over the defense establishments, even in wartime. This attitude is visible in the Soviet military exercises; and it was also reflected in the World War II command. But nuclear war, never fought before, may be launched and won or lost within minutes; such a confrontation could create circumstances in which the time available to political leaders of the two superpowers for decisions of immeasurable gravity could be reduced to the vanishing point.

Nuclear-Weapons Reactor Safety and Waste Dumping   The procedural, mechanical, and technical control and protection from the hazards of nuclear-weapons production facilities and the disposal of spent nuclear fuel. The problem with nuclear-weapons reactor safety and waste dumping has recently reached a menacing proportion. With over $24 billion in physical assets, and an annual budget of $8 billion, the U.S. program for nuclear weapons ranks toward the top of the Fortune 500 companies. For over four decades, a network of 280 facilities, with a land base larger than Delaware and Rhode Island combined—at 20 weapons-making sites—has produced massive quantities of highly radioactive waste. The United States Department of Energy runs these facilities mostly in secret, with practically no oversight from environmental agencies. The Energy Department has dumped billions of gallons of low-level radioactive wastes from the manufacture of bomb-grade material directly into soil and ground water, which will remain dangerous for thousands, even millions, of years. *See also* NUCLEAR RADIATION; RADIOACTIVE DECAY.

Significance   The scope of the problem of the nuclear-weapons reactor safety and waste dumping has become clearer with the completion, in December 1988, of the Department of Energy's first systematic environmental assessment of 17 of 20 weapons production sites around the country. Among the hundreds of abuses detailed in the study are these: (1) At the Portsmouth Uranium Enrichment Complex in Piketon, Ohio, workers dumped oil into the soil and plowed it under—failing to analyze it for cancer-causing solvents that have now contaminated the underground water and threaten drinking water supplies. (2) At the Savannah River Plant, near Aiken, South Carolina, wastes laden with radioactive and chemical pollutants were dumped into seeping lagoons. The solvents kept going into the ground water, threatening drinking water supplies in nearby communities. (3) At Pinellas Plant in Largo, Florida, toxic substances have been discharged into the county sewer system, which may have contaminated ground water. Crude dumping practices, mostly in violation of federal law, are already responsible for extensive environmental damage. The Energy Department estimates that the bill for cleanup costs would be at least $29 billion through the year 2010, and the cost of modernizing the aging weapons-making plants would be $52 billion over that period. This may force the Congress and the public to reconsider the long-term outlook for the nuclear weapons program in the United States.

Nuclear Winter   The theory that the result of a large-scale prolonged nuclear interchange would trigger a climatic catastrophe that would engulf the earth. The advent of a nuclear winter is a hypothetical scenario immediately following a nuclear war in which the world would undergo severe and perilous climatic changes. The term "nuclear winter" was coined in a 1983 article in the journal *Science*, by U.S. physicist Richard Turco. The article was coauthored by Thomas

Ackerman, James Pollard, Carl Sagan, and Owen Toon. According to these authors, a nuclear winter would involve the subjection of large areas of the planet to prolonged periods of darkness, below-freezing temperatures, violent windstorms, and persistent radioactive fallout. These subfreezing temperatures, according to the theory of nuclear winter, would produce a large blanket of dust and smoke, thrown up in the aftermath of many nuclear explosions, that would prevent the sun's rays from reaching the earth. It is believed that it would require only a fraction of the world's strategic arsenal—500 to 2,000 of the estimated 18,000 strategic warheads—to trigger such a climatic catastrophe. Since 1983, other scientists have claimed that the originally predicted temperature variations were too wide, and that the actual temperature decline during a nuclear winter would be less severe. *See also* BALANCE OF TERROR; GENERAL NUCLEAR WAR; NUCLEAR WAR.

Significance   A nuclear winter would last for several months and would imperil every survivor on earth. It would prevent crops from growing, resulting in widespread starvation and death. Fresh water supplies would freeze, and various forms of life would gradually be eliminated. Scientists also claim that a toxic smog, loaded with debris of burned cities, would circle the Northern Hemisphere; it would possibly bring havoc to the entire world. Although most scientists agree on the possibility of nuclear winter, there is disagreement over its extent and threshold. Specialists in nuclear war and in the effects of nuclear weapons often seek to allay the public's anxieties, arguing that the difference between nuclear war and conventional war is greatly exaggerated. Nevertheless, the notion that nuclear war would bring about the end of the world persists. The promoters of the nuclear winter concept speak as if, at last, the decisive argument has been found that will compel nations to support nuclear disarmament.

O

Offensive Nuclear Weapons   A nuclear weapon designed to attack and destroy enemy targets. An offensive nuclear weapon can be used either for aggressive or defensive purposes. The world's nuclear arsenal consists of about 50,000 offensive nuclear weapons. Most, or all, contemporary nuclear weapons are categorized as offensive. Nuclear weapons do more than create the offensive means of destruction. By packaging the destructive power capacity (compare a single thermonuclear weapon with a hundred thousand World War II bombs) offensive nuclear weapons, especially the thermonuclear variety, make delivering the destruction infinitely easier. A variety of plans for U.S. offensive nuclear weapons account for 11,500 tactical warheads (8,000 of these warheads are allocated for the North Atlantic Treaty Organization), 10,000 strategic warheads, 2,500 for antisubmarine warfare, and 4,000 comprise a strategic and tactical reserve. A few thousand warheads are reserved for strategic defense of the United States. All four U.S. military services use a wide variety of nuclear weapons from this arsenal. *See also* ANTIBALLISTIC MISSILE TREATY; COUNTERVALUE STRIKE; MUTUAL ASSURED DESTRUCTION (MAD); NUCLEAR WEAPON.

Significance   Offensive nuclear weapons form the central plank of nuclear deterrence, as envisaged under the 1972 Strategic Arms Limitation Talks (SALT I). On the one hand, the treaty limited each superpower to two antiballistic missile defense systems, later reduced to one each. On the other hand, it merely identified a ceiling for both superpowers, thereby establishing parity in offensive weapons. SALT I conceptualized an assured second-strike capability by each superpower, which guarantees mutual assured destruction (MAD) in case of nuclear war. This very fear is held to be the cornerstone of a stable nuclear deterrence. The theory is premised on the penetrability and survivability of offensive nuclear weapons through an enemy missile defense system, and the implicit delivery of unacceptable damage upon the adversary. This countervalue strategy envisions a mutual hostage situation in which the offensive nuclear weapons of both superpowers are given the spotlight in ensuring a stable world. In this way, offensive nuclear weapons function as defensive weapons because their mission is to prevent an adversary from launching an offensive attack.

On-Site Inspection   A direct method of verifying compliance with arms control agreements. An on-site inspection entails allowing representatives of other countries direct access to view weapons deployment and destruction or to certify a demilitarization or denuclearization. From the very beginning of the nuclear age, the United States was unwilling to accept any agreement that was not verified by on-site inspection. In 1955, attempting to solve this impasse between the superpowers, President Dwight D. Eisenhower offered the Open Skies Proposal as a confidence-building prelude to the negotiation of arms reductions. President Lyndon B. Johnson, in 1964, tried to open discussions on arms limitation by proposing a freeze on strategic weapons that would be monitored by on-site inspection. This proposal was rejected. Soviet opposition to on-site inspection has traditionally been attributed to fears that the process is a U.S. ploy for conducting spying operations within the Soviet Union. The Soviets have recently softened their opposition, and expressed a willingness to include on-site inspection in arms control treaties. The Intermediate-range Nuclear Forces Treaty (1987) is one example of mutual on-site inspections of the destruction of nuclear weapons by the two superpowers. *See also* INTERMEDIATE-RANGE NUCLEAR FORCES TREATY; NATIONAL TECHNICAL MEANS OF VERIFICATION (NTM); OPEN SKIES PROPOSAL.

Significance   An on-site inspection clashes with the notion of a country's sovereignty; it also arouses fear of losing valuable national security secrets. However, an on-site inspection can complement and strengthen national technical means of verification. Traditionally, the United States has been its proponent, and the Soviet Union its opponent, in arms control negotiations. Soviet opposition has been based on the allegation that on-site inspection would enable the U.S. inspectors to engage in espionage. Recently, however the Soviet Union has reversed its long-standing position at the urging of President Mikhail S. Gorbachev. This change of policy facilitated the signing of the Intermediate-range Nuclear Forces Treaty (1987) between the superpowers. Accordingly, each side has been allowed to verify the other's destruction of intermediate- and medium-range ballistic missiles by visiting and monitoring the missile sites with sophisticated equipment.

The question of on-site inspection probably accounts, more than any other single issue, for the lack of progress in certain critical arms control areas: chemical weapons and nuclear testing. In both cases the United States has demanded almost continuous access as essential to ensure compliance with arms control treaty provisions.

Open Skies Proposal   A proposal to reduce tension in the arms race and verify arms control agreements. The Open Skies Proposal called for the superpowers to exchange military information and to open national airspace to aerial reconnaissance flights. The proposal was developed by a group of governmental and private experts who met at the U.S. Marine Base at Quantico, Virginia. It was presented by President Dwight D. Eisenhower to the Geneva summit conference on June 21, 1955. The Soviets rejected the plan; they felt such flights would add little to their knowledge of the United States, but would allow the United States to gain considerable knowledge of the Soviet Union. However, the concept of this type of inspection on a bilateral basis, rather than under the auspices of an international body, was put into effect by the Antarctic Treaty (1959). The United States also conducted some aerial reconnaissance by high-flying U-2 aircraft in the late 1950s, but stopped when the Soviets shot down one such plane in their airspace in 1960. *See also* ANTARCTIC TREATY; BARUCH PLAN; STRATEGIC BALANCE.

Significance   The Open Skies Proposal was one of a series of arms control initiatives rejected by one or the other superpowers. The technology to monitor each other by satellite had not yet been developed in 1955 when the proposal was put forward. Aerial reconnaissance flights were considered both a surrender of one's sovereignty and the legalization of spying. In addition, the United States at that time had a five-to-one advantage over the Soviet Union in nuclear warheads. The proposal did not suggest a parity in the number of warheads, and the Soviets felt that by accepting President Eisenhower's idea they would be accepting a dramatic strategic asymmetry between the two superpowers. In effect, U.S. policymakers had rejected the idea of banning nuclear weapons, and were seeking, instead, other ways of controlling nuclear weapons. While some perceived arms control as a first step toward disarmament, most regarded it as a means of making life with nuclear weapons bearable and somewhat less dangerous.

Outer Space Treaty   An agreement outlawing the establishment of military fortifications in space, and limiting the use of all celestial bodies to peaceful purposes. The Outer Space Treaty prohibits the deployment of nuclear weapons—as well as any other weapons of mass destruction—in outer space. Its concepts, and some of its provisions, are modeled after the Antarctic Treaty (1959). The key to the Outer Space Treaty is Article I, which bans the signatories from placing weapons of mass destruction in orbit, on celestial bodies, or in outer space. In addition, Article VI of the treaty underscores the use of the moon and other celestial bodies for peaceful purposes, by all states. The Outer Space Treaty was opened for signature on January 27, 1967, in Washington, Moscow, and London. Major provisions of the treaty are: (1) prohibit placing nuclear or other weapons of mass destruction in orbit or on the moon and other celestial bodies; (2) ban military bases and maneuvers on the moon and other planets; (3) provide that all exploration and uses of outer space be for the benefit, and in the interests, of all countries; (4) forbid claims of national sovereignty in outer space; and (5) encourage international cooperation in the exploration of space by mutually assisting astronauts and space vehicles, and in the exchange of scientific information. *See also* ANTARCTIC TREATY; FREE-ELECTRON LASER WEAPON; STRATEGIC DEFENSE INITIATIVE (SDI).

Significance   The Outer Space Treaty is the second of the post-World War II demilitarization agreements, supplementing the Antarctic Treaty of 1959. The agreement did not include weapons of "limited destruction," such as lasers, particle beams, and nonnuclear explosives. Subsequent advances in technology, and the relatively restricted wording of the Outer Space Treaty, mean that outer space has not been fully denuclearized or demilitarized. The treaty also does not prevent the use of fractional orbital bombardments (a Soviet theoretical idea for deploying a nuclear warhead in orbit). Nor does it prevent the flight through outer space of intercontinental ballistic missiles carrying nuclear weapons. Because of the treaty's prohibition against stationing nuclear or other weapons of mass destruction in space, it is a continuing point of contention in negotiations that relate to the Strategic Defense Initiative (SDI); the U.S. position has been that SDI is not a negotiable subject. Nevertheless, the Outer Space Treaty has probably made a psychological difference. Without the treaty, a number of nuclear weapons could be placed in permanent earth orbit, and could be dropped on their targets during a war.

Overkill   The capacity of the superpowers to destroy each other's military, industrial, and population targets more than once. Overkill entails the nuclear capability in excess of what is adequate to destroy a specific target or groups of targets. The United States and the Soviet Union have nuclear overkill capacity in regard to the strategy of mutual assured destruction (MAD). This means that each of the superpowers has more nuclear weapons than necessary to ensure its second-strike capability, the central plank of a stable nuclear deterrence. Delivery systems such as long-range bombers, intercontinental ballistic missiles (ICBMs), and submarine-launched ballistic missiles (SLBMs) have turned this possibility into an unprecedented and certain destructive capability. A balance of terror between the two superpowers exists. Between them, the two superpowers have 50,000 nuclear weapons—more than enough to destroy every man, woman, and child on earth many times over. Scientists and other nuclear experts disagree on the extent of overkill capacity, but all agree that overkill exists. *See also* BALANCE OF TERROR; LETHALITY; MUTUAL ASSURED DESTRUCTION (MAD).

Significance   Overkill is a bizarre term that describes the ability of the superpowers to destroy each other many times. It also means that they could reduce their nuclear arsenals under a mutual agreement, without jeopardizing their second-strike capability. In an overkill scenario, the superpowers could, theoretically, negotiate away their redundant weapons without having to worry about upsetting the stable mutual hostage, or MAD, situation. This image is hardly reassuring to those who are concerned about the long-term survival of planet earth. The danger perhaps can be best understood with the realization that presently stockpiled nuclear explosives at the superpowers' disposal have a yield equivalent to 10 tons of TNT for every person on earth. Questions relating to this danger abound. What is a sufficient nuclear capability? How many of what kinds of nuclear weapons are needed? When will each superpower have "enough" nuclear warheads so that production can be stopped? Answers to each question involve the concept of overkill and the difficulties in controlling and reducing the arms race.

Overpressure   The transient pressure, usually expressed in pounds per square inch (psi), that is commonly used to determine the capability of an object to withstand a nuclear blast. Overpressure refers to the sea of compressed air created by a shock or blast wave in the aftermath of a nuclear explosion. It varies according to the yield and type of weapon detonated. Building collapse occurs at 6 psi overpressure. Humans can withstand up to 30 psi, but anything over 5 psi overpressure causes damaged eardrums and hemorrhaging. There are two kinds of overpressures: static and dynamic. Both are created in a nuclear blast. Static overpressure pushes objects down, much like a rolling pin flattening a lump of dough. Dynamic overpressure pushes objects outward in the same way as a strong wind, like a hurricane, knocks thing over in its path. While static overpressure is a vertical force, dynamic overpressure is a horizontal force. *See also* AIR BURST; FIREBALL; GROUND BURST.

Significance   Overpressure nuclear blasts are strong enough to destroy hardened silos or command bunkers. The overpressure resulting from the explosion of a one-megaton nuclear bomb over the center of New York City would collapse all buildings within 61 square miles at ground zero, the point at which the weapon is detonated. Overpressure collapses buildings, uproots trees, and crushes people. High winds that accompany overpressure hurl dangerous debris, such as bits of broken glass. It is such overpressure that would be responsible for flattening a city after a nuclear explosion. Although the greatest number of deaths and injuries from a nuclear explosion would be caused by the blast itself, a group of credible physicians holds that "the body, like many other structures, responds to the difference between the external and internal pressures. As a consequence, the injury caused by a certain peak overpressure depends on the rate of increase of the pressure at the blast wave front."[22] This means that if the pressure rise-time is short, as it is in a nuclear explosion, under appropriate terrain and burst conditions, the damaging effect of a given pressure will be correspondingly greater.

Ozone Depletion   Deterioration of ozone, a condensed form of oxygen, that may result from a nuclear explosion. Ozone is a special type of molecular oxygen that forms a thin layer ten to twenty miles in the stratosphere, where it absorbs a large fraction of the sun's ultraviolet (UV) radiation before it reaches the earth. A nuclear weapon explosion creates and disperses many substances that can reduce the protective ozone layer. Ozone depletion is a physical phenomenon that places an upper limit to the number of weapons that can be used in a nuclear war. The depletion of the ozone layer has already increased ultraviolet radiation at the earth's surface. The ozone layer in the stratosphere is vital to life on earth, but at ground level ozone is considered a toxic pollutant. Nature is a source of ozone. Evergreen trees emit hydrocarbons known as terpenes, which react with sunshine and nitrogen oxides in the air to form ozone. The word "ozone" comes from the Greek, meaning "to smell." *See also* AIR BURST; GROUND BURST; NUCLEAR TEST SITE.

Significance   The ozone depletion controversy entered the public debate in the 1970s with frightening suddenness. It is receiving substantial attention from environmentalists and scientists worldwide. Some experts estimate that a number of nuclear explosions within a short period of time could cause blindness and skin disease for humans and animals in the Northern Hemisphere. Others postulate that it could take as long as 30 years for the ozone layer to be reconstituted once it is destroyed. The increased radiation would cause skin burns, serious sunburn, harm some aquatic species, and damage crops. It is believed that life on earth could not have evolved without an ozone layer. Threat to the ozone layer has recently been identified in connection with the impact of supersonic transports and of nuclear weapons' explosions. In 1975, the National Academy of Sciences published a study called *Long-Term Worldwide Effects of Multiple Nuclear-Weapons Detonations.* This study estimated that in a 10,000-megaton nuclear war in the Northern Hemisphere, if many of the weapons exploded were one megaton or more, 30 to 70 percent of the stratospheric ozone layer could be destroyed in the Northern Hemisphere and 20 to 40 percent in the Southern Hemisphere.[23] In the 1980s, a warning of impending danger came from scientists who discovered a large "hole" in ozone layer in the Antarctic region.

P

Parity   An equivalent capability that produces constraint when two nations, or two groups of nations, find themselves in similar degrees of strategic effectiveness. Parity is the crucial element that helps restrain countries from fighting a nuclear war by providing a balance of terror. While parity is the stated goal of both superpowers in nuclear arms control negotiations, it does not necessarily imply equality. It is judged by the size of the retaliatory strike one nation can deliver against its opponent. Parity exists when each side has an assured retaliatory second-strike capability to prevent the other from attacking. In the 1950s and 1960s it was possible to explain the Soviet nuclear buildup as an effort to gain parity. When parity exists, it has to be preserved in order to maintain the basic position of equality. The two coequal superpowers can make equal reductions and eschew one-sided increases, if they choose. *See also* BALANCE OF POWER; BALANCE OF TERROR; COUNTERVALUE STRIKE; NUCLEAR PARITY.

Significance   Parity is one thing in theory, but it is another matter to assure it in practice. There are two main problems: first, it is not easy to count with accuracy, and to verify the number and types of weapons; and second, it is often controversial to try to relate and compare different weapons systems. While it is difficult to guarantee a parity, a perception of parity may help deter the superpowers from engaging in a nuclear conflict. The apparent nuclear parity that exists between the two superpowers, however, does not extend to the other nuclear weapons states. Arms control negotiations between the two superpowers have been concerned with establishing parity between the quality and quantity of their stockpiles. Negotiations on this matter inevitably have led to debate on the meaning of particular disparities. As negotiations have moved into more and more difficult areas, it has become apparent that the force structures of the two superpowers do not lend themselves to close comparisons. Also, questions arise

211

concerning the overkill capacity of each superpower and how it relates to the impact of parity on policy decisions in arms control negotiations.

Particle Beam Weapon   A theoretical weapon that would be part of a high-technology defense system. Particle beams would, theoretically, destroy a missile during its boost phase. The development that exists is ground-based; ultimately, scientists envision locating a system of particle beam weapons in space. Initial research was undertaken in the 1890s by Nikola Tesla. The idea of a particle beam weapon was not well received in the United States until 1977, when it was announced by the Department of Defense (DOD) that the Soviet Union had developed a "death ray." The Soviet particle beam weapon could, supposedly, neutralize U.S. intercontinental ballistic missiles and thereby alter the military situation, but no supportive evidence exists. Secondary types of particle beam weapons are presently under development, including electron beam weapons and neutral particle beam weapons. *See also* CHEMICAL LASER WEAPON (CLW); STRATEGIC DEFENSE INITIATIVE (SDI).

Significance   Development of particle beam weapons had a setback when using a proton beam—a nuclear particle with a positive charge equal and opposite to that of an electron; beams of charged particles such as protons bend in the earth's magnetic field and present targeting difficulties—because proton beams are susceptible to deflection from the earth's magnetic field. To overcome this handicap, neutron beams, unaffected by the earth's magnetic field, will be used. Their neutrality makes them immune to magnetic attraction. Thus they can maintain their speed and intensity over a long distance, but the technical problems involved are immense. The United States is currently conducting research in particle beam weapons under the Strategic Defense Initiative. All the U.S. military services were interested in the research oversight role for this project. In the way that the air force dominates research on laser weapons, the army won and now controls research on particle beam weapons.

Pastoral Letter on War and Peace   The letter entitled "The Challenge of Peace: God's Promise and Our Response," adopted by Catholic bishops of the United States in May 1983. The letter was drafted by a committee of five led by Joseph Cardinal Bernardin of Chicago. The bishops contend that nuclear war is an immoral act and that therefore arming for it is also immoral. They also support Pope John Paul II's judgment that deterrence may still be judged to be morally acceptable. The bishops made it clear that their complex, balanced letter, "in its entirety . . . (and) complexity," should be used as a guide and framework for church educational programs on war and peace. Similar statements have been issued by the German, French, and other Catholic hierarchies. The U.S. Catholic Conference, the National Catholic Education Association, and many representatives of peace and justice groups in the United States and other countries also call preparing for nuclear war immoral. *See also* NUCLEAR WAR.

Significance   The letter was overwhelmingly approved, adopted, and discussed in Roman Catholic congregations throughout the United States. It had two purposes: to help form individual consciences and to offer moral guidance in a public policy debate. The letter is a noteworthy and cautionary contribution to a contemporary theology and politics of peace that reclaims and develops the classic Catholic heritage. The Roman Catholic tradition on war and peace is a long and complex one, reaching from the Sermon on the Mount to the Church's teaching on peace, and at the center of all Roman Catholic social teaching are the transcendence of God and the dignity of the human person. Catholics approach the problem of war and peace with fear and reverence. They maintain that the Roman Catholic Church, as a community of faith and as a social institution, has a proper and necessary role to play in the pursuit of peace.

PAVE PAWS   A radar system designed to detect and warn of the approach of an attacking submarine-launched ballistic missile (SLBM). PAVE PAWS is an acronym that stands for Precision Acquisition of Vehicle Entry—Phased Array Warning System. It has 1,800 active transmitter-receiver elements embedded in its antenna face. To detect SLBMs, the early-warning satellites in the Western Hemisphere are complemented by PAVE PAWS radar stations at the Cape Cod Air Force Station, Massachusetts; Beale Air Force Base, California; Robins Air Force Base, Georgia; and San Angelo, Texas. They provide 360° coverage of SLBM corridors, which cannot be overflown. The PAVE PAWS radars have faces, each looking 120° away from the other, facing outward from the United States. The United States has installed PAVE PAWS–type radars (one each) at Thule, Greenland; Fylingdales, England; and Clear, Alaska. As phased array radar, the PAVE PAWS is equipped with extensive computer capacity. *See also* BALLISTIC MISSILE DEFENSE (BMD) SYSTEM; DISTANT EARLY WARNING (DEW); PHASED-ARRAY RADAR; RADAR.

Significance   The PAVE PAWS is a powerful radar system; many small stationary antennae are electronically controlled to aim the beam over a wide arc of ocean. With its electronic scanning, PAVE PAWS can track many targets simultaneously and perform accurate counting and trajectory predictions. PAVE PAWS is designed to notify decision makers if an enemy attack is under way so that appropriate action can be taken. An ideal sequence in which sensor data would appear at Command, Control, Communications, and Intelligence (C3I) centers is the following: submarine-launched ballistic missile and intercontinental ballistic missile launches detected by infrared satellites, close-in SLBMs detected by PAVE PAWS; high-altitude SLBM bursts detected by electromagnetic pulse sensors. In order to transmit these and forty other different communications systems to the C3I, an enormous network of global communications systems has been established—one that is controlled by the Worldwide Military Command and Control System.

Peace   A vague, general notion that is taken to mean the absence of war. Peace in the nuclear era refers, *inter alia*, to the absence of a nuclear war between the superpowers. It is based on the mutual hostage situation between the United States and the Soviet Union. This countervalue strategy has made nuclear aggression by either of the superpowers a suicidal mission.

Since the Middle Ages, philosophers and statesman have reflected systematically on the problem of peace. The political measures of modern times to make international peace more secure had their starting point in the Napoleonic wars. These wars destroyed the balance of power that had been the foundation of international peace and order since the end of the Middle Ages. International peace is the highest political goal of nation-states, and they seek it through their constitutional declarations. The main purpose for the establishment of the United Nations was, and remains, to maintain world peace and security. The absolute necessity of peace among the great powers in international politics is, however, a much newer development; most analysts date it to the invention and first use of nuclear weapons in 1945. To establish permanent peace through limitation, several devices have been used: collective security alliances, disarmament, judicial settlement, and diplomacy. *See also* BALANCE OF POWER; NUCLEAR WAR; WAR.

Significance   Peace is regarded as a blessing, and its opposite, war, as a scourge. Yet, despite its bad image, most nations prepare for war and many engage in it. In the post-World War II period, great power peace is based on nuclear deterrence. The fundamental and sole utility of nuclear weapons is to impress upon the adversary the futility of aggression. Peace is the devaluation of nuclear weapons. This means that their usefulness as an instrument for seeking foreign policy objectives has declined. The only utility of nuclear weapons is to prevent the outbreak of war. It is this shaky, fragile peace that is the hallmark of the nuclear era. Relations between the superpowers have had their ups and downs. Even if there are no serious political differences between the overt behavior of the United States and the Soviet Union, the existence of their massive nuclear arsenals is a source of great tension with the foreboding danger of ultimate war. The answer to this vexing problem may be mutual nuclear disarmament. Of course the superpowers are not the only players to be counted in the game. Other than the six overtly proclaimed nuclear nations, more states are bound to acquire nuclear weaponry. Thus the search for a more effective method of preserving peace reflects a new and ever-increasing urgency, which intensifies the quest. The old Roman maxim—*si vis pacem, para bellum* (if you seek peace, prepare for war)—is slowly giving way to ideas of disarmament and negotiated settlements.

Peaceful Nuclear Explosion (PNE) Treaty   A bilateral agreement between the two superpowers that limits the yields of nuclear explosions. The Treaty of Underground Nuclear Explosions for Peaceful Purposes (PNE treaty), signed in 1976, prohibits the United States and the Soviet Union from undertaking peaceful nuclear explosions with a yield greater than 150 kilotons. It is intended to monitor as well as encourage the nonmilitary use of nuclear detonations for such purposes as stimulating natural gas, recovering oil shale, diverting rivers, or excavating. For many years various explosives experts, such as Edward Teller—a distinguished U.S. physicist—have hoped to turn nuclear weapons to peaceful uses. For example, some engineers envisioned the creation of a bigger Panama Canal by the means of nuclear explosions. The U.S. Senate has not yet ratified the PNE treaty, although Washington, along with Moscow, has declared that it is abiding by the provisions of the treaty. *See also* LIMITED TEST BAN TREATY (LTBT); NONPROLIFERATION TREATY (NPT); OUTER SPACE TREATY; THRESHOLD TEST BAN TREATY (TTBT).

Significance   The PNE treaty sets useful guidelines for explosions for nonmilitary purposes. The treaty is similar to the 1974 Threshold Test Ban Treaty. The unratified treaty is not unacceptable to the signatories, since both parties abide by the treaty's provisions. Whereas the Threshold Test Ban Treaty is concerned with nuclear explosions for military purposes, the PNE treaty focuses on nuclear, nonmilitary explosions. The two treaties complement each other, and they both strengthen the Limited Test Ban Treaty (1963). Desire to include a loophole for peaceful nuclear explosions in various treaties has led to negotiation complications without equivalent benefits. Responsibility for the failure to ratify the PNE treaty rests mainly with the U.S. Senate, which has failed to give its consent.

Phased-Array Radar   A radar system designed to detect and identify airborne objects. A phased array is a sophisticated radar that can detect and track about a hundred objects simultaneously. It operates by beaming radio waves into the sky, which are then reflected back from the airborne objects. The radio waves are analyzed to discern the object's position, size, and speed. Phased-array radars, as their name implies, form beams by adjusting the phases of numerous small sources of electromagnetic energy called elements. The beam can then be steered by simply changing the relative phases of the elements. The advantage of the phased-array radar is that the phases necessary for steering the beam to any arbitrary position can be precalculated, stored in a computer, and called upon to switch the beam instantaneously anywhere within the coverage. Phased-array radars are more complex and more expensive than conventional radars. *See also* IMAGING RADAR; RADAR.

Significance   A phased-array radar can notify decision makers if an enemy attack is under way so that they can take appropriate action. This system has been developed by the superpowers for monitoring enemy nuclear attacks. The radar allows a country to retaliate under a strategy of launch-under-attack. However, they have been restricted to two (later reduced to one) by the Antiballistic Missile Treaty (1972). They can be deployed only on the periphery of a country's territory. Moreover, they must point outward, so that they can perform their function of warning of an incoming enemy. The U.S. Navy has deployed some phased-array radars to serve as a protective umbrella for a naval fleet. The downing of an Iranian Airbus in July 1988 demonstrated that the radar still has to improve its ability to distinguish different shapes, sizes, and speeds. In particular, it needs to master the technology to distinguish between friendly and enemy objects.

Plutonium Weapon   Arms made of a heavy man-made radioactive metallic element with the atomic number 94. This weapon uses plutonium 239, which is produced by neutron irradiation of uranium 238.

The metal is heavy, unstable, and can easily be split in a fission process. It is also highly radioactive and does not occur in nature but is created in nuclear reactors (by the neutron bombardment of uranium 238). It may be used as reactor fuel, but its main use is as fissile material for nuclear weapons. Since all of the isotopes (one of two or more atoms) are produced synthetically, the atomic weight depends on the particular isotopic composition of any given sample, which in turn depends on the source of the sample. Plutonium was discovered at the University of California at Berkeley in late 1940 and early 1941. A group of scientists at the university produced the isotope with mass number 238 of the 94-proton element, which they named plutonium, after the planet Pluto. Only a few isotopes are suitable for fueling a nuclear weapon. It is critical to have the correct isotope if the weapon is to work. *See also* HYDROGEN BOMB; NAGASAKI; THERMO-NUCLEAR WEAPON; URANIUM.

Significance   The plutonium weapon is highly radioactive; exposure to even a minute particle is extremely dangerous. Fallout from the detonation of a plutonium weapon can severely damage the environment. The vast majority of nuclear weapons in the arsenals of the superpowers are plutonium-made. The Nonproliferation Treaty (1968) attempted to restrict the transfer of plutonium, in an effort to limit the spread of nuclear weapons. It is easier to construct and operate a dedicated plutonium-production reactor than an electrical power-producing reactor. Investment costs for the simplest type of graphite-moderated reactor—giving enough plutonium 239 for one or two weapons annually (10 kilograms of plutonium)—are estimated to be over $13 million to $26 million. There are further expenses of warhead assembly and weapons testing. Because of the evolution of sophisticated technology, electronics, chemical engineering, and the like, the actual cost of developing plutonium weapons is now less than it was in 1945. Plutonium weapons comprise the vast majority of nuclear armaments in the world, and together they have 1,000 Nagasakis of striking power. Nagasaki was obliterated by a 10,000-pound, 20-kiloton TNT equivalent plutonium bomb in 1945, whereas the bomb dropped on Hiroshima several days earlier utilized uranium 235 as its main source of explosive power.

Post-Attack Command and Control System (PACCS)   The aircraft that could function as a U.S. command post during a nuclear war. The Post-attack Command and Control System would serve as a backup to the land-based command centers, which may be destroyed in a nuclear attack. The PACCS consists of especially modified Boeing 707 airliners. These aircraft are kept airborne 24 hours a day. The PACCS was established in 1961, code-named "Cover All" or "Looking Glass." It would be fully alerted in an intense crisis prior to enemy attack. A scenario of a nuclear attack could be visualized as follows: The PACCS fleet would take up positions across the United States and loiter within line-of-sight range of one another, allowing transmission of necessary data and voice conferencing from the National Emergency Airborne Command Post (NEACP) near Washington, D.C., through the Strategic Air Command (SAC) in Omaha, Nebraska, to the west coast of the country—and thence to the Minuteman ICBM (intercontinental ballistic missile) fields and, farther, toward the Soviet Union. At various times and locations the PACCS would try to maintain contact with the SAC and the National Command Authorities (NCA). *See also* ALTERNATE MILITARY COMMAND CENTER (ANMCC); NATIONAL COMMAND AUTHORITIES (NCA); NATIONAL EMERGENCY AIRBORNE COMMAND POST (NEACP); STRATEGIC AIR COMMAND (SAC).

Significance   The Post-attack Command and Control System operates primarily as an airborne command post for the commander of the Strategic Air Command. Its aircraft maintain a direct communications link with the Joint Chiefs of Staff (JCS). It has facilities to order the launch of nuclear weapons. The PACCS is a subsystem within the general command system—it operates at the battlefield level, rather than at the policy-planning stage. At high altitudes the PACCS have some clear advantages as command centers; they have line-of-sight radio contact with other airborne command posts and bombers, and to wide areas of the country. These aircraft are capable of remaining in the air through the crucial early hours of a major nuclear attack. They can land on surviving airfields and return to the air quickly, if their special communications capabilities are needed. The aircraft currently used in the PACCS fleet require runways 10,000 feet long. There are presently 232 such runways in the United States.

Preemptive Strike   A surprise attack that involves hitting the enemy before he hits you. A preemptive strike assumes the other side is preparing a mammoth blow and that by preempting the initiative the advantage can be gained. This concept was developed by Soviet military experts during the 1950s. A preemptive strike is aimed at seizing the initiative to gain advantage of a sudden and surprise blow against an enemy. It is assumed that the mutual vulnerability of strategic command and control satellites would increase the incentives to use nuclear weapons first, in the belief that ASAT (antisatellite) attacks would provide a decisive advantage at the outset of hostilities.

A disarming preemptive strike may be understood as one in which the victim is unable to retaliate to any considerable degree. Such a surprise attack might be triggered by false or misleading intelligence data. Military analysts believe that coequality of nuclear power between the superpowers has all but eliminated the chances of preemption, for fear of mutual annihilation. *See also* FIRST STRIKE; LAUNCH-ON-IMPACT (LOI).

Significance   A preemptive strike is an attack against the enemy before he has a chance to be alerted to the danger. This type of attack, which seeks to destroy an enemy's strategic capabilities, is not a rational strategy for either side under any circumstances; it can be said that preemption will be abandoned as a possible alternative by the nuclear states. It seems strange to many that Soviet strategy in the 1950s was to preempt the United States at a time when the Soviet nuclear arsenal was much inferior to that of the United States. But preemption was central in Soviet policy at that time because Moscow was not sure of its ability to launch a retaliatory strike against a sudden attack by the United States. To be effective, a preemptive strike must come when it is not expected. Some Western analysts believe that if the superpowers' military balance ever should tip decisively in the Soviets' favor, the Soviets may then choose to press their advantage.

President   The chief executive of the United States. The president is the administrative head of the executive branch of the U.S. government, which includes numerous agencies, both temporary and permanent, and 14 executive departments. Article II, Section 1, of the United States Constitution provides that "the executive Power shall be vested in a President of the United States of America. He shall hold his Office during the Term of four Years, . . . together with the Vice President, chosen for the same Term. . . . " In addition to the powers set forth in the Constitution, statutes have conferred upon the president specific authority and responsibility covering a wide range of governmental affairs. His constitutional responsibility can be grouped under six categories: chief executive, commander in chief of the armed forces, chief foreign-policy maker, chief lawmaker and executor of law, head of his party, and head of state. As chief executive, the president is responsible for administering the affairs of the country. As commander in chief, he can use armed forces abroad to defend U.S. interests and at home to maintain law and order. He is responsible for formulating and implementing the foreign policy of the country. As chief lawmaker and executor of law, he shapes the congressional agenda and can veto legislation. As head of his party, he influences the direction of the party. As head of the state, he receives dignitaries, confers honors, undertakes goodwill tours, and grants pardons. *See also* COMMANDER IN CHIEF; NATIONAL COMMAND AUTHORITIES (NCA).

Significance   The president exercises a broad array of powers, some specifically provided by the Constitution and statute, others based on custom, tradition, and those inherent to the nature of the office. The presidency has also been shaped by the experiences, personality, and philosophy of the various presidents since George Washington. One of the most demanding duties and functions of a president is to serve as the manager of a vast civilian and military establishment that employs over five million people who serve in 1,900 federal agencies, and spends over one trillion dollars annually. Although assisted by federal officials, the president is responsible for running the country and receives public credit or blame for the actions of his administration. It is a tremendous responsibility, and an awesome burden. As political scientist Richard E. Neustadt says, "from outside or below, a president is many men or one man wearing many 'hats,' or playing many 'roles'."[24] This is further evidenced by the fact that the president alone, and ultimately, has the authority to order the use of nuclear weapons.

Presidential Directive 59   An executive order promulgated by President Jimmy Carter in 1980, which redefined U.S. strategic doctrine. Presidential Directive 59 emphasized selectivity in what was to be targeted by nuclear forces, and highlighted the priority assigned to military targets. It called for 40,000 targets in the Soviet Union; emphasized the need to target in a timely, redundant, and flexible manner; and outlined the weapons potentially needed. The directive described a prolonged nuclear war lasting for weeks or months, and provided for a "secure strategic reserve"—that is a missile force in reserve, not to be used in the early stages of the conflict. There were three major foci in the directive: (1) targeting was substantially changed from economic to military; (2) leadership and command changes were instituted; and (3) political targets were established. Presidential Directive 59 recognized that the Command, Control, Communications, and Intelligence (C3I) system was inadequate to support a policy of extended nuclear fighting, and noted that the strategic policy outlined in the directive required improvements in C3I. *See also* COMMAND, CONTROL, COMMUNICATIONS, AND INTELLIGENCE (C3I); COUNTERFORCE STRATEGY; COUNTERVALUE STRIKE.

Significance   Presidential Directive 59 included flexibility for attacking tactical military or strategic civilian targets. It provided an increased orientation toward counterforce strikes. President Carter was prepared to use nuclear weapons to thwart an attack on NATO (North Atlantic Treaty Organization) members, and would back efforts to regain any territory lost through invasion. The U.S. defense doctrine had been changing since 1974, when Secretary of Defense James Schlesinger launched his ideas about counterforce and limited war-fighting. Presidential Directive 59 codified this restated doctrine and gave guidance for further evolution in planning and defense acquisition. The current U.S. nuclear policy was thus set by the Carter administration. Although the Reagan administration appeared to change it, the policy nevertheless has remained basically the same.

Qualitative and Quantitative Limitation   Restrictions on the capabilities and numbers of weapons. Respectively, issues of qualitative
and quantitative limitations play a major role in arms control negotiations. While an exact quantitative balance may not be essential, a
qualitative parity is considered the bedrock of an acceptable arms
control agreement. Nevertheless, one can identify quantitative limitation as a subsystem of a qualitative limitation. This may mean that,
after reaching an understanding on the types of armaments systems
that are to be restricted, comes the detailed business of agreeing on
the numbers of weapons in these systems. A comprehensive weapons
limit, much reinforced by sublimits and payload-related collateral limits, could serve a number of arms control objectives. First, it would
produce a considerable reduction of armaments—for which there is
strong public support. Second, it would prevent either side from attempting to impose major unilateral changes on the other. Finally, it
would allow modifications in existing forces that would increase stability without perpetuating an unending arms race. *See also* STRATEGIC
ARMS LIMITATION TALKS (SALT I); STRATEGIC ARMS LIMITATION TALKS
(SALT II).

Significance   A qualitative and quantitative limitation played a crucial role in the arms control talks between the United States and the
Soviet Union in the 1970s. The Antiballistic Missile Treaty (1972)
imposed qualitative limitations on the type of defense systems the
superpowers are allowed to deploy. Accordingly, they may deploy a
ground-based missile defense system, but are barred from building
space- or sea-based defense systems. The Antiballistic Missile Protocol
(1974) imposes a quantitative limitation of one missile defense system
for each of the superpowers. Whereas a quantitative limitation restricts the actual number of weapons deployed, a qualitative limitation
restricts the capabilities and available technology of weapons. A global

ceiling—counting nuclear explosives carried in each intercontinental ballistic missile (ICBM) and submarine-launched ballistic missile (SLBM) and those carried in heavy bombers—would equate very different weapons with no recognition of their individual capabilities. Thus, in seeking an overall quantitative weapons limit, there is a strong case for also seeking some qualitative constraint on the destructive potential of the forces of the superpowers. Qualitative limits, because of their nature, tend to be harder to negotiate than quantitative ones.

Quick Reaction Alert (QRA)   A condition in which specified numbers of aircraft and missiles are readied to deliver nuclear strikes on very short notice. The quick reaction alert implies that a certain number of U.S. and North Atlantic Treaty Organization (NATO) bombers and missiles are maintained on alert status, so that they can be launched quickly. The U.S. and NATO aircraft, loaded with 150 nuclear weapons, are routinely kept on quick reaction alert. The peacetime QRA by one ground-launched cruise missile (GLCM) flight will be on a main-operating base and in a hardened shelter. A wartime, or crisis, alert will be directed to dispersed sites in concealed positions. In addition, the United States has earmarked 1,400 of the nuclear gravity bombs for use by 320 U.S. aircraft, so it could easily act alone to increase the number of QRA weapons. F-111s are on nuclear-armed QRA at all times at two British bases; these aircraft are on board for all-weather nuclear attack, including terrain-following and ground-mapping capabilities. Their low-level navigation and weapons delivery capabilities allow bombing at night and in adverse weather. *See also* GROUND-LAUNCHED CRUISE MISSILE (GLCM); NORTH ATLANTIC TREATY ORGANIZATION (NATO).

Significance   The quick reaction alert sites are not considered to be survivable, and missiles must reach covert field firing positions to avoid detection. Each missile on QRA holds a series of targets. Targets are generated at three mission planning centers: one in Britain, two in the United States. Each flight's launch-control center maintains an additional series for various targets. Twenty U.S. and allied bases are used, each with a secure QRA area. Tactical aircraft—the F-111, F-4, and the Tornado—stand with weapons loaded, behind double-guarded barbed wire fences, whose gates can only be unlocked with two keys by two officers. Actually, it takes about 15 minutes to launch. The backbone of the system is the artillery of nuclear weapons, deployed in Europe under U.S. supervision. These can be used by U.S. forces and by NATO.

R

Radar   Radio detection and determination of the distance, speed, and direction of flying objects. Radar is an acronym derived from the initial letters of the phrase "radio detecting and ranging." It became operational in 1935, and today it permits ground defenders to track incoming missiles and bombers that are hundreds of miles away. Radar operates by transmitting radio waves at an object and analyzing the electromagnetic energy reflected back from that object. There are two major kinds of radars in use: line-of-sight radar and over-the-horizon radar. Line-of-sight radar has a relatively short vision: its range is limited to the horizon. In contrast, over-the-horizon radar is not restricted by the curvature of the earth, and has an operating range beyond the horizon. Usually, line-of-sight radars are ground-based, and over-the-horizon radars are airborne. One could point to a third kind—the phased-array radar, which is noted for its ability to track about a hundred objects simultaneously. Verification of a satellite early warning situation is provided by back-scatter, over-the-horizon radar system, Ballistic Missiles Early Warning System, Perimeter Acquisition Radar, Phased-Array Radar, Stealth Bomber Characterization System, and large-phased radars, among others. *See also* AIRBORNE WARNING AND CONTROL SYSTEM (AWACS); BALLISTIC MISSILE DEFENSE (BMD) SYSTEM; DISTANT EARLY WARNING (DEW); PAVE PAWS.

Significance   Radar is useful for a variety of peaceful and military purposes. Strictly peaceful uses of radar include the guidance of civilian airliners. It is also used to gather information for military purposes, including detection of missiles' test flights and any threat of an enemy nuclear attack. The threat of a Soviet missile attack against the United States has changed the rationale for warning. Emphasis has shifted from a warning of air attack to that of a missile attack, to ensure that U.S. bombers and airborne command posts can be flushed from their bases to activate the U.S. retaliatory forces. Combat aircraft today are routinely equipped with a variety of devices that jam enemy radar, making it look as though there are more defensive weapons than there are, or that the retaliation forces are somewhere else, or heading in a different direction. The bomber technology makes it difficult to detect by enemy radar because of various new features, such as the extensive use of exotic composite materials, some of which absorb, rather than reflect, radar waves.

Radioactive Decay   A decrease, with the passage of time, of a radioactive substance due to spontaneous emission of particles and corresponding transformation of the atoms into a nonradioactive substance. Radioactive decay proceeds through a series of steps, changing to a different element each time a substantial amount of radiation is emitted. For example, uranium 235—a radioactive isotope—undergoes 15 separate transformations until it finally becomes lead, a nonradioactive element. Radioactive decay may continue over a very long period of time; the duration depends on the half-life of the element that is decaying. Uranium 238 has a half-life of 4.5 billion years; and over a time span of 24,000 years plutonium 239 loses just half of its radioactivity. There are three major types of radioactive decay: alpha, beta, and gamma. While alpha decay involves the release of a positively charged helium nucleus, beta decay emits negatively charged electrons. In contrast, gamma decay involves neutral gamma rays. Radiation from beta decay is more penetrating than radiation from alpha decay; emission from gamma decay is more penetrating than either of the others. *See also* DELAYED RADIOACTIVE FALLOUT; HALF-LIFE; NUCLEAR RADIATION; THERMAL RADIATION.

Significance   Radioactive decay takes place in the by-products of a nuclear detonation. They are sucked into the atmosphere in the mushroom cloud and spread in the fallout that attends such an event. Radioactive decay is harmful to people and animals; the energy released can destroy or deform living cells. It can cause radiation sickness, cancer, genetic defects, and death. Accurate assessment of these risks would require scientists, statisticians, and physicians to monitor large populations over a long period of time, which may present insuperable problems. Interpretation of the data gathered may prove to be an extremely arduous and controversial business. Depending on who prevails in the end—scientists, statisticians, public health officials, nuclear workers, and the public—the controversy over hazards of radioactive decay is likely to continue indefinitely.

Reentry Vehicle (RV)   The portion of a missile that carries and houses the warhead, reenters the earth's atmosphere, and, if accurately guided, hits the target. The reentry vehicle on a ballistic missile carries the nuclear warhead. These vehicles are designed to minimize environmental factors, such as wind and atmospheric density, that accompany the missile's reentry. All ballistic missiles systems may carry one or several reentry vehicles, which may be independently targeted. If the missile system carries several RVs that are not independently targetable, it is simply referred to as a multiple reentry vehicle. Separate warheads are delivered by separate RVs. The systems with more than one warhead are labeled by the acronyms MRV (multiple reentry vehicle), MIRV (multiple independently targetable reentry vehicle), and MARV (maneuverable reentry vehicle). The MX missiles will be able to carry from ten to fourteen warheads the size of the current Minuteman warhead (Mk 12A). *See also* MANEUVERABLE REENTRY VEHICLE (MARV); MULTIPLE INDEPENDENTLY TARGETABLE REENTRY VEHICLE (MIRV); MULTIPLE REENTRY VEHICLE (MRV).

Significance   The shape and construction of a reentry vehicle are chosen to minimize drag upon atmosphere reentry, thus maintaining accuracy under varying weather conditions and rendering the high-speed RV difficult to counter. The transit time of the missile over intercontinental range is about half an hour. Reentry vehicles are distinct from single nuclear warheads because, although they contain a nuclear warhead, they are specifically released in outer space and then reenter the earth's atmosphere *en route* to their targets. During the reentry through the atmosphere, the payload is protected against burnup from friction with the air, and may be guided toward the target by control flaps or by shifting weights inside the reentry vehicle. It is expected that improvements in accuracy will be coupled with further developments in the technology of RVs. The effects of such improvements in reentry technology will allow the United States and the Soviet Union to put more reentry vehicles with warheads in a missile.

S

Satellite   A small object revolving around a larger one; a secondary planet or moon. Satellites are man-made space capsules and instrument packages that are propelled into space for scientific and exploratory purposes. They orbit the earth, another planet, or the sun. There are over 5,000 artificial satellites in orbit around the earth, deployed by many nations. Peaceful uses of satellites include weather forecasting, provision of telecommunications, and relaying television signals. Satellites broadly fulfill the following functions: they provide global communications, early warning of long-range attack, tactical warning of low-level attack, surveillance of events on the ground and at sea, electronic intelligence, navigational reference, the monitoring of nuclear tests, arms control verification, and assistance in guiding missiles to their targets. A U.S. spy satellite, called Atlantis, launched in December 1988, is unofficially estimated to cost $500 million; this satellite is capable of producing detailed images of 80 percent of the Soviet Union's land area, regardless of weather conditions. *See also* ANTISATELLITE WEAPON; ARMS CONTROL.

Significance   Satellite reconnaissance has become one of the most stabilizing technologies in the arms race, since it provides detailed information about the enemy's actual weapons inventory. The United States relies on satellite reconnaissance for intelligence-gathering of Soviet weapons developments and deployment. The Atlantis, code-named "Lacrosse," uses radar waves bounced down to earth and back to the satellite to compose high-tech pictures with computer enhancement. These images can show objects the size of a man. Atlantis can view the Soviet Union at night and through clouds. This photo satellite can take pictures of objects as small as a basketball during the day. Thus, a major gap in monitoring arms control has been filled by this satellite. The air space above a country is considered part of its sovereign territory and cannot be violated—but this is not the case for

227

satellite intrusion. When the Soviet Union launched its Sputnik I satellite in 1957, it did not ask for overflight permission from other nations. This set a precedent in international affairs, which has remained since the launching of this first artificial unmanned satellite. Satellite reconnaissance photography has also become an acceptable practice in international politics.

Scowcroft Commission   A presidential commission appointed in 1983 by Ronald Reagan to review the U.S. strategic forces program. The Scowcroft Commission was charged specifically with evaluating the future of land-based intercontinental ballistic missiles (ICBMs) and to provide recommendations for greater stability. Known as the Commission on Strategic Forces, it was chaired by Lieutenant General Brent Scowcroft (USAF, ret.), who had been President Gerald Ford's National Security Adviser. In its report to President Reagan on April 6, 1983, the commission made the following recommendations: first, the United States must continue to improve its Command, Control, Communications, and Intelligence systems; second, the bomber, submarine, and cruise missile programs need to be continued; third, the country must modernize its ICBM forces by, *inter alia,* the development of 100 new MX missiles with 10 warheads for each missile, basing them in existing Minuteman silos; and four, developmental work on a small, single warhead ICBM (the Midgetman) should be continued. Finally, there is a need for a major research effort in strategic defense and on ways to increase the survivability of U.S. land-based forces. *See also* CRUISE MISSILE; COMMAND, CONTROL, COMMUNICATIONS, AND INTELLIGENCE (C3I); INTERCONTINENTAL BALLISTIC MISSILE (ICBM); STRATEGIC BALANCE.

Significance   The Scowcroft Commission was designed to help the Reagan administration determine the best way to deploy the MX missile. With a MIRV (multiple independently targetable reentry vehicle) capability, the MX is the most modern of the U.S. ICBMs. By recommending the deployment of MX missiles in existing Minuteman silos, the commission attempted to resolve the debate over their basing mode. The commission decided that MIRVs are likely targets for a surprise nuclear attack. By shifting back to smaller, single-warhead ICBMs, they hoped to introduce greater stability into nuclear deterrence. Thus the commission advised the building of 1,000 smaller Midgetman missiles. In addition, the commission put to rest the fear of the "window of vulnerability" (perceived weakness of one superpower's nuclear arsenal) of U.S. land-based ICBMs. In November 1983, the U.S. Congress approved a plan based on the commission's recommendations, and deployment of the MX was to begin in 1986. The Scowcroft Commission was, in part, a device to achieve a compromise acceptable to different elements on Capitol Hill. One consequence of the debate over basing the MX has been the proposal to build Midgetman, a corollary recommendation of the commission.

Sea-Bed Treaty   An agreement that prohibits the emplacement of nuclear and other weapons of mass destruction on or under the ocean floor. The Sea-Bed Treaty bans the deployment, testing, and storage of all weapons of mass destruction on the world's ocean floor outside the 12-mile territorial waters. Concluded by the United States and the Soviet Union in 1971, the United Nations also endorsed the Sea-Bed Treaty. Most nations have signed and ratified the treaty, including the three major nuclear states—the United States, the Soviet Union, and the United Kingdom. France and China did not sign the treaty. All NATO and Warsaw Pact littoral states also acceded to the treaty. The Sea-Bed Treaty does not prohibit the militarization of the seabed, only the emplacement of nuclear and other weapons of mass destruction on it, or within its subsoil, and the deployment of bottom-crawling vehicles specifically designed to carry nuclear weapons. *See also* ANTARCTIC TREATY; TREATY OF RAROTONGA; TREATY OF TLATELOLCO.

Significance   The Sea-Bed Treaty preserves the oceans as zones permanently free of weapons of mass destruction. Neither superpower wanted to extend the arms race into the new environment for its own reasons of high cost and questionable effectiveness; but each faced the possibility that its opponent might be tempted to do so, and thus it might be compelled to follow suit. The treaty prevented the extension of the competition into new areas. However, the treaty is weakened by not banning deployment of weapons of mass destruction within the 12-mile territorial waters boundaries. (For the first time, the United States agreed to extend the territorial waters jurisdiction from the traditional 3-mile to a 12-mile limit). Another weakness of the treaty is that it does not forbid ships and submarines from carrying nuclear and other weapons of mass destruction. However, judging from the fact that the multilateral arms control agreements have generally been concerned with preventing the introduction of nuclear weapons in specific environments, and controlling the testing of the nuclear weapons, the Sea-Bed Treaty may be viewed as a success.

Sea-Launched Cruise Missile (SLCM)   A cruise missile capable of being launched from a submarine or a ship. A sea-launched cruise missile can serve both strategic and conventional uses; the former can carry a nuclear warhead for a range of about 1,500 nautical miles. It is a slow, low-flying, highly accurate missile that resembles a pilotless airplane. The United States has deployed the sea-launched Tomahawk missile since 1984. It has a range of 2,500 kilometers and delivers a yield of 200 kilotons. The Soviet Union deploys six types of SLCMs. First introduced in the early 1960s, SS-N-3 Shaddock, which is deployed on submarines, is the oldest Soviet SLCM. It has a range of 450 kilometers and carries a 350 kiloton nuclear warhead. Since 1973 the Shaddock is being replaced by SS-N-12. This missile has a longer range—1,000 kilometers—but carries a warhead of the same yield as a Shaddock. The SS-N-12 will also be placed on aircraft carriers. First operationalized in 1968, the SS-N-7 has a much smaller range of 45 kilometers. Introduced in 1974, the SS-N-14 Silex has a comparable range of only 55 kilometers. Whereas the Silex contains one-kiloton Midgetman equipment, the Siren is a 200-kiloton heavy missile. Also while the Siren is deployed on submarines, the Silex is placed exclusively on ships. SS-N-19 has a range of 500 kilometers and is deployed on both submarines and aircraft. *See also* AIR-LAUNCHED CRUISE MISSILE (ALCM); GROUND-LAUNCHED CRUISE MISSILE (GLCM).

Significance   Placed on submarines, a sea-launched cruise missile can be launched from a position very close to an enemy shore, making radar detection more difficult. Until their air-breathing engines could be turned on, long-range cruise missiles would be boosted above the surface of the ocean by small rockets. Then the missile would fly low above the ocean surface until reaching land, where it would use a TERCOM (Terrain Contour Matching—a cruise missile guidance system) system to fly to a predesignated target with extreme accuracy. The maximum 2,500-kilometer range of the present generation of U.S. cruise missiles makes them relatively unsuitable as sea-launched strategic retaliatory missiles; the launching submarine would have to hide close to shore in order to enable the missile to reach the interior of the enemy's territory. Recently, with the development of engines capable of very long range, cruise missiles have reemerged as strategic weapons.

Second Strike   A retaliatory attack in response to an enemy strike. A second strike entails the ability to absorb the enemy's initial strike and still retaliate with devastating, unacceptable damage to the enemy. This arrangement works only if the superpowers have equal capability. A second-strike capability is also called strike-back capability. A second strike is ensured by the strategic triad: the land-based intercontinental ballistic missile (ICBM), the submarine-launched ballistic missile (SLBM), and the long-range bomber. The objective is to make each leg of the triad independent of the others. In this way if one leg fails to maintain parity in the superpower strategic balance, there are still two more legs to ensure deterrence stability. A missile attack may be launched by mobile MX and the highly accurate Trident II. When both sides have achieved a balance of second-strike capability, then they are deterred from attacking each other because an attack would be suicidal. *See also* BALANCE OF TERROR; FIRST STRIKE; INTERCONTINEN-TAL BALLISTIC MISSILE (ICBM); LONG-RANGE BOMBER.

Significance A second-strike capability by the superpowers is the essence of the MAD (mutual assured destruction) deterrence doctrine. In its turn, the MAD doctrine has been the cornerstone of post-World War II stability. A credible second-strike capability is fundamental to a stable nuclear deterrence; this means the United States must have secure second-strike forces. The characteristics of such forces are that they must be capable of surviving any initial attack, remaining cap-able of launch and penetration to their targets in the Soviet Union. It implies, to introduce another term from the strategic lexicon, that the United States has the ability to "ride out" the Soviet attack and still retain operating forces to strike back. This is further defined as sec-ond-strike counterforce capability: the use of surviving missiles to strike back at military targets. Further, to avoid destruction of second-strike capability, the superpowers have emplaced intercontinental missiles in hardened silos, dispersed their nuclear weapons delivery systems, and constantly maintain some of their strategic bombers in the air.

Secretary of Defense The cabinet officer who heads the U.S. Department of Defense (DOD). The secretary of defense is a civilian, appointed by the president with Senate approval. He is assisted in the administration of the department by a deputy secretary of defense who acts for, and exercises the powers of, the secretary and is respon-sible for the supervision of the activities of the department as directed by the secretary. In addition, the secretary of defense is assisted by the executive secretary of the department, the under secretary of defense, and many assistant secretaries. The National Security Act of 1949, as amended in 1974, unified the armed forces under the control of the secretary of defense. He oversees the Joint Chiefs of Staff (JCS), and the secretaries of the army, navy, and air force. *See also* DEPARTMENT OF DEFENSE (DOD); JOINT CHIEFS OF STAFF (JCS); PRESIDENT.

Significance   The secretary of defense is the chief assistant to the president in matters concerning the defense of the United States. Under the direction of the president, the secretary of defense exercises control of the Department of Defense, the largest department in number of employees and amount of money spent. The secretary of defense is by law a civilian, yet many people doubt the effectiveness of civilian supremacy over a vast and powerful military establishment of over 2 million on active duty and another 2.5 million on reserve (the department has about one million civilian employees). He ranks after the secretaries of state and treasury as cabinet adviser to the president and in the line of succession to the presidency. The secretary of defense serves as the focal point for policy planning on strategic international security matters concerning the affairs of Europe and the North Atlantic Treaty Organization, strategic and theater nuclear force planning, and all matters concerning nuclear and conventional weapons, and bilateral and multilateral negotiations on arms reduction, defense, and space negotiations.

Sensor   A device used to detect objects or environmental conditions. Sensors monitor activity in the Soviet Union and at sea and assess whether an attack is under way. Examples of sensors are: radars, infrared detectors, sonar, and seismographs. Sensors act as extensions of human sense organs. There are many different types of sensors, responding to different kinds of energy. Radar sensors "see" by detecting radio waves reflected off objects. Seismic sensors "feel" disturbances by detecting shock waves in the earth's crust. Heat sensors "smell" heat being given off by an object. The United States has sought to exploit space for surveillance and warning; it has flown radars in space with favorable results, and the Soviets have followed suit. U.S. designers of a space-based infrared system intend to provide warning of an intercontinental ballistic missile (ICBM) and submarine-launched ballistic missile (SLBM) attack. To maintain such a system on continuous alert would involve very substantial procurement and operating costs. *See also* DISTANT EARLY WARNING (DEW); GROUND-BASED ELECTRO-OPTICAL DEEP SPACE SURVEILLANCE (GEODSS); NATIONAL TECHNICAL MEANS OF VERIFICATION (NTM).

Significance   The sensor system plays a critical role in nuclear weapons technology. It is used both to detect incoming warheads and to guide outgoing ones to their targets. Data for these kinds of information are gathered at a distance, calling upon the technologies for sensing electromagnetic radiation. Such technologies include active and passive sensors—radio waves, microwaves, millimeter waves, infrared waves, visible waves, and ultraviolet waves. Active sensors are radars at radio frequencies, and radars at infrared and optical frequencies. Passive sensors are radio receivers and optical detectors of various types. It is pertinent to consider combinations of these sensor systems. Because of multiple susceptibilities—to physical attack, jamming, natural interference, malfunction—it is desirable to have redundant sensors which will serve in different ways and under different conditions.

Short-Range Ballistic Missile (SRBM)   A ballistic missile with a range of 1,100 kilometers or less. The short-range ballistic missile has less target distance capability than medium-range, intermediate-range, and intercontinental ballistic missiles. The United States deploys three types of SRBMs: Honest John, Pershing Ia, and Lance. The Soviet Union has four types: Frog-7, SS-21, SS-22, and SS-23. France has two types: Pluton and Hades. China possesses the DF-1. Honest John has a range of 30 kilometers, and delivers a single .01- to 15-kiloton warhead. Since 1972 it is being replaced by Lance, which has a range of 125 kilometers and carries a single 1- to 100-kiloton warhead. Pershing Ia has a longer range and larger payload. It can travel up to 740 kilometers and deliver a single 60- to 400-kiloton warhead. The Soviet Frog-7 has a range of 70 kilometers, and carries a 200-kiloton warhead. With a range of 120 kilometers, the SS-21 is replacing the older Frog-7 missiles. The SS-22 has a greater range of 900 kilometers, and SS-23 has a range of 500 kilometers. The French Pluton has a range of 120 kilometers, and the Hades—with a range of 240 kilometers—will replace the Pluton in 1992. The Chinese DF-1 has a range of 650 kilometers. *See also* CRUISE MISSILE; INTERCONTINENTAL BALLISTIC MISSILE (ICBM); INTERMEDIATE-RANGE BALLISTIC MISSILE (IRBM); MEDIUM-RANGE BALLISTIC MISSILE (MRBM).

Significance   Short-range ballistic missiles are generally categorized as tactical nuclear weapons. The U.S. Honest John must be heated to 77 degrees Fahrenheit for one to two days before launching. Except for those based in Greece and Turkey, Honest John is being replaced by Lance in all NATO forces. The Pershing Ia was deployed in West Germany; it was replaced by Pershing II in the early 1980s, which, along with SRBMs, were later dismantled under the Intermediate-range Nuclear Forces Treaty (1987). The Soviet's Frog missiles have been replaced by the more advanced SS-21, which is targeted at both Western Europe and China. In 1984 the Soviet Union deployed SS-22 missiles in East Germany and Czechoslovakia, in response to NATO's Tomahawk cruise missiles and Pershing II missiles in Western Europe.

Among the other nuclear powers, Britain has no short-range ballistic missiles.

Single Integrated Operational Plan (SIOP)   The strategic master plan for U.S. operations in a general nuclear war. The Single Integrated Operational Plan is an all-embracing top-secret military contingency plan that covers the deployment and detailed use of U.S. nuclear forces. It includes plans for the use of the entire nuclear arsenal: missiles deployed both on land and on submarines and those in Europe are included in SIOP. The first SIOP was a development of the Strategic Air Command (SAC) targeting plans assembled by a succession of SAC commanders in the 1950s. First completed in 1960 under the Eisenhower administration, SIOP was revised under the Kennedy administration as SIOP-62, and again under the Nixon administration in 1972. The current plan, SIOP-5D, was issued in 1980, the result of Jimmy Carter's Presidential Directive 59. SIOP-5D has increased the 4,000 targets of 1962 to 40,000 targets, even though an estimated 232 targets are expected to cripple the Soviet Union. However, even at maximum strength and efficiency the United States can master only 10,000 warheads capable of reaching the Soviet Union. SIOP—pronounced "sigh-op"—is aimed in large part at the Soviet war-making potential. *See also* COMMAND, CONTROL, COMMUNICATIONS, AND INTELLIGENCE (C3I); NATIONAL MILITARY COMMAND CENTER (NMCC); NATIONAL MILITARY COMMAND SYSTEM (NMCS); NUCLEAR FOOTBALL; STRATEGIC AIR COMMAND (SAC).

Significance   The Single Integrated Operational Plan is so secret that it has its own security classification: Extremely Sensitive Information (ESI). It is periodically revised to adapt to changing needs. SIOP takes into account all the individual U.S. strategies for waging a nuclear war in specific geographical areas. Great Britain's war plans are also included in SIOP. The integrated plan not only involves predicting the ability of U.S. missiles to destroy their targets, but also coping with the destruction of targets within the United States by Soviet missiles. In addition, it aims to ensure the coordination of the U.S. communications network in a nuclear war. SIOP takes into account nuclear weapons of all branches of the U.S. military; integrates all the nuclear contingency plans of the regional commands in the Atlantic, Europe, and the Pacific; and employs the president's nuclear code book ("Football") containing the instructions for the release and execution of the plan. Once an option is selected, execution of the complex military operations under the SIOP will unfold as planned— insofar as enemy action permits.

Stealth Bomber   A long-range aircraft that will incorporate technology intended to permit the plane to evade radar detection. The Stealth, or Advanced Technology Bomber, includes sharp aerodynamics contours and special coating materials that prevent radar from detecting airborne objects. The effect is achieved through a continuation of electronic countermeasures technology. First, the airframe is covered with a plastic material that absorbs radar waves. Then the aircraft is shaped in such a way as to eliminate flat surfaces and sharp angles off which radar reflect. The B-2 Stealth bomber, costing $516 million per plane, is scheduled to go into operation in the early 1990s along with the F-19—a plane designed to be used as a fighter or for short-range reconnaissance—which was also flight tested in 1988. The Stealth bomber is designed to fly five times the speed of sound, or more than 3,800 miles an hour. It will fly higher than 100,000 feet and, with aerial refueling, will be limited in range only by the crew's endurance. *See also* BALLISTIC MISSILE DEFENSE (BMD) SYSTEM; LONG-RANGE BOMBER.

Significance   The Stealth bomber is almost invisible to enemy radar. As of 1985, programs have been initiated to enable both the Advanced Technology Bomber and BI-B to acquire and engage relocatable targets, notably Soviet SS-20 and SS-X-245 mobile missiles. The existence of the Stealth bomber remained classified until a leak revealed the new aircraft in 1980. Finally, the U.S. Air Force displayed the flying-wing-shaped aircraft to selected viewers in the fall of 1988. This Advanced Technology Bomber allows the U.S. Air Force to penetrate the Soviet air defenses by evading radar detection. Just how many of this aircraft will be built is not yet clear, and will depend on the outcome of the future arms control negotiations between the superpowers, and the impact of efforts by the Bush administration to balance the national government's budget.

Strategic Air Command (SAC)   The branch of the U.S. Air Force dedicated to nuclear warfare, including bombers and intercontinental ballistic missiles (ICBMs). The responsibility of the Strategic Air Command includes a force of Minuteman III and Titan II missiles. Its bomber fleet comprises 165 B-52G and 190 B-52H aircraft. Under a war alert, SAC would operate from its underground bunker at its headquarters at Offutt Air Force Base in Omaha, Nebraska. It would also operate from the Looking Glass—an alternate airborne command post—which is a duplicate of the bunker. The Emergency Rocket Communications System (ERCS), giving automatic preprogrammed launch orders from the atmosphere, is an additional responsibility of SAC. The SAC will supervise the Post-Attack Command and Control System. SAC is also responsible for strategic reconnaissance. Such missions are carried out by the SR-71 (Blackbird), TR-1 (an updated version of the U-2s of the 1950s) high-flying planes, and air force satellites. SAC places a major emphasis on Command, Control, Communications, and Intelligence (C3I). As a deterrent to a surprise attack, SAC keeps one of its Looking Glass aircraft on airborne alert 24 hours a day. In 1962, during the Cuban missile crisis, SAC flew one-eighth of its B-52 bombers on airborne alert continuously for weeks. *See also* COMMAND, CONTROL, COMMUNICATIONS, AND INTELLIGENCE (C3I); LONG-RANGE BOMBER; POST-ATTACK COMMAND AND CONTROL SYSTEM (PACCS); SINGLE INTEGRATED OPERATIONAL PLAN (SIOP).

Significance   The Strategic Air Command oversees the Joint Strategic Target Planning Staff in designing and implementing the Single Integrated Operational Plan (SIOP)—the primary strategic nuclear war plan. The planning staff selects the targets for retaliation by the U.S. nuclear strike force, and creates a general war plan. Together these evolve into the series of SIOP that becomes the essence of overall U.S. military planning. As the bombing division of the U.S. Air Force, SAC would carry out nuclear strikes on cities and industrial districts inside the Soviet Union. This responsibility is of utmost concern to many specialists, who are worried about the vulnerability of U.S. strategic forces.

Strategic Arms Limitation Talks (SALT I, 1972)   Agreements signed between the United States and the Soviet Union to place a ceiling on the number of strategic nuclear weapons. The SALT I treaty, signed by President Richard M. Nixon and Soviet President Leonid Brezhnev in May 1972, in Moscow, has four components. Two of the best-known agreements included in SALT I are the Antiballistic Missile Treaty and the Interim Agreement on Offensive Weapons. The ABM treaty allowed each superpower to deploy only two (later limited to one by the 1974 Nixon-Brezhnev agreement) defensive weapons systems. One of these was to protect the national capital, the other to defend a missile site. The Soviet Union deployed its system—"Galosh"—around Moscow; the United States placed "Safeguard" to protect a missile site in Grand Forks, North Dakota. The Interim Agreement on Offensive Weapons set a numerical ceiling on the number of strategic missile launchers that each superpower could deploy over the next five years—before October 3, 1977. The United States was limited to 1,054, and the Soviet Union was restricted to 1,618 ICBM (intercontinental ballistic missile) launchers. The accompanying protocol allowed the United States 710 and the Soviet Union 950 SLBM (submarine-launched ballistic missile) launchers. The United States agreed to let the Soviet Union have more nuclear weapons to compensate for U.S. technological superiority. *See also* ANTIBALLISTIC MISSILE TREATY; BALLISTIC MISSILE DEFENSE (BMD) SYSTEM; INTERCONTINENTAL BALLISTIC MISSILE (ICBM); STRATEGIC ARMS LIMITATION TALKS (SALT II).

Significance   The Strategic Arms Limitation Talks made operational the mutual assured destruction (MAD) doctrine, which advocates a stable nuclear deterrence between the superpowers on the basis of a second-strike capability by each side. SALT I emphasized offensive over defensive weapons to achieve global stability. The essence of this concept of peace is mutual vulnerability; this, in turn, is premised on the penetrability and survivability of attacking warheads against the target country's missile defense system. Thus, while SALT I drastically restricted defensive systems, it merely placed a ceiling on offensive weapons. Even though SALT I did not envision an actual reduction of nuclear weapons, it was the first concrete step toward arms limitation between the superpowers. It established a rough equivalency in the number of strategic weapons; this was a move toward acknowledgment of the undesirability of numerical strategic superiority for either side.

Strategic Arms Limitation Talks (SALT II, 1979)   An agreement between the United States and the Soviet Union to put a restraint on the nuclear arms race. The Strategic Arms Limitation Treaty (SALT II) was signed by President Jimmy Carter and Soviet President Leonid Brezhnev in Vienna on June 22, 1979. The treaty had three parts: a treaty, effective until the end of 1985; a protocol, of three years duration; and a Joint Statement of Principles. It provided for an equal aggregate limit on the number of strategic nuclear delivery vehicles. Initially, the ceiling would be 2,400, as agreed at Vladivostok; it would be lowered to 2,250 by the end of 1981. Second, there would be an equal aggregate of 1,320 on the total number of launchers of MIRVed (multiple independently targetable reentry vehicle) ballistic missiles and heavy bombers with long-range cruise missiles. Third, there would be an equal aggregate limit of 1,200 on the total number of launchers of MIRVed ballistic missiles. Finally, the treaty imposed an equal aggregate limit of 820 on launchers of MIRVed intercontinental ballistic missiles. *See also* ANTIBALLISTIC MISSILE TREATY; BALLISTIC MISSILE DEFENSE (BMD) SYSTEM; INTERCONTINENTAL BALLISTIC MISSILE (ICBM); STRATEGIC ARMS LIMITATION TALKS (SALT I).

Significance   The Strategic Arms Limitation Treaty (SALT II) implemented the principle of equal aggregate total, established under the 1974 Vladivostok Accord. Thus, SALT II further facilitated the establishment of parity between the superpowers, by placing numerically equal limits on their nuclear arsenal. This numerical equality was a positive development beyond SALT I. In addition, each side agreed to limit the modernization of existing weapons systems; both also agreed to develop only one new type of intercontinental ballistic missile (ICBM). Finally, a limitation was placed on the number of nuclear missiles equipped with more than one warhead. Even though the superpowers refused to ratify SALT II, both agreed to abide by its terms. By 1986, however, both countries were funding weapons programs that led to the charge of violating the provisions of SALT II. The SALT II treaty failed because opponents of the agreement in the United States convinced many people that the Soviets were taking actions to make monitoring of the agreement very difficult. Under these circumstances, and because of the Soviet invasion of Afghanistan, the U.S. Senate did not give its approval for ratification. The Soviets, who had been waiting for U.S. ratification, did not ratify SALT II either.

Strategic Arms Reduction Talks (START)   Negotiations between the United States and the Soviet Union to limit strategic nuclear forces. The Strategic Arms Reduction Talks began in June 1982, in Geneva. President Ronald Reagan outlined his formula for START negotiations on May 9, 1982, in a speech at Eureka College. He renamed the Strategic Arms Limitation Talks (SALT) as the Strategic Arms Reduction Talks. His proposals, like those made earlier by President Jimmy Carter, contained three steps: (1) the reduction of ground- and submarine-based ballistic missiles to one-third below current level, for each category, which amounts to 5,500 warheads, down from 8,500 warheads; (2) cutting down to one-half the total number of ballistic missiles deployed on each side; and (3) placing an equal ceiling on other elements of U.S. and Soviet strategic forces. The Soviet Union proposed a reduction of all strategic systems on both sides to 1,800 strategic launchers. After the Soviets walked out of the START talks in November 1983, there were no arms control negotiations between the superpowers on strategic weapons for more than a year. New talks began in March 1985 and have continued since; no agreement has been reached to reduce strategic arms. *See also* ANTIBALLISTIC MISSILE TREATY; INTERCONTINENTAL BALLISTIC MISSILE (ICBM); STRATEGIC ARMS LIMITATION TALKS (SALT I); STRATEGIC ARMS LIMITATION TALKS (SALT II).

Significance   The Strategic Arms Reduction Talks reveal the differing perceptions of the two superpowers in regard to nuclear arms control. On the one hand, the United States has the larger inventory of submarine-launched ballistic missiles (SLBMs), but the Soviet Union has the larger arsenal of land-based intercontinental ballistic missiles (ICBMs). Each desired to maintain its own area of strength while wishing to see a reduction in the relative position of the other: the Soviet Union wanted to see a reduction in U.S. SLBMs and the United States pressed for a reduction in Soviet ICBMs. A mix of unrealistic demands, U.S. in-fighting, presidential-congressional politics, and, above all, the intransigent national aspirations and strategic doctrines of the superpowers, depotentiated START. As superpower relations have begun to improve considerably in recent years, prospects for renewed progress in the negotiations—culminating in the conclusion of a treaty to reduce strategic weapons—remain a possibility.

Strategic Balance   An equilibrium relating to the nuclear strength of the superpowers. A strategic balance refers to the forces that are capable of threatening massive destruction to each country, such as intercontinental ballistic missiles (ICBMs), submarine-launched ballistic missiles (SLBMs), and strategic bombers. Although it can include the number of delivery vehicles, strategic balance is commonly measured by each side's total number of nuclear warheads. A more thorough analysis would include many or all of the following indices: (1) the number of strategic delivery vehicles; (2) total explosive energy yield of strategic nuclear warheads, measured in trillions of joules (amount of energy taken as standard); (3) throw-weight or payload; (4) the number of warheads; (5) warhead lethality: two-thirds power of the warhead yield divided by the square of the circular error probability of the delivery system; (6) military expenditures; (7) equivalent weapons on the basis of certain known targets and the stockpile of nuclear weapons. *See also* BALANCE OF POWER; BALANCE OF TERROR; MUTUAL ASSURED DESTRUCTION; NUCLEAR WEAPON.

Significance   A strategic balance implies a scenario in which each superpower has an equal ability to fight a nuclear war. A prudent assessment of strategic balance must incorporate diverse factors, including the types and technology of nuclear weapons, geographical position of each country, and some considerations of the human factor. The myriad of factors to be considered leads to different opinions as to whether there is a balance in superpower nuclear capabilities. Often what is considered a stable balance is in fact a favorable balance to one side's advantage; it depends on perception. Some defense analysts believe that the strategic balance is off-center, favoring the Soviet Union. They argue that the apparent state of near-equality is deceptive: it overestimates the contribution of the U.S. lead in strategic bombers and number of warheads because Soviet air defenses would prevent many U.S. bombers from reaching their targets. However, the crucial task in a strategic balance is to deter the initial use of nuclear weapons, and this is unlikely to be influenced by the total inventory. In a general nuclear war, 50 percent (the second half) of the weapons fired would most likely be used against targets of relatively little military use. Weapon counts and simple exchange models typically used in describing the weapons balance fall short of measuring strategic balance.

Strategic Bomber   An aircraft with intercontinental range, equipped with nuclear weapons. A strategic bomber is capable of taking off from the home base of one superpower and delivering nuclear weapons against the other superpower's home territory. It would take about ten hours to reach its target. Intermediate-range bombers can serve as strategic bombers if they are equipped for in-flight refueling or sent on one-way missions. The long-range bomber is not the only component of a strategic bomber force; there are two other legs of the triad—the intercontinental ballistic missile (ICBM) and the submarine-launched ballistic missile (SLBM). The U.S. strategic bomber forces would carry the following weapons: short-range attack missile (SRAM) —a guided missile with a range of 75 miles; (2) air-launched cruise missile (ALCM)—a long-range guided missile whose flight path remains within the earth's atmosphere; and (3) air-to-surface ballistic missile (ASBM)—when deployed, it would have a target up to several thousands miles. There are 18 air force bases in the United States that use B-52, B-1, and FB-111 aircraft for strategic bombing missions. Thirty percent of the bomber forces are always kept on 15-minute alert. *See also* INTERMEDIATE-RANGE BOMBER; LONG-RANGE BOMBER; STEALTH BOMBER; STRATEGIC BALANCE; TRIAD.

Significance   The strategic bomber force refers to the air-component of the U.S. triad. Because of their relatively low speed, strategic bombers are considered the most vulnerable leg of the triad. However, this very slowness allows them to be called back during flight. In this sense, their alert readiness during a crisis plays a crucial symbolic role in sending signals to the adversary about a country's resolve to defend its national interest. The objectives of the United States in modernizing the strategic bomber force are to maintain a capability to penetrate Soviet airspace with high confidence, and to deliver

weapons more accurately. To do this the United States is install-
ing air-launched cruise missiles on B-52s, completing deployment of
the B-1B bombers, developing the Stealth, or Advanced Technology
Bomber, the B-2, and pursuing an advanced cruise missile (ACM)
program.

Strategic Defense   Forces and weapons designed primarily to protect a country or its allies from an attack. It is becoming increasingly
apparent that "strategic" does not mean only "nuclear" and that "nuclear" does not mean only "Soviet." Strategic defense encompasses
defense against land-based, air-launched, and submarine-based missiles and long-range bombers. The Antiballistic Missile Treaty (1972)
between the United States and the Soviet Union limits strategic defense. It restricts strategic defense systems deployed in the air, at sea,
in space, or on the ground. President Ronald Reagan's March 1983
speech initiated a research program to develop an effective strategic
defense program. Strategic defense is distinct from strategic offense,
which encompasses nuclear weapons designed to attack an enemy.
The idea to defend the United States against a nuclear attack has
recurred occasionally in policy and academic debates, more recently
in conjunction with President Reagan's Strategic Defense Initiative
(SDI). *See also* BALANCE OF TERROR; COUNTERDETERRENCE; MUTUAL AS-
SURED DESTRUCTION (MAD); STRATEGIC BALANCE; STRATEGIC DEFENSE
INITIATIVE (SDI).

Significance   Strategic defense has been underpinned by the doctrine of mutual assured destruction (MAD), which emphasized a
credible second-strike capability by both superpowers for a stable deterrence. The Antiballistic Missile Treaty (1972) reduced the number
of missile defense systems to two for each superpower (later reduced
by agreement to one each). Stability was based on offensive weapons,
creating a mutual hostage situation. President Reagan's SDI program
intends to swing the pendulum in favor of strategic defensive measures for a stable world. However, for certain technology weapons,
such as space-based lasers, the offense-defense distinction becomes
blurred. This has renewed concern for stability through strategically
defensive weapons. There is no acceptable body of opinion that suggests security can be achieved by strategic defense alone. Any current
agreements between the superpowers should not preclude work toward a viable strategic defense; on the other hand, such work must
not block offensive reduction. However, as one side begins to make
substantial progress in the area of strategic defense, the other side will
likely develop new weapons capable of defeating the strategic defense.

That has been, and will probably continue to be, the nature of the superpowers' arms race.

Strategic Defense Initiative (SDI)   A major research program designed to develop advanced technologies to build an effective defense against incoming intercontinental ballistic missiles (ICBMs). The Strategic Defense Initiative program is being conducted within the United States and in Western Europe. Many commentators, both supporters and critics, refer to the SDI as "Star Wars," after the science fiction film of the same name, which portrays high-technology battles in outer space. The first major step in the direction of the SDI was taken by President Ronald Reagan in his speech on March 23, 1983, in which he urged the scientific community to render missile-delivered nuclear weapons impotent and obsolete. In December 1983, the National Security Council approved a fund of $26 billion, over a five-year period, for SDI research. In 1984, the Strategic Defense Initiative Organization (SDIO) was created as an agency of the Department of Defense, to oversee the diverse research programs. The program of SDI inaugurated not merely an expensive research-and-development effort, but a heated new strategic debate, which continues. In the fall of 1988, the Department of Defense (DOD) announced that in the initial phase it intends to cut in half the number of space-based weapons costing an estimated $69 billion—thus reducing the previous estimate also by one-half. The SDI program differs from the past antiballistic missile (ABM) systems in that it plans to intercept Soviet missiles during all three phases of missile flight—the boost phase, the midcourse phase, and the terminal phase, using new laser and particle beam technologies. *See also* ANTIBALLISTIC MISSILE TREATY; BALLISTIC MISSILE DEFENSE (BMD) SYSTEM; HIGH FRONTIER; MUTUAL ASSURED DESTRUCTION (MAD); OUTER SPACE TREATY.

Significance   The Strategic Defense Initiative envisions a long-term multibillion-dollar missile-proof space "shield" against attacking enemy ballistic missiles. Proponents assert the eventual technological feasibility of such a missile defense system. They contend that even a 95 percent efficiency is better than no defense in case of nuclear war. Also, it would offer some security if a Soviet missile were accidentally launched. Supporters of SDI allude to the possibility of a third country attack, or nuclear blackmail. They point to the moral imperative and humane nature of a strategy of mutually assured survival. Opponents claim that the SDI is technologically impossible, even in the long run. It can never be a foolproof system, but might encourage a nuclear first strike by one of the superpowers; thus the SDI is strategi-

cally destabilizing. There are others who do not question this necessary technological development in the long run. These cautious opti-
mists also do not question the stabilizing effect of a missile defense,
once it is in place. They are, however, concerned about the unstable
transitional period from a doctrine of mutually assured destruction to
one of mutual assured survival. SDI offers the U.S. negotiating leverage for arms control and arms reduction talks.

Strategic Weapon   Nuclear arms with intercontinental range, and
the consequent ability to destroy targets in the enemy's home territory. The strategic weapon includes the warheads, its long-range
delivery system, and ancillary equipment designed primarily for general war responses. Long-range ballistic missiles and bombers make
up the strategic weapons armory, though it is the former type that
is commonly referred to as the strategic weapon. The three principal
strategic weapons are: intercontinental ballistic missiles (ICBMs), submarine-launched ballistic missiles (SLBMs), and strategic bombers.
Together they form the U.S. strategic triad. Both superpowers are
creating adjuncts to their triads by developing advanced cruise missiles that can be land-based or carried by submarines and aircraft. As
of the late 1980s, the superpowers had huge arsenals of strategic weapons with sufficient range to hit each other's home territory. The United
States had 1,000 ICBMs with 2,170 warheads; the Soviet Union had
1,373 with 6,395 warheads; the United States had 640 SLBMs with
5,632 warheads; the Soviet Union had 983 with 2,495 warheads; and
the United States had 340 strategic bombers with 3,028 warheads; the
Soviet Union had 300 with 600 warheads. *See also* INTERCONTINENTAL
BALLISTIC MISSILE (ICBM); STRATEGIC BOMBER; SUBMARINE-LAUNCHED
BALLISTIC MISSILE (SLBM); TACTICAL NUCLEAR WEAPON (TNW); TRIAD.

Significance   The strategic weapon is particularly relevant to warfare between the United States and the Soviet Union, because of the
great geographical distance between the two superpowers. Strategic
weapons can be launched from underground missile silos, submarines,
or bombers. These weapons are the central element of a superpower's
second-strike capability. It has been strategic weapons that basically
have ensured nuclear deterrence and global stability. The power of
strategic weapons in the arsenals of the superpowers is difficult to
grasp, although the number of nuclear weapons (both strategic and
nonstrategic) in their possession is quite well known (30,000 for the
United States and 20,000 for the Soviet Union). In view of the size of
these arsenals, many analysts maintain that it really does not matter
who is ahead, or if there is an equal balance, as long as both sides

have enough strategic weapons to destroy the other over and over again. The increased accuracy of weapons, and the development of intermediate-range weapons, mean that the line between strategic and tactical, or theater, nuclear weapons has blurred.

Submarine-Launched Ballistic Missile (SLBM)   Any ballistic missile launched from a submarine. The submarine-launched ballistic missile is carried underwater by a submarine and propelled into the upper atmosphere by booster rockets. Once the rockets burn out, the missiles fall through the atmosphere, pulled by gravity to their targets. The United States deploys three types of SLBMs: (1) Poseidon, (2) Trident I (C-4), and Trident II (D-5). Poseidon is an advanced form of the Polaris missile, with a diameter of 6 feet 2 inches and 34 feet in length. It has a range of 4,000 kilometers and carries ten 40-kiloton warheads. Poseidon missiles are gradually being replaced by Trident missiles. Trident I (C-4) has a range of 7,400 kilometers and carries eight to fourteen 100-kiloton warheads. This missile will also be replaced by Trident II in the early 1990s. Trident II (D-5) is under development as a follow-up missile for the Trident submarine force. *See also* INTERCONTINENTAL BALLISTIC MISSILE (ICBM).

Significance   The submarine-launched ballistic missile is a delivery vehicle for nuclear weapons. Even though an individual submarine may be vulnerable to attack, the SLBM system, as a whole, has the powerful advantage of virtual invulnerability as long as the submarines are travelling undetected. The SLBM has a more tenuous communication link with the National Command Authorities (NCA). On the credit side, the SLBM has extremely low vulnerability to preemptive attack. It is considered to be the strongest leg of the triad (the basic structure of the U.S. strategic deterrence force comprised of the intercontinental ballistic missile [ICBM], the submarine-launched ballistic missile [SLBM], and the strategic bomber) for assured retaliatory capability. The charge that U.S. nuclear forces are vulnerable to a Soviet first strike appears to be unfounded, given the vast destructive power of SLBMs in each submarine, and the ability of submarines to be elusive and evasive.

Supreme Allied Commander Europe (SACEUR)   The military officer responsible for the defense of the European members of the North Atlantic Treaty Organization (NATO). The Supreme Allied Commander Europe administers the area extending from the North Cape to the Mediterranean, and from the Atlantic to the eastern border of Turkey. The command is headquartered in Belgium, which is known as SHAPE (Supreme Headquarters Allied Powers Europe). The SACEUR's main functions are to prepare and finalize defense plans for the area under his command, and to ensure combat efficiency in the event of a war of forces assigned to him. He also makes recommendations to the Military Committee on matters likely to improve the organization of his command. In wartime, the SACEUR would control land, sea, and air operations in his area. Always an American, the SACEUR and his two deputy commanders are assisted by political and scientific advisers in addition to their military staff. All the NATO countries, except France and Iceland, maintain national military representatives at SHAPE. NATO has planned on using nuclear weapons on the battlefield from the beginning of the agreement in 1949 and in a general strike plan under the SACEUR. *See also* EUROGROUP; EUROMISSILES; NORTH ATLANTIC TREATY ORGANIZATION (NATO); WARSAW PACT.

Significance   The Supreme Allied Commander Europe has full authority in a war situation to carry out such operations as he considers necessary for the defense of any part of the area under his command. However, internal defense and defense of coastal waters remain the responsibility of the national authorities concerned. France was the first country to raise questions about the U.S. dominance of NATO in general and SACEUR in particular. The French, often in variance with the U.S. agenda, consider U.S. preponderance in SACEUR as a subjugation of their interests. This disapproval caused President Charles de Gaulle to remove French troops from NATO; and the organization's headquarters were subsequently moved from France to Belgium. Even though France is not formally a member of the NATO military structure, it remains a party to the North Atlantic Treaty and almost always chooses to organize military exercises that are called for in the alliance contingency plans. There is little doubt that SACEUR is both NATO's supreme commander and the U.S. commander in Europe.

Surface-to-Air Missile (SAM)   A ground- or ship-launched missile employed to counter airborne threats. The SAM missiles generally combine some guidance from the ground or ship during the initial phases of their flight, with built-in terminal guidance in the last phases of the interception. The United States deploys three types of surface-to-air missiles with nuclear warheads. (1) Nike-Hercules is a surface-to-air guided missile, with four rear-mounted fixed wings, and is controlled by means of four small pivoted fore-planes that are indexed in line

Significance; air missiles with wings. It can be equipped with either a conventional or nuclear warhead. Nike-Hercules has a range of 160 kilometers and delivers a single 1- to 20-kiloton warhead. (2) A Terrier missile is launched from aircraft carriers and destroyers. It has a range of about 37 kilometers and delivers a single 1-kiloton warhead. All Terrier missiles currently deployed have nuclear warheads. (3) Standard has a range of 104 kilometers and delivers a single, low-yield warhead. It can be armed with either a conventional or nuclear warhead and is launched from cruisers. *See also* BALLISTIC MISSILE DEFENSE (BMD) SYSTEM.

Significance   Surface-to-air missiles are primarily defensive weapons, launched at attacking aircraft and missiles. The SAM system covers a broad spectrum—from shoulder-fired heat-seeking missiles to long-range radar-controlled interceptors carrying nuclear warheads and operating in an automated mode. The SAM problem is easier than the ballistic missile defense (BMD) because of the slower speed and greater vulnerability of aircraft, but more difficult than BMD because aircraft try to evade the interceptors and must be detected. No nation has developed an unambiguous scheme for defining an effective SAM system without a BMD capability.

During the 1973 Arab-Israeli war, the SAM series of antiaircraft missiles had shown impressive results, but a success of this type might also be ascribed to the Israeli war strategy and the timing of Israel's retaliation against her enemy. The SAM-6 missiles caused an overall loss rate of 1 to 1.5 percent per mission. In Afghanistan, the shoulder-fired heat-seeking missiles are credited by many observers with being responsible for the Soviet withdrawal because of their deadly impact on Soviet helicopters and aircraft.

Surface-to-Surface Missile (SSM)   A ground- or ship-launched missile designed to attack targets on the surface. Most nuclear missiles are surface-to-surface missiles. Pershing is a primary example of a U.S. tactical, land-based nuclear SSM. The Soviet counterparts are Scud and Frog. Naval SSMs include the U.S. Harpoon (nonnuclear) and the Soviet Styx and Shaddock missiles. The development of Pershing started in 1958 to replace the U.S. Army missile Red Stone, which was double in weight and size. The Pershing entered the U.S. Army service in 1962. A train of four M-174-tracked vehicles can transport the Pershing with its support and firing equipment, and is controlled by three movable tailfins at the first stage, and is powered by solid propellent rocket motors. It is armed with a nuclear warhead. The length of the Pershing missile is 34 feet 6 inches, body diameter 3 feet 4 inches and the weight 10,000 pounds. Its ranges vary from 115 to 460 miles, and it can reach a peak of 3,000 miles per hour. Some of the other Soviet SSMs are: Sandal, Savage, and Scamp. *See also* GROUND-LAUNCHED CRUISE MISSILE (GLCM); SURFACE-TO-AIR MISSILE (SAM).

Significance   The surface-to-surface missiles (Pershing and others) are easy to transport and quickly assembled to the firing position. Pershing is a short-range ballistic missile, and its most impressive new feature is its extremely high accuracy. The United States deployed 108 Pershing II ballistic missiles in Europe in the 1980s, in response to the Soviet's 210 SS-20s deployed against North Atlantic Treaty Organization (NATO) targets. It was argued (mostly by Europeans) that the deployment of the Pershing II intermediate-range ballistic missiles (IRBMs) in Europe was to enable the United States to fight a limited nuclear war in Europe in which North America would not suffer. The Reagan administration claimed that its deployment in Europe was aimed at goading the Soviets into agreeing on a joint withdrawal of all such missiles from both Eastern and Western Europe. Such agreement came to pass in the ratification, in 1988, of the Intermediate-Range Nuclear Forces Treaty between the two superpowers to eliminate both Pershing and SS-20 and other intermediate-range and shorter-range missiles in Europe.

T

Tactical Nuclear Weapon (TNW)   A battlefield weapon as distinguished from a long-range strategic operation. Tactical nuclear weapons are small, highly specialized nuclear weapons, and are designed to travel relatively short distances. They were first developed by the United States in the early 1950s as a substitute for conventional forces in Europe. Some of the tactical nuclear weapons include the U.S. Army's Lance MGM-52C, the Lance II and Nike-Hercules MIM-14 artillery missiles, and a number of artillery-fired atomic projectiles. The U.S. Air Force holds one air-to-air nuclear armed missile—the Genie AIR-2A. The U.S. Navy has a number of ship-to-ship and ship-to-air missiles: specifically, the Terrier RIM-20, the Standard 2 RIM-67B. The Soviet Army deploys the Frog-7, the Scud (SS-1B/SS-1C), and Saleboard SS-12. The Soviet Navy carries a large number of submarine-launched cruise missiles (SLCM) in a ship-to-ship role, although they can be adapted for a ship-to-ground use. Great Britain has the Lance missile. *See also* NUCLEAR WEAPON; THEATER NUCLEAR WEAPON (TNW).

Significance   Tactical nuclear weapons are less powerful and cannot strike the home territory of the superpowers. At this point a distinction between a tactical and strategic weapon must be made. While tactical weapons are used by forces in battle, strategic weapons are directed at the enemy's basic means of support, such as the economy, supplies of raw materials, industrial installations, and civilian populations. Many of the atomic scientists who had been responsible for the development of the first atomic bombs, which were dropped on Japan, were distressed by the extent of the destruction on Hiroshima and Nagasaki and deaths of thousands of people there. As a future alternative, the leader of this liberal group of physicists, J. Robert Oppenheimer, argued for the development of tactical nuclear weapons that military commanders could deliver with precisely controlled force—

on the right spot at the right time. The objective was to minimize collateral damage while maximizing military effectiveness. These views contributed to the origin of tactical nuclear weapons, which were basically adaptations of the new atomic weapons to battlefield needs.

Telemetry   Transmission to earth of electronic signals from an in-flight missile. Telemetry is used by analysts to evaluate missile performance and to verify arms control agreements. Satellites record the telemetry data sent back from the missile to the ground-control stations, such as the burn times of the various stages, the maneuverings of the bus, and the launching of the multiple independently targetable reentry vehicles (MIRVs), in order to obtain information about the size, throw-weight, and the number of MIRV warheads. Telemetry is the set of signals by which a missile, a stage of a missile, or a missile warhead, sends data back to earth about its performance during a test flight. These data relate to such features as structural stress, rocket motor thrust, fuel consumption, guidance system performance, and the physical condition of the environment. Some of the most advanced technical developments of telemetry are utilized in the space program. An unmanned orbiting vehicle is the site of measurements of surface temperatures and other variables necessary in the scientific investigation. In a manned vehicle, it monitors such signals as the astronaut's pulse rate, blood pressure, and respiration rate. *See also* ENCRYPTION; SATELLITE; VERIFICATION.

Significance   Telemetry aids in evaluating a weapon's performance and provides a way of verifying weapons tests undertaken by an adversary. Intercepted telemetry can provide intelligence on such questions as the number of warheads carried by a given missile, the range of the missile, its payload and throw-weight, and hence the probable size of its warheads and their accuracy. Encryption (coding) of telemetry is banned under the provisions of Strategic Arms Limitation Talks (SALT I). But the Soviets have, from time to time, scrambled or otherwise put into code their missile telemetry in order to inhibit remote eavesdropping by the United States. How can the United States be confident that the Soviet Union is abiding by SALT I if Moscow codes its telemetry? It can't. The United States has also used encryption to deprive foreign intelligence services of telemetric information about the testing of U.S. weapons. The superpowers listen to each other's telemetry regularly for purposes of espionage and for arms control.

Terrain Contour Matching (TERCOM)   A cruise missile terminal guidance system. The terrain contour guidance matching has accuracies several times better than those derived from the inertial guidance systems on land-based intercontinental ballistic missiles (ICBMs). The vehicle flies part of the time under control of its inertial guidance system, but at various points along its flight path reorients itself with respect to the ground. The on-board computer compares this actual ground reading with an altitude map stored in a computer memory. TERCOM compares the actual terrain under the missile with the predicted information in the missile's computer. TERCOM gives cruise missiles a 100 percent kill probability against military targets. Because it allows the cruise missile to skim so low over the ground, TERCOM can evade radar detection. When the system operates correctly, the results are spectacular. There have been reports of air-launched cruise missiles (ALCM) landing within 200 feet of the target over a 2,000-kilometer flight. *See also* MAGNETIC CONTOUR MATCHING (MAGCOM); NAVSTAR.

Significance   Terrain contour matching guidance requires accurate radar maps of selected portions of an opponent's territory. It promises an accuracy limited only by the ability of the on-board computer to process the altitude data. Before a new missile can be deployed with any degree of confidence, it must first be test-fired 10 or more times. Likewise, before a terrain contour matching system in a cruise missile can be judged satisfactory, it must be test-flown repeatedly. If TERCOM maps required active radar sounding, one could monitor this activity with high confidence. However, this is not the case, since terrain altitude data obtained from surveys can be transformed into synthetic TERCOM maps. TERCOM continually compares its map, which is programmed into each missile according to its target, with the path the flight is actually taking. The maps themselves, which include an estimated 100 million references—at a cost of about $1 billion for the entire cruise program—are produced by the U.S. Defense Mapping Agency.

Theater Nuclear Weapon (TNW)   A nuclear weapon deployed in particular regions, or "theaters of operation," such as Europe and the Pacific. Theater nuclear weapons do not have intercontinental range, and they can be launched from underground missile silos, bombers, naval vessels, and trucklike vehicles. The TNW is usually of longer range and larger yield than a tactical weapon (short-range battlefield nuclear weapon), which can be used in theater operations. They include bombs and depth charges on nonstrategic aircraft, cruise missiles (air-, sea-, and land-based), short-range ballistic missiles used in surface-to-surface and surface-to-air missiles, artillery projectiles, and nuclear land mines. The TNW includes U.S. F-111 strike fighters, Pershing II and cruise missiles and Soviet Backfire, Blinder, and Badger bombers and SS-20 and SS-4 missiles. These weapons represent a category that is intermediate between tactical and strategic weapons (long-range); their range lies between that of tactical and strategic weapons. *See also* INTERMEDIATE-RANGE NUCLEAR FORCES TREATY; NUCLEAR WEAPON; TACTICAL NUCLEAR WEAPON (TNW).

Significance   Theater nuclear weapons are designed to be used within a theater of war. For example, in Europe, the U.S. and North Atlantic Treaty Organization (NATO) strategy is based on the border of Soviet-controlled Eastern and Southern Europe, with large U.S. bases in Turkey and Germany; TNWs need only be short- to medium-range to penetrate the Soviet Union itself. The Soviets cannot threaten U.S. targets the same way, although an attack with theater weapons from Kamchatka could certainly penetrate Alaska. U.S. theater nuclear weapons were integrated into NATO defense plans for Western Europe as early as 1955, to compensate for inferior NATO manpower levels. The TNW modernization included increased long-range capability, mobility, and dispersal, and more precise guidance and targeting capabilities. The original idea of deploying 15,000 nuclear weapons in Europe was reduced to 7,000 under Secretary of Defense Robert S. McNamara. In 1979, the number of nuclear weapons was further cut by 1,000, and was reduced in 1984 by another 1,400. The Intermediate-range Nuclear Forces Treaty (1987) requires the United States to eliminate 436 intermediate- and medium-range nuclear weapons in Europe in exchange for the elimination of 1,565 Soviet nuclear weapons in Europe. Unless political and arms control developments intervene, TNWs are likely to continue to play their limited role in regional defense.

Thermal Radiation   Electromagnetic radiation released in a nuclear detonation. Thermal radiation is emitted from the fireball by a nuclear explosion, and can cause burns, blindness, and fires. A nuclear explosion will release a range of radiation isotopes from the products of its own fission. Various types of weapons and conditions produce different mixes of radiation—neutrons, gamma rays, X-rays, and alpha and beta particles. A neutron is a neutral particle with no electrical charge. Gamma rays are electromagnetic radiation (thermal radiation) of high photon energy, having no mass or charge. X-rays are also photons, and can be emitted in nuclear decays. An alpha particle consists of two photons and two neutrons. And a beta particle has mass and electronic charge equal to an electron. In addition to the powerful pulse of initial radiation, consisting mainly of neutron and gamma rays, there is still deadly danger persisting from residual radiation, even when all other effects of a nuclear explosion have ceased. *See also* IONIZING RADIATION; NUCLEAR RADIATION.

Significance   Thermal radiation is one of the most destructive effects of a nuclear explosion. The effects of radiation depend on the size of the weapon and the distance from where it is detonated. Those killed immediately are mainly either crushed or burned to death. Most of the survivors of Hiroshima and Nagasaki were still alive at the end of 1945 (the atomic bombs were dropped on these cities in early August of that year), and appeared to be reasonably healthy. But later a variety of illnesses—including eye diseases, blood disorders, malignant tumors, leukemia, and psychoneurological disturbances—began to appear. Because nuclear weapons have so many yields, sizes, and designs, the proportion of the energy given off as blast, heat, and radiation can differ very considerably, and the death, disability, and other casualty rates can vary also. The danger from radiation cannot be stressed too much. Nobody can see, hear, smell, taste, or feel radiation, and yet it can instantly deliver a lethal blow. When radiation fails to kill immediately, it can still leave its devastating mark on living cells.

Thermonuclear Weapon   The most destructive nuclear device that utilizes a fission-fusion process of hydrogen atoms to release tremendous explosive power. A thermonuclear weapon uses very high temperatures to cause the fusion of light atoms, releasing great amounts of energy. A thermonuclear bomb, also referred to as a fusion or hydrogen weapon, is usually defined as an atomic weapon. Only at 10 to 100 million degrees Kelvin (the interior of the sun is 14 million degrees Kelvin) are the rates sufficiently high to make a fusion bomb possible. A thermonuclear weapon is exploded in a two-step process: (1) an atom-splitting (fission) reaction generates very high temperatures, and (2) this heat triggers the combining of atoms (fusion). The required temperatures at the density of the fusion materials are achieved with a fission explosion. There is an optional third step to increase the destructive power of the weapon, the fission of the Tamper, the uranium shell that surrounds the core of the bomb. Thermonuclear weapons were developed by the superpowers in the early 1950s. *See also* FISSION; FUSION; HYDROGEN BOMB.

Significance   A thermonuclear weapon is the most destructive type of nuclear weapon. It derives its tremendous power primarily from the energy released in the forced combination (fusion) of small, light nuclei. The current strategic arsenals of the superpowers are made up mostly of thermonuclear weapons. The thermonuclear weapons are considered most dangerous, both for their enormous destructive power and also because of the lethal and long-lasting radioactivity they create upon explosion. The bombs used on Japan in World War II had the power equivalent to 12,000–15,000 tons (Hiroshima uranium bomb) and 20,000 tons (Nagasaki plutonium bomb) of TNT. A standard size of thermonuclear weapon—a one megaton bomb—is many times the size of the World War II bombs, and the largest U.S. warheads (20 megatons) are 1,000 times more powerful. In the 44 years since the first use of two small atomic bombs, the world has not yet experienced a thermonuclear war—although on several occasions humanity has been threatened with nuclear confrontation. Since men and machines are fallible, we live constantly under the threat of self-annihilation.

Threshold Test Ban Treaty (TTBT)   An agreement between the United States and the Soviet Union limiting underground nuclear weapons tests to a yield of 150 kilotons each. The Threshold Test Ban Treaty was signed in 1974 to reduce the amount of environmental damage caused by nuclear testing. It is the second arms control treaty between the superpowers involving nuclear testing. The first accord, the Limited Test Ban Treaty, was reached between the superpowers (along with Britain) in 1963, and prohibited nuclear testing in the atmosphere, in outer space, and under water. Agreement on the TTBT was reached during the Moscow Summit. Both nations agreed to: prohibit, prevent, and not conduct underground nuclear weapons tests having a yield exceeding 150 kilotons; limit the number of their underground nuclear weapons tests to a minimum; and continue negotiations toward solution to the problem by the cessation of all underground nuclear weapons tests. Assurance of compliance is by a National Technical Means of Verification, and a protocol to the treaty requires the signatories to exchange the following data for further verification of compliance: the geographic coordinates of the boundaries of each test site; the geology of the testing areas of the sites; the geographic coordinates of underground nuclear weapon tests after they have been conducted; and yield, date, time, depth, and coordinates for two nuclear weapons tests from each geographically distinct testing area where tests have been or are to be conducted. *See also* LIMITED TEST BAN TREATY (LTBT).

Significance   The Threshold Test Ban Treaty has not been ratified by the U. S. Senate, but both superpowers have agreed to abide by its terms. The unratified TTBT is a small step toward a nuclear weapons freeze; a comprehensive test ban (CTB) treaty would be a major move to block proliferation of nuclear weapons. A commitment by the superpowers to end nuclear weapons testing would bring the pressure of the community to bear against other nuclear nations to ban their own testing. Proponents of a CTB argue that a complete end to the superpowers' testing would contribute much to stopping nuclear proliferation in the world. Opponents focus on the problems of verifying a zero-based test ban because some nuclear explosions are not clearly detectable by the other side. The most basic of the undebated assumptions about the nuclear threshold is the public belief that the superpowers adhere to treaty provisions.

Throw-Weight   The maximum weight that can be carried by a missile over a particular range. Throw-weight includes the weight of the reentry vehicles, penetration aids, and their release devices. Ballistic missile throw-weight is the maximum useful weight that is placed on a trajectory, toward the target, by the central boost phase of the missile. Throw-weight is distinguished from payload, which is the weight of the explosive material contained in a nuclear warhead. The United States has miniaturized its bombs so that they use the available throw-weight more efficiently. The readiness rate of U.S. strategic missiles is about 98 percent, while the Soviet readiness rate is about 75 percent. The reliability of U.S. missiles is about 75 to 80 percent; Soviet missiles have about 65 to 75 percent. Recent improvements in U.S. missiles place them within a 0.12 nautical mile radius, while Soviet missiles have a circular error probability of about 0.5 nautical mile radius. *See also* INTERCONTINENTAL BALLISTIC MISSILE (ICBM); MULTIPLE INDEPENDENTLY TARGETABLE REENTRY VEHICLE (MIRV); STRATEGIC ARMS REDUCTION TALKS (START).

Significance   Throw-weight is one criterion for determining the strength of a nation's nuclear arsenal. The Soviet Union deploys heavier and larger missiles, which have a considerable throw-weight advantage over the United States. The United States has a smaller number of missiles, and these do not carry the large fraction of the total payload that the Soviet intercontinental ballistic missile (ICBM) force carries. The United States has high reliability, high accuracy, and high penetrability potential against the antiballistic missile (ABM) defenses through multiple independently targetable reentry vehicle (MIRV) warheads. Soviet missiles are believed to lack high accuracy. The quantitative parameter of actual throw-weight in tons (of both U.S. and Soviet ICBMs) has been a bone of contention between them during nuclear arms control negotiations. The Soviets are reluctant to accept throw-weight as a useful definition of relative strength, and thus are unwilling to limit their throw-weight. This has been one of the vexing problems facing the U.S. arms control negotiators in attempting to set a standard that would limit Soviet power.

Tomahawk Cruise Missile   A cruise missile deployed on ships, submarines, and aircraft. Tomahawk cruise missiles—initially deployed by the North Atlantic Treaty Organization (NATO) in Western Europe in the early 1980s—have two versions: a shorter-range, conventionally armed antishipping missile; and a longer-range, nuclear-armed missile aimed at land targets. Both versions use the same cylindrical airframe to permit launching from a torpedo tube. In the United States, all three military services are deploying cruises. Originally deployed by the navy as an antiship sea-launched cruise missile (SLCM), the Tomahawk has been modified so that it can be launched from the ground and the air. The ground-launched cruise missile (GLCM)—also a Tomahawk missile—is known popularly as the Cruise. The small size of the Cruise permits a variety of possible launching platforms, including an air-launched cruise missile (ALCM). The Tomahawk has a range of 2,500 kilometers, and carries one warhead with a yield of 10 to 50 kilotons in the GLCM, or 200 kilotons in the SLCM. *See also* AIR-LAUNCHED CRUISE MISSILE (ALCM); CRUISE MISSILE; GROUND-LAUNCHED CRUISE MISSILE (GLCM); SEA-LAUNCHED CRUISE MISSILE (SLCM).

Significance   Tomahawk cruise missiles are exceptionally accurate, capable of striking the exact location of target. Because of their extraordinary capabilities, and because they are different in kind from bombers, ICBMs, or SLBMs, cruise missiles are sometimes considered a "fourth leg" of the U.S. strategic triad (which includes intercontinental ballistic missiles, submarine-launched ballistic missiles, and strategic bombers). The nuclear-armed Tomahawk is conceived as a theater nuclear weapon intended for use against targets outside the Soviet Union, such as in Eastern Europe. It does not require the launching ships to be available continuously in order to deliver nuclear strikes. However, it is not currently envisioned as playing a strategic nuclear role, except insofar as it would constitute an ultimate strategic reserve. The only strategic nuclear application for the Tomahawk at the present is the possibility of developing an air-launched version—Tomahawk air-launched cruise missile, or TALCM. The Tomahawk cruise missile represents a major increase in nuclear capabilities within tactical naval forces. Although designated as a part of the "strategic reserve force," it is also designed as an antiship and land-attack weapon. One of the features that makes it a dangerous attack weapon is its ability to penetrate at low altitude beneath enemy radars.

Treaty of Rarotonga   An agreement to establish a nuclear-free zone in the South Pacific. The Treaty of Rarotonga is the world's second agreement to provide for the military denuclearization of a populated area; the first was the Treaty of Tlatelolco, authorizing a Latin American nuclear-free zone. In 1985, the 13 members of the South Pacific Forum—Australia, the Cook Islands, Fiji, Kiribati, Nauru, New Zealand, Niue, Papua New Guinea, the Solomon Islands, Tonga, Tuvalu, Vanuatu, and Western Samoa—concluded the Treaty of Rarotonga. It prohibits the manufacture, testing, and stockpiling of nuclear arms in the region. The treaty also embodied a clause that guaranteed the passage of nuclear-armed or nuclear-powered vessels; each signatory was left to decide whether it would allow such passage in its territorial waters. The agreement has three protocols that would restrict nuclear weapons states from nuclear activities in the zone. *See also* NONPROLIFERATION TREATY (NPT); NUCLEAR FREE-ZONE (NFZ); TREATY OF TLATELOLCO.

Significance   The Treaty of Rarotonga covers a vast region in which none of the signatories have their own nuclear weapons, or, as in the North Atlantic Treaty Organization (NATO) and the Warsaw Pact, have accepted them under the controls of nuclear weapons states. The various protocols to the treaty met with complicated responses from the nuclear weapons states. A protocol banning testing was directed at France, and it was unacceptable to her; another protocol permitting ships from nuclear weapons states to carry nuclear weapons in the South Pacific was initially unacceptable to the Soviet Union. However, Moscow subsequently ratified the Treaty of Rarotonga. China has also expressed support for the South Pacific nuclear-free zone. The United States has so far refused to ratify any of the treaty's protocols. The United States has refused to sign the treaty on the ground that proliferation of nuclear-free zones may weaken U.S. deterrence policy. The conclusion of the Treaty of Rarotonga (the capital of the Cook Islands) coincided with the collapse of the ANZUS military pact between Australia, New Zealand, and the United States after New Zealand barred U.S. ships carrying nuclear weapons from entering its ports. Like the Treaty of Tlatelolco, the Treaty of Rarotonga has a mechanism for on-site inspections. Presumably, findings of violations could be taken to the United Nations, as in the Tlatelolco case. The Treaty of Rarotonga remains in effect indefinitely.

Treaty of Tlatelolco   Establishes all of Latin America and the Caribbean as a nuclear-free zone. The Treaty of Tlatelolco bans nuclear weapons in an area spanning more than 7.5 million square miles of Latin America. Signed in Mexico City in 1967, the treaty is a mainstay of the international nonproliferation regime in Latin America and the Caribbean. The Treaty of Tlatelolco, the first such agreement to provide a nuclear-free zone in a populated region, is now in force for 22 Latin American and Caribbean countries. Cuba is not a party to the treaty. Argentina has signed the treaty, but has not ratified it; Brazil and Chile have ratified it, but the treaty is not in force for them due to reservations attached to their ratification. The treaty has two protocols. Protocol I applies to nations outside the treaty zone who have possessions within it. The United States ratified the protocol in 1981, promising to abide by the treaty in the Panama Canal Zone, Guantanamo Bay Naval Base, Puerto Rico, and the U.S. Virgin Islands. The Protocol also applies to Britain and the Netherlands. Protocol II applies to nuclear weapons states; they undertake not to use or threaten to use nuclear weapons against parties to the Treaty of Tlatelolco. *See also* NONPROLIFERATION TREATY (NPT); NUCLEAR-FREE ZONE (NFZ); TREATY OF RAROTONGA.

Significance   The Treaty of Tlatelolco laid the foundation for the world's first nuclear-free zone. This contains the most extensive nuclear weapons restrictions adopted to date. The treaty not only makes Latin America and the Caribbean a nuclear-free zone but also (in a protocol signed by all the nuclear weapons states) establishes the principles of (1) nonintrusion by nuclear weapons states in the area and (2) no first use of nuclear weapons by nuclear weapons states signatories to the Treaty of Tlatelolco against any members of the treaty. The United States fully supports the goals and objectives of this treaty. It is the only post-World War II arms control agreement in force to which all five major nuclear weapons states are parties. Whether the treaty will succeed in keeping Latin America and the Caribbean free of nuclear weapons permanently is open to question. Because of his contribution to this United Nations disarmament negotiation, Mexico's Alfonso Garcia Robles was awarded the Nobel Peace Prize in 1982, along with Alva Myrdal of Sweden.

Triad   The U.S. strategic force, composed of three units: land-based intercontinental ballistic missiles (ICBMs), submarine-launched ballistic missiles (SLBMs), and strategic bombers. Triad evolved from an allocation of national resources and priorities in order to meet certain strategic objectives, primarily to deter nuclear conflict. When the Soviet Union proceeded to develop its ICBMs as the primary means of delivery, concern over the vulnerability of the U.S. bomber force arose. The result of this development, and the uncertainty of the ability of U.S. bombers to penetrate Soviet air defenses, was the decision to create a multiforce triad. Since the early 1960s, the United States has developed a nuclear arsenal based on specific components on the ground, in the water, and in the air. At the time of the Cuban missile crisis in 1962, all three components of triad were in place. Under the triad concept, each of the three units should be able to impose unacceptable damage upon the Soviet Union. The defense planners recognize that each element in the triad has particular advantages and disadvantages. The bomber force is slow, and vulnerable on the ground. With land-based missiles, the main disadvantage is that their positions are fixed—everyone knows their location. ICBMs are most accurate. SLBMs are virtually undetectable, and therefore the most survivable; their disadvantage is that they are less accurate, and more difficult to command and control. *See also* INTERCONTINENTAL BALLISTIC MISSILE (ICBM); SUBMARINE-LAUNCHED BALLISTIC MISSILE (SLBM); STRATEGIC BOMBER.

Significance   Triad is the basic structure of the U.S. strategic deterrent forces, which relies upon somewhat varied means of survival; hence it decreases an enemy's potential for a successful first strike. Diversity of forces is useful. But is there something magical about the U.S. triad? Probably not, but it has become part of the bedrock of U.S. defense policy. The continuing need for all three components has been challenged by defense critics. Such interservice rivalry has become acute, and as underground silos have become more vulnerable to acute missile strikes, such criticism has increased. Still, preserving the triad has remained a part of official U.S. defense planning. By maintaining an effective triad, the United States compels the Soviet Union to disperse its military resource against three components, as opposed to concentrating on the defeat of only one or two. The three components complement each other, and the strength is believed to be in this mix. Bombers can quickly respond to any warning and still be recalled; land-based missiles can strike precisely; and submarines will survive to retaliate.

Trinity Test   The first test atomic bomb explosion carried out in the desert near Alamogordo, New Mexico. Code-named "Trinity Test," it was conducted on July 16, 1945, to test the design of the bomb to make sure that it would work. The Manhattan Project—which produced the bomb—was headed by General Leslie Groves; many scientists, including J. Robert Oppenheimer, Enrico Fermi, and Niels Bohr, were associated with the project. The project cost $2 billion, and drew upon the work of specially built laboratories all over the United States. For this first explosion every available gram of plutonium was collected from the Los Alamos laboratory. The Trinity atomic explosive device, called the Gadget, had a plutonium core weighing about 13.5 pounds (6.1 kilograms), which was imploded by some 5,000 pounds of high explosive. The test was conducted at the Trinity site's 100-foot tower at 5:30 A.M. "Fat Man," the bomb dropped on Nagasaki on August 9, 1945, was based on the same design as the Gadget. *See also* ATOMIC WEAPON; FAT MAN; MANHATTAN PROJECT.

Significance   The Trinity test was the result of intensive efforts of the Manhattan Project. That massive operation was created under President Franklin D. Roosevelt, and successfully completed its work during the Truman administration. The design assembled for the first test shows neither its complexity nor its awesome power. The sight of the Trinity test reminded Oppenheimer, "the father of the atomic bomb," of Shiva, the Hindu god of destruction. "I have become death, the destroyer of worlds," Oppenheimer quoted from the Bhagavad Gita (Hindu Scripture) as he witnessed the explosion. At that instant the United States initiated the atomic age. It ushered in the possibility, and the ultimate reality, of the manufacture of explosives of unprecedented mass destruction—threatening the very survival of humankind. For the first decade of the atomic age the United States monopolized the ability to fight a nuclear war. The United States ended World War II by using its first two atomic weapons against Japan, dropping them on Hiroshima and Nagasaki.

Tritium   A highly perishable radioactive gaseous form of hydrogen used in the manufacture of most U.S. nuclear weapons. Tritium has an atomic number of 1, an atomic weight of 3, and a nucleus containing a proton and two neutrons. It is mildly radioactive, with a half-life of 12.3 years. Tritium can be produced artificially via lithium transformation (by neutron bombardment) in pressurized nuclear reactors, or in the fusion fuel capsules of thermonuclear weapons. There are only three tritium production reactors (at Savannah River, near Aiken, South Carolina) which meet U.S. requirements for nuclear weapons. The amount of tritium needed to keep the U.S. stockpile of weapons operational is classified. The Savannah reactors are more than 30 years old, and have developed dangerous safety hazards resulting in the closure of all production plants in August 1988. Secretary of Energy John S. Herrington proposed in 1988 construction of two tritium production reactors, at a cost of $6.8 billion, to replace the aging Savannah plant. *See also* PLUTONIUM WEAPON; URANIUM.

Significance   Tritium is used to boost the explosive power of thermo-nuclear warheads. Unlike plutonium, a nuclear bomb's other main fuel, which is not in short supply, tritium decays at a rapid rate, by 5.5 percent a year. In so doing it turns into helium, which is useless in weapons production. The speedy decay means that supplies of new tritium must be readily available. The amount of tritium that the United States has on hand is classified. The long delay in restarting the reactors, and possibly the cost, is a test of how the Bush adminis-tration plans to address the environmental and safety concerns at the nation's nuclear weapons plants. In the meantime, a political battle has been brewing over how best to construct nuclear processing plants to supply the tritium the United States needs for national defense.

U

Underground Nuclear Tests   Nuclear weapons experiments below the ground. Nuclear tests are conducted underground to protect the atmosphere from radioactive material, even though such experiments cause some above-ground radioactivity. In 1963, the superpowers concluded the Limited Test Ban Treaty, which prohibits above-ground nuclear testing. They have also agreed to halt nuclear tests under water and in outer space. In 1974 and 1976 the superpowers also agreed to treaties limiting the size of underground nuclear explosions. While negotiating the Threshold Test Ban Treaty (TTBT) in 1974, the United States and the Soviet Union recognized the need to establish a parallel agreement to govern underground nuclear explosions for "peaceful purposes." The negotiation resulted in the Treaty of Underground Nuclear Explosions for Peaceful Purposes (PNE treaty). Signed in 1976, the signatories agreed not to carry out at any place under their jurisdiction or control: (a) an individual explosion having a yield exceeding 150 kilotons; (b) a group explosion having an aggregate yield exceeding one and one-half megatons; (c) a group explosion having an aggregate yield exceeding 150 kilotons, unless the individual explosions in the group could be identified and measured by agreed verification procedures; and (d) an explosion that does not carry out a peaceful application. The PNE treaty was signed by the United States, but has not been ratified by the Senate. *See also* LIMITED TEST BAN TREATY (LTBT); THRESHOLD TEST BAN TREATY (TTBT).

Significance   An underground nuclear test occurs initially during the research and engineering phase of nuclear weapons development. The test must be conducted in suitable environments, that is, where the geologic structure is exceedingly stable—as in Nevada. Restraint on nuclear testing has long been considered an essential step toward controlling nuclear arms competition. Since the 1950s, successive U.S. governments have sought verifiable limitations on nuclear testing that would contribute to arms control while providing the means to maintain an adequate deterrent. These efforts have been pursued through a variety of channels, including the United Nations and tripartite negotiations involving the United States, the Soviet Union, and the United Kingdom. Agreement on more comprehensive limits has been inhibited by concerns about the proper relationship of a nuclear test ban to other arms control issues, and the overall East-West military balance. There is also disagreement over how best to guarantee compliance with specific testing limitations and prohibitions. During the early 1980s, the Soviets unilaterally stopped all testing for a long period, but failure of the United States to follow this lead led to a resumption of Soviet testing in the late 1980s.

United Nations Disarmament Commission (UNDC)   A United Nations arena for discussing and debating disarmament issues. The U.N. Disarmament Commission includes every member of the United Nations. Since its establishment in 1952, the UNDC has been meeting at U.N. headquarters in New York, usually in May and June of each year. The commission operates under its own rules and procedures, and reports to the United Nations General Assembly. The UNDC is convened in full session on rare occasions; it has been called into plenary session on two occasions—in 1960 and 1965. The purpose of these sessions was to create momentum to the disarmament movement, and to provide occasions for expression of world concerns over the arms race, the threat of nuclear war, and for achieving general and complete disarmament. From 1965 to 1978 the commission remained dormant, but was revived following the U.N. Special Session on Disarmament. Reconstituted at the initiative of the nonaligned nations, this special session of the General Assembly charged the Disarmament Commission with giving consideration to "the elements of a comprehensive programme for disarmament." The Second Special Session on Disarmament (SSOD II) was convened in 1982. *See also* DISARMAMENT; NUCLEAR DISARMAMENT; UNITED STATES ARMS CONTROL AND DISARMAMENT AGENCY (USACDA).

Significance   The United Nations Disarmament Commission is a deliberative (rather than negotiating) body, formed to give Third World nations an opportunity to deal with issues of disarmament. It functions primarily as a forum for world opinion, in order to influence the policies of the five major powers armed with nuclear weapons: China, France, the Soviet Union, the United Kingdom, and the United States. The fact remains that meaningful progress toward the goals of reducing nuclear arsenals and negotiating in good faith for general and complete disarmament has been slow and inadequate. Prime responsibilities fall on the nuclear weapons states to undertake specific disarmament measures and to reduce their reliance on nuclear deterrence—if they are to discourage horizontal proliferation. A great deal also depends on the half-dozen or so threshold states yet unwilling to commit themselves, by treaty, to a renunciation of the nuclear option in the absence of tangible progress by the nuclear powers to reduce their own nuclear stockpiles. Critics of the United Nations can point to many shortcomings in the achievements of the UNDC. But it has accomplished much that remains unpublicized. Like the United Nations itself, it has been serving as a forum for the ideas and concerns of the interested parties. The two U.N. special sessions on disarmament spoke on behalf of humankind as a whole.

United States Arms Control and Disarmament Agency (USACDA)
The major agency charged with responsibility for formulating and implementing the arms control and disarmament policies of the United States. The U.S. Arms Control and Disarmament Agency conducts long-range research on arms control methods and prepares position papers for consideration by the National Security Council (NSC). The agency, nicknamed "The Peace Agency," was established in 1961, in response to congressional feeling that U.S. arms control and disarmament policy could best be formulated and performed in a manner promoting the national security by a central organization given primary responsibility for arms control and disarmament. USACDA (also known as ACDA) conducts research and provides advice relating to arms control, and manages U.S. participation in international arms control and disarmament negotiations. The ACDA provides for a General Advisory Committee, not to exceed 15 members, to advise the president and secretary of state. The agency participates in discussions and negotiations with the Soviet Union and other countries on such issues as strategic arms control limitations, mutual force reductions in Europe, and prohibition of chemical weapons. *See also* DISARMAMENT; NATIONAL SECURITY COUNCIL (NSC); NUCLEAR DISARMAMENT; UNITED NATIONS DISARMAMENT COMMISSION (UNDC).

Significance   The United States Arms Control and Disarmament Agency is staffed by arms control and foreign policy experts and physicists. The director of the ACDA is, by law, the president's principal adviser on arms control and disarmament; in practice, he has not always served in that capacity. The director does not have the freedom to advocate policies independently of the secretary of state; although the agency is not technically under the direction of the secretary, he nevertheless has primary responsibilities within the government on arms control and disarmament matters. USACDA is considered a presidential agency—one that is oriented toward presidential control, and does not directly affect congressional constituencies. ACDA is concerned with preventing the spread of nuclear weapons to nations not now possessing them, and with monitoring arms control negotiations abroad. By placing an active role in negotiations and ratification of the Outer Space Treaty (1967), Nonproliferation Treaty (1968), Sea-Bed Treaty (1971), Intermediate-range Nuclear Forces (INF) Treaty (1987), USACDA has endeavored to achieve a greater measure of arms control, one that leads to eventual disarmament.

Uranium   A heavy silvery white metallic element that is used as a basic raw material for nuclear weapons. Two isotopes, uranium 235 and uranium 238, are used in power generation and in nuclear weapons. Discovered in 1789 and first obtained in pure form in 1841, uranium proved essential to the development of nuclear physics. Uranium exists in nature in two varieties: U-235 and U-238. Almost all (99.3 percent) naturally occurring uranium is U-238, which cannot sustain a nuclear reactor. The percentage (.7 percent) of U-235, which can fuel a nuclear reaction, must be increased; this process is called enrichment. It is through this process that uranium is enriched to weapons-grade level. The bomb dropped on Hiroshima in 1945 contained 60 kilograms of highly enriched uranium. It is never found in its elemental state, but rather is always combined with other elements in about 150 known minerals. It must be extracted from those containing less than 0.1 percent uranium. The largest quantities of uranium ore are mined from the Blind River area of Canada. Other considerable uranium deposits have been found in South Africa, Australia, France, and the United States. Relatively minor amounts of uranium are found in the basaltic rocks, which form the floors of oceans. *See also* ATOMIC WEAPON; ENRICHED NUCLEAR FUEL; PLUTONIUM WEAPON.

Significance   Although uranium is usually regarded as one of the rarer elements, it is actually present in considerable amount in the earth's crust. The bulk of U.S. uranium is obtained by either open-pit or underground mining. The open-pit uranium-producing states are Wyoming, New Mexico, and Texas, and underground mining is carried out mainly in New Mexico, Colorado, and Utah. To establish an open-pit mine, the topsoil must be stripped away and the ground water table lowered, a process that can devastate the local environment. The effects of mining uranium, whether open-pit or underground, do not differ qualitatively from those resulting from the extraction of other minerals. What is unique to the uranium industry is the radioactive nature of the materials involved. Uranium ores contain radium, which decays into radon gas. The greatest biological hazard in working with uranium is the possibility of developing lung cancer. Uranium has few uses outside of nuclear technology. It is used in nuclear technology because it fissions (splits into two smaller nuclei of approximately equal size) and is radioactive. For these reasons it is used to make atomic weapons, to fuel nuclear reactors, and to produce radioactive isotopes for medical and industrial purposes.

V

Verification   The process of determining, to the extent necessary to safeguard national security, that the other side is complying with an agreement. Verification entails three distinct purposes: (1) it serves to detect violations of an agreement, and hence to furnish timely warning of any threat to a nation's security; (2) by increasing the risk of detection and complicating any scheme of evasion, it helps to deter evasion; (3) it serves to build internal and external confidence in the viability of an arms control agreement. The terms defining verification in existing arms control treaties vary from practically no provision, as in the case of the Sea-Bed Treaty (1971), to the generous verification provisions in the Antarctic Treaty (1959). Emphasis has recently been placed on verification by National Technical Means (NTM is a technical network that includes satellites, radar, and seismic stations). On-site inspections are examples of cooperative means of verification of arms control agreements. Verification for nuclear arms control treaties is carried out by the spy satellites of each superpower. *See also* NATIONAL TECHNICAL MEANS OF VERIFICATION (NTM).

Significance   Verification of arms limitation agreements must be adequate to ensure that any evasion of the limits cannot drastically affect the balance. After a treaty has been negotiated, signed, and ratified, verification must determine, on a regular basis, the extent to which provisions are being met. There is a two-step verification process. First, before the conclusion of an arms control treaty, involved parties must forecast whether the adversaries could evade detection. Second, after the signing of the agreement, verification must determine the extent to which terms are being complied with. Verification matters more to the United States than to the Soviet Union, for the simple reason that the former releases a greater quantity of defense information into the public record. By contrast, the Soviet Union is a closed society, and has been unwilling to share its military secrets. The

United States emphasizes that an arms control agreement with the Soviet Union must be verifiable. Underlying this policy is mistrust of the Soviets. Efforts to negotiate arms control and disarmament agreements have always faced the problem of how each side can verify—to its own satisfaction—the capabilities of the other side. This means that in the final analysis, the task of verifying compliance with the specific agreement is not merely a technical problem; it is, in a very real sense, a political problem. If any major power is politically unwilling to accept the level of intrusion that effective on-site inspection presupposes, then it can dilute a treaty's effectiveness by interposing political obstacles.

Vertical Proliferation   The upward spread of nuclear weapons. Vertical proliferation is distinct from horizontal proliferation, which refers to the expansion of nuclear weapons to nonnuclear nations. Vertical proliferation is seen as the expansion of existing nuclear weapons or the development of new arsenals. In 1945, only the United States owned two nuclear bombs, and those were dropped on Japan. Today, at least six nations—the United States, the Soviet Union, United Kingdom, France, China, and India—possess nuclear weapons. This proliferation did not begin immediately following the end of World War II, the first (and so far the last) war in which nuclear weapons were used. In 1947 the United States had an arsenal of 13 atomic bombs. The great proliferation in the United States began in 1949 when the Soviet Union exploded its first nuclear weapon. The destructive power of the U.S. nuclear arsenal increased dramatically when it developed the first thermonuclear or hydrogen bomb in 1952. Because nuclear weapons offer a cheap substitute for conventional defense, the vertical proliferation of the former was attractive to President Dwight D. Eisenhower. This policy of proliferation still continues, and the United States has 30,000 nuclear weapons today, while the Soviet Union arsenal consists of 20,000 weapons. To this superpower proliferation, one may add several hundreds of nuclear weapons in the arsenals of the United Kingdom, France, China, and India. *See also* HORIZONTAL PROLIFERATION; NUCLEAR PROLIFERATION.

Significance   Vertical proliferation of nuclear armories of the superpowers continues unabated. About 98 percent of the world's nuclear weapons are in the arsenals of the superpowers. With the increase in the number of nuclear weapons, many delivery systems and warheads have been added to them. The delivery systems are vehicles such as missiles and bombers. They also include silos that house the missiles and the radar that guides the missile to its target. Nuclear warheads are cruise missiles, artillery shells, ballistic missiles, and bombs carried by aircraft. A reentry vehicle is a warhead that is designed to reenter the atmosphere from space. Why do the super and major powers stock such a huge arsenal? As well as serving the needs of self-interest and national defense in the minds of state leaders, nuclear weapons are bureaucratically and politically attractive. They give nuclear nations super or major power status in the world. On the political level, persuading all nations to sign the nuclear nonproliferation treaty has not succeeded—France, China, India, and more than a half-dozen nonnuclear nations refused to accede to the agreement.

W

War   An armed clash between nations or between factions in the same nation; a state of hostility or military conflict undertaken by means of armed force. War, in a legal sense, exists when one, two, or more states officially declare that a state of open hostilities exists between them. Hostilities may range from war utilizing nuclear, bacteriological, chemical, and radiological weapons of mass destruction, to a small and more limited war confined to the use of conventional land, sea, and air forces. The causes of war are many and complex. They may include political, economic, territorial, ideological, religious, linguistic, chauvinistic, irredentist, and personal factors. Most of the 1,500 wars in the last 6,000 years have been fought on one or more of these grounds; the United States has been involved in more than 200 military actions abroad, but no wars have been fought in the United States since the U.S. Civil War (1861–1865). Accidents of history, geography, and the nature of U.S. political and economic systems—all contribute to the low level of domestic warfare in the United States. *See also* ACCIDENTAL NUCLEAR WAR; NUCLEAR WAR.

Significance   A war is *not* taken to be the absence of peace, but peace is considered as absence of war. The asymmetry lies in what we do about war and peace: we try to eliminate war rather than produce peace. As war is not the obverse of peace, removing war is not a guarantee that peace will follow. Where humankind stands in regard to the range of moral, political, economic, and strategic dilemmas forced upon it by the development of nuclear weapons may be determined by each nuclear nation and the nuclear threshold states. Different nations may resolve such dilemmas in different ways. But if the solutions are to have any effect, they must address the critical problems of the nuclear age; these cannot be ignored simply because wars appear nonexistent between the superpowers. Although wars have made major contributions toward the development and integration of civilizations, they have also been responsible for their eventual disintegration and destruction. Even though a third world war, and the suspected consequent use of nuclear weapons, has been avoided, the mere feeling of "living with nuclear weapons," and the constant thought that such a devastating arsenal of weapons can be unleashed at any moment by the decision of one or two persons, is frightening. World War III carries the threat of annihilation for our entire civilization.

War Powers Act   A new policy that limits the authority of the president to wage and conduct war. The War Powers Act also gives Congress the right to participate, with the president, in making decisions to use armed forces abroad. War powers are expressly granted by the Constitution, implied in it, or inherent in the duty of the president to protect the country. Although the Constitution expressly vests in Congress the power to declare war, only five of the eleven major wars fought by the United States were officially declared by Congress. Yet, in each of these five wars—the War of 1812, the Mexican War, the Spanish-American War, World War I, and World War II—Congress declared them only in response to the president's request. The first and second war powers acts were passed in 1941 and 1945 respectively giving the president additional power to deal with war situations. The third war powers act, passed in 1973, limited the president's authority by imposing a duty on him: in the absence of a declaration of war by Congress, the president must report to Congress within 48 hours after U.S. armed forces have been committed into conflict. The War Powers Act of 1973 gave the president the authority to conduct a war—conventional or nuclear—for 60 days without congressional approval. Within this period, Congress can take action to terminate use of U.S. forces. The president is required, however, to submit a report to Congress, explaining his action within 48 hours of dispatching U.S. troops into combat. *See also* COMMANDER IN CHIEF; JOINT CHIEFS OF STAFF (JCS); PRESIDENT; SECRETARY OF DEFENSE.

Significance   The War Powers Act has not really been tested in a situation in which the president deployed U.S. forces on a large scale and for a long period of time. It remains to be seen whether Congress will refuse to approve a president's use of the military and authorize such use beyond 60 days. Under the Constitution, Congress has the power to declare war, but, as commander in chief, the president has the primary responsibility for the defense of the nation. Recognition of the facts of modern warfare, and the existence of nuclear weapons that could strike targets in the United States within minutes, the decision to wage a war or launch nuclear weapons must reside with one person—the president. In vetoing the act, President Richard M. Nixon asserted that the act was blatantly unconstitutional; Congress overrode the veto. But presidents since 1973 have refused to comply with some provisions of the War Powers Act, holding it to be unconstitutional.

Warhead The part of a missile, bomb, projectile, torpedo, rocket, or other munition that contains either the nuclear, thermonuclear, conventional, chemical, or biological materials intended to inflict damage. Warheads can be delivered to their targets by means of shells, bombs, or missiles. They can be fired from silos, aircraft, submarines, and even huge guns. Figures on the U.S. stockpile of nuclear warheads of all sorts stand at about 30,000. As with delivery systems, warheads themselves are constantly being replaced and modernized. Four types of nuclear weapons have been withdrawn from the U.S. arsenal: atomic land mines, Nike-Hercules SAMs, B53 strategic freefall bombs, and Titan II 9-megaton warheads. Ten more types are being replaced, including artillery shells. Many new warheads have been produced, such as the W 78 Minuteman III warhead, the W 80 cruise missile series, and the W 70 MOD 3 ER (enhanced radiation) warhead for Lance missiles. More are planned for production. The total number of warheads could grow to 32,000 or more in the 1990s. Nuclear warheads are produced in multiple stages—beginning in laboratories in New Mexico and California, and ending at the Pantex assembly plant in Texas. *See also* MANEUVERABLE REENTRY VEHICLE (MARV); MULTIPLE INDEPENDENTLY TARGETABLE REENTRY VEHICLE (MIRV); MULTIPLE REENTRY VEHICLE (MRV); NUCLEAR WEAPON.

Significance Many types of warheads are being produced to enhance the effectiveness of U.S. nuclear capability. For example, the B 83 modern strategic bomb is a major new nuclear weapon; it is capable of destroying a hardened Soviet ICBM (intercontinental ballistic missile) silo. Separate warheads are delivered by separate reentry vehicles. Systems with more than one warhead refer to the multiple reentry vehicle (MRV), multiple independently targetable reentry vehicle (MIRV), and maneuverable reentry vehicle (MARV). The MRV was developed to penetrate ABM (antiballistic missile) defenses. The MIRV system gives a single missile the ability to strike several independent targets, several hundred kilometers apart. The MARV adds maneuverability to each separate reentry vehicle. The U.S. advantage in strategic bombers provides for rough equality between the superpowers in total numbers of strategic nuclear delivery vehicles. Because of its more advanced MIRV, the United States still holds a lead in the number of ballistic missile warheads. On the whole, the Soviet Union equals or surpasses the United States in most quantitative but not qualitative measures of nuclear capability.

Warsaw Pact   A mutual assistance treaty between the Eastern European communist nations, including the Soviet Union. The Warsaw Pact, signed in 1955, served as the basis for the establishment of the Warsaw Treaty Organization (WTO) as a military-political structure to counter the North Atlantic Treaty Organization (NATO). The pact was formed as a formal response to the rearmament and entrance of West Germany as a full member of NATO. The text of the Warsaw Pact nearly duplicates the wording of many of the clauses of NATO. The Warsaw Pact commits the Soviet Union, Albania, Poland, Hungary, East Germany, Czechoslovakia, Bulgaria, and Romania to the joint defense of their European territories. It establishes a unified military command for the armed forces of the member nations, with headquarters in Moscow. The Pact commits each signatory to give immediate aid, by all means considered necessary, including the use of armed forces, to any member attacked. The Soviets have also signed bilateral status-of-force agreements with East Germany, Poland, Hungary, and Czechoslovakia that provide for the stationing of Soviet troops in these countries. There are a series of high-level military and political consultative bodies associated with the Warsaw Pact; all are thoroughly dominated by the Soviet Union. *See also* NORTH ATLANTIC TREATY ORGANIZATION (NATO); SUPREME ALLIED COMMANDER EUROPE (SACEUR).

Significance   The creation of the Warsaw Pact seemed designed for a larger purpose than merely to offset any gains NATO had made in balancing Soviet military power in Central Europe. It has a massive numerical superiority in weapons. As of 1988 the figures for individual arms systems for the Warsaw Pact nations with comparable figures for NATO (in parentheses) indicate the disparity: main battle tanks, 51,500 (16,424); infantry fighting vehicles, 22,400 (4,153); other armored vehicles, 71,000 (35,351); artillery, 43,400 (13,857); antitank weapons, 44,200 (18,240); air defense systems, 24,400 (10,109); helicopters, 3,700 (2,419); combat aircraft, 8,250 (3,977); and personnel, 3 million (2.2 million). In the military organization of the Warsaw Pact, all key positions are held by the Soviet Union, which is the only country among its allies to possess nuclear weapons. Nor have the Soviets supplied any nuclear warheads to their Eastern European allies. Deployment in the 1980s of new Soviet nuclear systems in Eastern Europe in the wake of NATO's decision to deploy Pershing II missiles and ground-launched cruise missiles (GLCMs) appeared to have re-kindled resentment among non-Soviet Warsaw Pact states over their lack of input on nuclear issues. Support for the intermediate-range Nuclear Forces (INF) Treaty, which will eliminate such weapons over a period of years, appears to be general among Warsaw Pact members. Basically, the Warsaw Pact created a political and military structure to maintain Soviet hegemony in Europe.

Weapons-Grade Nuclear Fuel   Refined uranium that can fuel nuclear weapons. Weapons-grade nuclear fuel can be used in nuclear weapons, nuclear energy, and research reactors. Uranium exists in nature in two forms: uranium 238 (U-238) and uranium 235 (U-235). More than 99 percent of the natural element consists of U-238, which has 146 neutrons in the nucleus together with 92 protons. Nearly all remaining natural uranium consists of isotope 235, which has only 143 neutrons in each nucleus. To make a weapon from uranium, the unstable isotope of uranium, having a total of 235 protons and neutrons in its nucleus (U-235) is used. The process is known as enrichment. Uranium enriched to about 90 percent is considered weapons-grade nuclear fuel. Enriched uranium can also be used as a fuel in nuclear power or research reactors. Uranium enrichment plants have been built in many countries, including the nuclear nations. The three United States plants are in Oak Ridge, Tennessee; Portsmouth, Ohio; and Paducah, Kentucky. They are owned by the Department of Energy but operated by private industry under U.S. government contracts. There are tremendous problems facing U.S. policymakers in the projected $100 billion or more cleanup and revitalization costs of processing plants. *See also* ENRICHED NUCLEAR FUEL; URANIUM.

Significance   Weapons-grade nuclear fuel is produced by an extremely complex process, and requires considerable investment. That is why the uranium enrichment route has been generally considered a less likely path to nuclear proliferation than the plutonium option (all nuclear reactors produce plutonium as a by-product). Nations wishing to obtain enriched uranium need to do the following: (1) discover their own uranium deposits or obtain it from outside the country; (2) establish a uranium mill for processing uranium ore containing less than one percent uranium into uranium oxide concentrate, or yellow-cake; (3) develop a conversion plant for purifying yellowcake and convert it into uranium hexafluoride, the material processed in the enrichment plant; (4) build an enrichment plant for enriching the uranium hexafluoride gas in the isotope U-235; and (5) demonstrate a capability for converting the enriched uranium hexafluoride gas into solid uranium oxide or metal. Leonard Spector chronicles the potentiality of development of weapons-grade enriched uranium by such nations as South Africa, Argentina, Pakistan, Israel, and Brazil.[25] India already has the capability, as evidenced by her test of a "nuclear device" in 1974; many developed nations have the capability to produce enriched uranium. This chain of events indicates that nuclear proliferation is about to enter a new and dangerous phase.

Window of Vulnerability   A phenomenon of perceived weakness when each side's nuclear arsenals are increasingly at the mercy of the other. The window of vulnerability is a destabilizing concept that either superpower might start a nuclear war. General Edward Rowney used the term at the Strategic Arms Limitation Talks (SALT II). In the SALT II treaty the Soviet Union emerged with an approximate 5:2 advantage in intercontinental ballistic missile (ICBM) and in ballistic missile throw-weight. To General Rowney this meant an unacceptable strategic imbalance and potential U.S. vulnerability. In the 1980 U.S. presidential elections, the Reagan campaign committee appointed Rowney as a foreign policy adviser, and candidate Ronald Reagan used the term "window of vulnerability" in his campaign against Jimmy Carter. The implication of the window of vulnerability was that the Soviets could strike at the United States with their greater number of ICBMs. However, the presidential Commission on Strategic Forces, headed by Brent Scowcroft, dismissed the concept in 1983. *See also* INTERCONTINENTAL BALLISTIC MISSILE (ICBM); SCOWCROFT COMMISSION; THROW-WEIGHT.

Significance   To some extent, the "window of vulnerability" is a matter of perception rather than fact. Many people would probably agree that mutual fear of one another's military capability is the driving force behind the arms race. Thus the fact of even a theoretical vulnerability logically raises the question of what to do. Some alternatives have been discussed: (1) reach agreement to dismantle the ICBM force; (2) protect the ICBM force more thoroughly; (3) develop a corollary capability; and (4) free ICBMs from their fixed sites and make them mobile. The principal reason for the vulnerability of the ICBMs is that their locations are both known and static. In the area of modernization, President Ronald Reagan proposed deployment of the MX ("Peacekeeper") missile, a program that he inherited from the Carter administration. Controversy over basing and mobility has prevented implementation of the MX program. The increasing accuracy of Soviet warheads—coupled with the additions to their numbers—increases the vulnerability of the U.S. ICBM force. Should it be followed by some new Soviet technological breakthrough that could result in the vulnerability of one or both of the remaining triad of strategic forces, U.S. security would be placed in serious jeopardy.

Worldwide Military Command and Control System (WWMCCS)
The principal communications channels for conveying instructions to U.S. conventional and nuclear forces throughout the world. The Worldwide Military Command and Control System is the command and control arm of Command, Control, Communications, and Intelligence (C3I), which links the National Command Authorities (NCA) to the National Military Command System (NMCS). The latter system executes orders through channels of command to the armed forces. WWMCCS consists of the National Military Command Center (NMCC, or the war room) in the Department of Defense in the Pentagon; the Alternate National Military Command Centers (ANMCC) in underground hardened bunkers in Virginia, Maryland, and Pennsylvania; and the National Emergency Airborne Command Post (NEACP). The Worldwide Military Command and Control System is used by the president, the secretary of defense, the chairman of the Joint Chiefs of Staff (JCS), the Strategic Air Command (SAC), and the regional military commanders. All these command authorities and centers receive, assess, and issue orders based upon information from the North American Aerospace Defense Command (NORAD), which has the overall responsibility of watching any hostile missile or bomber attacks against the United States (and Canada). Established in 1962, WWMCCS is linked with the Defense Communications System (DCS), the Minimum Essential Emergency Communications Network (MEECN), the Automatic Voice Network, the Automatic Secure Voice Communications, the Automatic Digital Network, the Diplomatic Telecommunications System, and the Defense Satellite Communications System. *See also* COMMAND, CONTROL, COMMUNICATIONS, AND INTELLIGENCE (C3I); NATIONAL COMMAND AUTHORITIES (NCA); STRATEGIC AIR COMMAND (SAC).

Significance   The Worldwide Military Command and Control System, made up of many computers and command centers, will be used to instruct launching of nuclear warheads and conventional weapons. Despite the apparent efficiency of the WWMCCS, its computers have been vulnerable to failure. The system has been used to oversee and respond to many international crises, and on each occasion its effects have been flawed. Constant attempts are being undertaken to improve the efficiency and accuracy of WWMCCS, but due to the excessive complexity of the system, it lacks real cohesion, and the program is fraught with the potential for disastrous consequences. It appears that the system, designed to maximize U.S. security and war effort, may be likely to plunge the nation and the world into a catastrophe. The General Accounting Office (GAO) concluded in 1979 that the computer system in the WWMCCS was in bad shape, could not be repaired by piecemeal modernization, and needed replacement. President Ronald Reagan decided to spend $18 billion to modernize the entire C3I system as part of a program to improve WWMCCS and nuclear capability. Former Defense Secretary Frank C. Carlucci in his report to the Congress said, "Our strategic command, control, and communications (C3I) modernization program has corrected many serious deficiencies in warning sensors, command centers, and communications links. Some of these improvements are already in place."[26]

X

X-Ray Laser Weapon   A potential weapon that could be part of a high-technology system for protection against attacking nuclear warheads. An X-ray laser weapon would generate X-rays rather than infrared, ultraviolet, or visible light. The energy for this component would come from the explosion of a nuclear device. It is sometimes called a "third-generation" nuclear weapon—the first generation being the atomic or fission bomb and the second generation being the nuclear fusion weapon. A considerable amount of the energy produced by a nuclear detonation is released as X-rays. Some of these X-rays are pumped into suitable lasting rods to produce focused X-ray energy beams that would travel at the same speed as beams from ordinary lasers. The power of this weapon would enable it to destroy a missile, or a warhead, instantaneously. Because the X-ray laser cannot penetrate deeply into the atmosphere, it would be most useful against offensive nuclear weapons. X-ray laser weapons could be deployed from the ground and could be based in space. In 1987 a study group of the American Physical Society (APS) concluded that nuclear explosion-pumped X-ray lasers present many physics and engineering problems, but they are still being examined. What has not been proven is whether it will be possible to make a militarily useful X-ray laser. *See also* KINETIC ENERGY WEAPON (KEW); STRATEGIC DEFENSE INITIATIVE.

Significance   An X-ray laser would be much more efficient than a second-generation nuclear arsenal, just as a second-generation weapon is much more efficient than a first-generation bomb. Advocates of X-ray lasers, such as the proponents of the Strategic Defense Initiative (SDI) headed by Edward Teller, the "father of hydrogen bomb," believe that laser beams emerging from the rods could be used to attack enemy missiles. They maintain that these weapons are defensive. The proposed X-ray laser ballistic missile defense would consist of a smaller battlestation, since its power source would be a compact nuclear weapon, instead of tanks containing chemicals. A single X-ray laser explosion would be capable of directing beams at, and destroying, several ICBMs. But there is a profound split in the scientific community about the efficacy of this weapons system. Most scientists believe that even if the pulse of X-rays reached the missiles in the boost phase, the enemy could protect his missiles from damage. X-rays of short wavelengths are rapidly absorbed by matter, actually making it easy to protect missiles from damage. Nevertheless, scientists at the Lawrence Livermore National Laboratory, California, where SDI research is making progress, are enthusiastic about the testing success of the X-ray laser weapons system.

Y

Yield   The total energy released in a nuclear explosion. The yield is generally measured in terms of the kilotons or megatons of TNT (trinitrotoluene) required to produce the same energy release (1 megaton equals 1,000 kilotons, and 1 kiloton equals 1,000 tons of TNT). The destructiveness of nuclear weapons increases with larger yields and through the use of multiple warheads. The Hiroshima bomb, called "Little Boy," produced three pounds overpressure over an area of four square miles. Produced some 25 years later, one Minuteman III can destroy over 10 times that area; the new MX, with 10 warheads, can destroy over 50 times the Hiroshima area (Little Boy had one warhead). There are two basic types of nuclear bombs—fission or atomic bombs, and fusion or hydrogen bombs; fission bombs were used on Japan in 1945. Both superpowers decided to develop hydrogen bombs because fusion weapons are enormously more destructive than fission bombs. There is an inherent upper limit to the explosive power, called "yield," that a fission bomb can have, but this is higher for fusion weapons. The yield of the Hiroshima bomb was the equivalent of 12,000–15,000 tons of TNT, or 12–15 kilotons, but hydrogen weapons are measured in millions of tons of TNT, or megatons. *See also* HIROSHIMA; HYDROGEN BOMB.

Significance   Yield is one measure of a nuclear weapon's strength. Larger yields, improved accuracy, and larger numbers of sophisticated multiple warheads all combine to give the superpowers a higher kill possibility against each other's targets. The technological revolution has allowed weapons to be totally destructive. Coupled with this is the simple fact that the number of nuclear weapons which has now increased to some 30,000 in the United States and about 20,000 in the Soviet Union. Typically, the United States has developed a more destructive weapon or a more efficient system for its delivery, only to have the Soviet Union produce a similar device within several years.

The largest weapon ever tested released an energy approximately 4,000 times that of the atomic bomb dropped on Hiroshima, and there is, in principle, no upper limit to the explosive yield that may be attained. The total strength of the present nuclear arsenals in the world is equivalent to about one million Hiroshima bombs, that is, 12–15 billion tons of TNT. This amount is considered equivalent to three tons for every human being on earth. As we dwell among proliferating nuclear arsenals, the gravity of the destruction becomes nightmarish to contemplate.

Z

Zero Option   A policy calling for the elimination of all intermediate-range nuclear weapons deployed by the superpowers in Europe. Zero option, as proposed by the United States in 1981, involved the removal of existing SS-4, SS-5, and SS-20 Soviet missiles in exchange for a U.S. pledge not to deploy Pershing II and Tomahawk cruise missiles in Europe. When the Soviets rejected the U.S. zero option, the Reagan administration decided to deploy Pershing II and Tomahawk missiles in Europe in 1983. Originally, the concept of zero option, or *Null-Lösung,* was mooted by West German Chancellor Helmut Schmidt in early 1981. He suggested that if the Soviet Union removed their intermediate-range nuclear weapons from Euro-bases, the United States would have no need to proceed with emplacing Pershing II and Tomahawk missiles. At first, the United States deplored the West German plan of zero option, but, in late 1981, it changed its position, and President Ronald Reagan offered zero option as his proposal, prior to the first round of intermediate-range nuclear forces (INF) negotiations. This time the Soviets rejected it. Compromises were also discussed, and the INF talks dragged on inconclusively until December 8, 1987, when a treaty to dismantle INF forces in Europe was signed in Washington by the two superpowers. *See also* INTERMEDIATE-RANGE NUCLEAR FORCES TREATY.

Significance   The U.S. zero option proposal created negotiating problems with the Soviets, but, in retrospect, it was a reasonable and fair proposal following the conclusion of the INF treaty. With a few exceptions, earlier negotiations between the superpowers in the field of nuclear weapon limitations had been broad-based. The INF talks, lasting over six years, were concerned mainly with the European theater, in which the large-scale introduction of new Soviet weapons created a disequilibrium for the North Atlantic Treaty Organization's objective of maintaining a strategic superiority in Europe. During the period of difficult INF negotiations, the superpower relations returned to an antipathetic position, reminiscent of the Cold War era of the 1960s, and both sides began to attach new political conditions to the proposed treaty. The delicate issues of arms control became a political treadmill. Finally, when the superpowers felt that reaching an agreement was more beneficial for them, both politically and economically, than rejecting it, they concluded the INF treaty. This can be viewed as a "zero plus" agreement. The success of the zero option negotiation is a display of even-handedness between the leadership of the two countries; the sagacity and ease with which the INF treaty was concluded provides hope for success in negotiating substantial reductions in other nuclear arms categories.

NOTES

The United States Government Manual 1988/89 (Washington, D.C.: U.S. Government Printing Office, 1988) was a valuable resource for information on departments and agencies of the U.S. government. Other sources, cited in the text, are included in the notes below.

1. Jonathan Schell, *The Fate of the Earth* (New York: Knopf, 1982), 163–164.
2. Walter S. Jones, *The Logic of International Relations* (Glenview, Ill.: Scott, Foresman/Little, Brown, 1988), 522.
3. Theodore A. Couloumbis and James H. Wolfe, *Introduction to International Relations: Power and Justice* (Englewood Cliffs, N.J.: Prentice-Hall, 1986), 234.
4. Ibid.
5. Harvard Nuclear Study Group, *Living with Nuclear Weapons* (Toronto: Bantam Books, 1983), 33–34.
6. Dietrich Schroeer, *Science, Technology, and the Nuclear Arms Race* (New York: John Wiley & Sons, 1984), 270.
7. Jeffrey M. Elliot and Sheikh R. Ali, *The Presidential-Congressional Political Dictionary* (Santa Barbara, Calif.: ABC-CLIO, 1984), 38–39.
8. Herman Kahn, "Thinking about the Unthinkable," in William Evan and Stephen Hilgartner, eds., *The Arms Race and Nuclear War* (Englewood Cliffs, N.J.: Prentice-Hall, 1987), 108.
9. Gilbert R. Winham, "Negotiation as a Management Process," *World Politics,* 30 (1977), 87–114.
10. Philip Noel-Baker, *Bulletin of the Atomic Scientists,* 33 (September 1977), 19.
11. Helen Caldicott, *Missile Envy: The Arms Race and Nuclear War* (Toronto: Bantam Books, 1984), 16.
12. Paul R. Ehrlich et al., *The Cold and the Dark: The World after Nuclear War* (New York: W. W. Norton, 1984), 9–11.
13. Christopher Campbell, *Nuclear Weapons: Fact Book* (Feltham, Middlesex, England: Hamlyn Publishing, 1984), 12.
14. Schroeer, 65.
15. John Hersey, *Hiroshima* (New York: Knopf, 1946); and Michihiko Hachiya, *Hiroshima Diary* (Chapel Hill, N.C.: University of North Carolina Press, 1955).

16. Leonard S. Spector, *Going Nuclear* (Cambridge, Mass.: Ballinger, 1987).

17. Joseph J. Kruzel, "Military and Diplomatic Signals," in Ellen P. Stern, ed., *The Limits of Military Intervention* (Beverly Hills, Calif.: Sage Publications, 1977), 83–99.

18. Caldicott, 82.

19. Ibid.

20. Robert Ehrlich, *Waging Nuclear Peace* (Albany, N.Y.: State University of New York Press, 1985), 213.

21. Ibid., 228.

22. Christine Cassel et al., *Nuclear Weapons and Nuclear War: A Source Book for Health Professionals* (New York: Praeger, 1984), 93.

23. National Academy of Sciences, *Long-Term Worldwide Effects of Multiple Nuclear-Weapons Detonations* (Washington, D.C.: National Academy of Sciences, 1975), 14.

24. Richard E. Neustadt, *Presidential Power: The Politics of Leadership* (New York: John Wiley & Sons, 1960), viii.

25. Spector.

26. Frank C. Carlucci, *Annual Report to the Congress, Fiscal Year 1989* (Washington, D.C.: U.S. Government Printing Office, 1988), 241.

INDEX

In this index, references in **bold** type indicate pages where terms in this dictionary are defined. Page numbers in roman type are used for places with further information about these terms and for other subjects that may interest the reader.

285